ETERNAL NUGGETS

ETERNAL NUGGETS

TIMELESS TRUTHS FOR A DYNAMIC WORLD

MARK NYARKO

To order additional copies of this book, contact:
Xlibris
800-056-3182
www.Xlibrispublishing.co.uk
Orders@Xlibrispublishing.co.uk
779897

CONTENTS

ABOUT THE BOOK

It is generally known that the spirit realm is the transcendent or absolute reality that actually gave birth to our temporal reality or what we know to be physical material dimension. Because our existence owes its source to the spirit realm, the latter is actually what dictates events in our realm. It takes no effort to realise that not only is the bible an integrated message system, but one with its origins in another dimension of existence. Have you wondered how the bible accurately described scientific phenomena millennia before science arrived on the planet? How on earth did Moses know how the world was created when no man was on the scene at the beginning. It does not take a genius to fathom that there has to be a supreme being, a God out there, who is the source and sustainer of all life. That is why it is important that we understand this realm and cooperate with it to get it to work with and for us.

Paul wrote in 2 Corinthians 4:18:

> *while we do not look at the things which are seen, but at the things which are not seen. For the things which are seen are temporary, but the things which are not seen are eternal.*

He is saying that our focus should be on the unseen, eternal realm which is the real or parent reality because that is permanent as opposed to this realm. The need to focus on the things which do not change becomes even more crucial because of the sheer amount, speed and complexity of change in our day. Changes in technology, science, medicine, careers, education and the work place are so fast and complex that we need something strong and enduring enough to provide the necessary moorings to hold our lives in place and provide the necessary foundational balance to our lives if we are not to be swept away by the change. Even though change can be unsettling, disruptive and scary, even good change, it brings opportunities and progress at the same time. So how do we maintain our sanity and embrace the necessary change. It is my conviction that we do this by turning our focus on the things that do not change. These may include God and His word, our humanity, our biological make up and sexuality, family, society, relationships, parenting etc. Of course the way these may be defined may change over time, but the fact is that they are there, and we need an enduring point of reference on all these to make sense of our very lives and humanity.

This is why it is important to access the right information from the source realm, the spirit dimension, to influence and direct our lives in our realm of existence. This is why it is important to know God's truth on every issue of life and apply it accordingly. Now the bible says that Jesus is the only legitimate door to the spirit realm according to John 10:9-10

> *I am the door. If anyone enters by Me, he will be saved, and will go in and out and find pasture. The thief does not come except to steal, and to kill, and to destroy. I have come that they may have life, and that they may have it more abundantly.*

He is the only authorized dealer mandated by God to take people into the Father's presence and hence the only mediator between God and man, according to:
1Timothy 2:5

> *For there is one God and one Mediator between God and men, the Man Christ Jesus,*

God wants to be active in our lives with His blessing and protection. He does these through His word, prayers, worship, meditation or declaration. These are our means of inviting Him to get involved in our lives. This is the purpose of this book: to get you to know the person of Jesus Christ in His many offices and ministries, and to underlie the importance of the word of God, and how to apply it in our lives.

In Psalm 1, we learn that the person who delights in God's word is firmly rooted, prosperous and fruitful in all he or she does, irrespective of the prevailing climate.

Psalm 1:1-3 puts it this way:

> *Blessed is the man*
> *Who walks not in the counsel of the ungodly,*
> *Nor stands in the path of sinners,*
> *Nor sits in the seat of the scornful;*
> *But his delight is in the law of the LORD,*
> *And in His law he meditates day and night.*
> *He shall be like a tree*
> *Planted by the rivers of water,*
> *That brings forth its fruit in its season,*
> *Whose leaf also shall not wither;*
> *And whatever he does shall prosper.*

As you embrace the truths enshrined in this book, understand that you are calling on a power greater than yourself, from a source beyond this temporal realm, to intervene in your life and that of your family. Make the truths enshrined in Eternal Nuggets your truths by incorporating them into your life and see the invisible but real hand of God move in your life to bring much needed blessing, peace and contentment into every area of your life. See this as a 'how to manual' for Christian living.

THE POWER OF YOUR DECLARATION

'And God said, Let there be light and there was light,' according to Genesis 1:1. Your declaration or bold confession holds the key to your breakthrough and destiny. God is the God of the bold declaration. His commands are his declarations of his will and intentions as we see in Genesis 1:1. The creation account in Genesis is punctuated with 'and God said, and God said' and repeated all through the Bible. He declared what he wanted to see done, and it was so.

Colossians 2:6 declares,

> As you therefore have received Christ Jesus the Lord,
> so walk in him.

This is really saying you are to live your Christian life the same way you received Christ as Lord and Saviour. You received Christ by confession or declaration, so live by the same rule. Confess or make bold declarations of the Word of God because that is the way God operates, and he responds to bold declarations or confessions made in faith.

In Luke 7:1, Jesus had a busy day ahead of him in Capernaum, but he will wait at the gate of the city and finish all his sayings or declarations before entering the city. 'Now when He concluded all His sayings in the hearing of the people, He entered Capernaum.'

He would not enter the city until he had finished his sayings or declarations in the hearing of the people. His declarations were his expression of faith, his notice of intent to the ruling spirits over the city, and notification of his Father of his readiness for the assignment ahead. It was his declarations that unlocked the door to the city of Capernaum and allowed him access. Some doors would never open to you without a command. You literally have to command them to open to you before they will yield. As a Christian seeking to sponsor the preaching of the gospel, the door to prosperity and wealth will not open to you without going to war with bold declarations. This is because the devil will contest your plan and seek to frustrate and block them at every turn.

When the door opened to him, of course, he entered the city. Your declarations will open the doors for you to enter your city of wealth, healing, prosperity, marriage, and destiny. When he entered, there was a big and challenging ministry assignment awaiting him. A centurion, a Roman military officer, who needed healing for his servant heard about him. Possibly, word had gone ahead of him into the city from the crowd who heard his declarations at the gate of the city. So the declarations had literally prepared the ground for him. But you can overrun his plans and overturn his efforts with your bold declarations of faith.

This centurion sent elders of the Jews to Jesus. Why elders, you may ask? He sent elders because elders know how to speak, how to present an issue in a measured and convincing fashion to get the desired response. Very often you need people who know how to go before God on your behalf to present an issue that will get God's attention. The elders also came with a declaration; they came saying that the one who sent them was worthy or deserving. What made him, a Gentile military officer, worthy or deserving to receive from the God of the Jews? They understood the fact that the God of their fathers has promised to bless anyone who blesses Abraham and his descendants. This man, they said, 'loves our nation, and has built us a synagogue.' Jesus readily went with them without any further questions, thus agreeing with their conclusion that the officer was deserving of God's blessing. You see, when you come to God with the right attitude and the right declaration in your mouth, he will cancel all other appointments, if he has to, to attend to you. God cannot resist faith-filled words declared in boldness, because that is his modus operandi.

Well, you are equally worthy or deserving because of the blood of Jesus shed on the cross for you. You are deserving of a good marriage, wealth, and victory over sickness and decease. In fact, he says in Colossians 1:12 that he has qualified you to share in his inheritance with all his children.

> Giving thanks to the Father who has qualified us to be partakers of the inheritance of the saints in the light.

And you are left to give him thanks for that because it is a done thing. In fact, our problem is not with the blessing or provision on God's part because he has already accomplished his part as he declares in Ephesians 1:3; Romans 8:17; 2 Corinthians 8:9; 9:8; and Deuteronomy 8:18.

> Blessed be the God and Father of our Lord Jesus Christ, who has blessed us with every spiritual blessing in the heavenly places in Christ,

> And if children, then heirs—heirs of God and joint heirs with Christ, if indeed we suffer with Him, that we may also be glorified together.

> For you know the grace of our Lord Jesus Christ, that though He was rich, yet for your sakes He became poor, that you through His poverty might become rich.

> And God is able to make all grace abound toward you, that you, always having all sufficiency in all things, may have an abundance for every good work.

> And you shall remember the LORD your God, for it is He who gives you power to get wealth, that He may establish His covenant which He swore to your fathers, as it is this day.

From all the above scriptures, it is clear that we do not have a problem with his provision. Our problem is with appropriation of the provided blessing. It is about learning how to get the blessing to move from the invisible realm into the visible material realm where it benefits us.

Before Jesus could get to him, the centurion sent *friends* to him. He sent elders and then friends. Some have elders but not friends, whilst others have friends but not elders. You need both. Have you got friends that can go before God on your behalf? Sometimes you may not be in a position to go before God yourself because of the circumstance you may be in. This is when you need sincere friends who will go before God on your behalf. Oh yes, many will say they are praying for you, but more often than not, these are mere pleasantries, publicity stunts, meant to appease your emotions.

The centurion said, 'Lord it is not necessary for You to come under my roof, but just say the word, and my servant will be healed.' This man, unencumbered by the Law, understood the dynamics of faith and the power of declaration. He is saying it is not always necessary to lay hands on the sick to get them healed. He is saying there is no distance in the spirit realm, so you do not have to be on the scene to pray to make a difference. And most importantly, he is saying, 'I know the power of making a faith declaration to effect the necessary change.' He is saying, 'Jesus, I know the authority you carry over sickness and disease and death. I know that any condition in the spirit realm will bow before your word, just the same way the soldiers under my command hearken unto my word.' Breathtaking stuff indeed. No wonder he was one of only two people in all of the New Testament Jesus said had great faith. The other was the Syrophoenician woman. And both were Gentiles who were not under the Law of Moses. You see, the Law is not of faith, and the Law is actually a killer of faith, as it is mechanical and does not help you know God or please him. So declaration is great faith. The bible declares that without faith it is impossible to please God, and those who come to him must first believe that he is and that he is a rewarder of all those who diligently seek him. It is crucial to believe that God is able and willing to change your circumstance for the better, whatever it happens to be, once you seek his face in faith. Settle this in your heart.

Jesus obviously made the declaration, and the centurion's servant was healed that instant, according to Luke 7:9.

Jesus declared his resurrection well in advance before his crucifixion as explained in several places in the gospels including Mark 8:31; 10:34; and John 2:19–21. He needed to do this in advance of his crucifixion and death.

> And He began to teach them that the Son of Man must suffer many things, and be rejected by the elders and chief priests and scribes, and be killed, and after three days rise again.

By the same token, you may be single today, but you could be praying, rather should be praying for your marriage and even unborn children before they happen. You don't wait for your children to fall sick before you pray for them. Pray and declare protection, health, and healing over them before they fall sick. We learn from this that declarations made today do not disappear into thin air but are stored in God's prayer archive until they are needed and activated. For want of a better analogy, it is akin to freezing one's eggs until they are needed to be fertilized to produce a healthy baby.

God created all things by his declaration, according to the Genesis account. And the Bible says that you and I have been made in his image and likeness. It means, amongst other things, that we are to operate the same way he does, to be co-creators of destinies with him, by our declaration as demonstrated by the example of the Old Testament Patriarchs according to Hebrews 11:3. These giants of faith literally changed the course of human history by their bold, uncompromising, faith-filled declarations and actions.

'By faith we understand that the worlds were framed by the word of God, so that the things which are seen were not made of things which are visible.'

The heavens and the earth have ears and can be entreated to align with our cause by our bold declarations.

According to Deuteronomy 32:1; Ezekiel 36:8; and Judges 5:20, the heavenly bodies have ears and can be summoned to our cause with our declarations.

> Give ear, O heavens, and I will speak; And hear, O earth, the words of my mouth.

> But you, O mountains of Israel, you shall shoot forth your branches and yield your fruit to My people Israel, for they are about to come.

> They fought from the heavens; The stars from their courses fought against Sisera.

The heavens and the earth and the created order have ears and can hear the command of your voice and respond accordingly. In most of the wars that ancient Israel had to fight, they lost or won depending on what transpired in the heavenlies. Most of their victories were won in the heavenlies before hostilities actually began. In the same way, too, at the individual level, you win or lose the fight in the heavens.

In Exodus 14:25, it is reported that God himself fought for the children of Israel against the Egyptian army in the midst of the sea.

> And He took off their chariot wheels, so that they drove them with difficulty; and the Egyptians said, 'Let us flee from the face of Israel, for the LORD fights for them against the Egyptians.'

One can only imagine the terror and panic of the Egyptian army when they realised that the God of Israel himself was fighting for Israel against the Egyptian army. They should have known this all along from the way their nation had been devastated with plague after plague prior to the departure of the Jews from Egypt. How could they assume God was going to abandon them in the wilderness? In the same way, we can get the forces of heaven and nature on our behalf through our declarations of his Word.

According to Isaiah 45:2–3, God promises us of his personal presence and intervention in the battles we have to fight, thus,

> I will go before you. And make the crooked places straight;
> I will break in pieces the gates of bronze. And cut the bars of iron.
> I will give you the treasures of darkness. And hidden riches of secret places,
> That you may know that I, the LORD, Who call you by your name,
> Am the God of Israel.

There are bronze gates that are so stubborn they only have to be destroyed and broken in pieces and bars of iron that can only be cut asunder. There is no key to these gates and bars, so the only recourse is to destroy them completely, which can only be done by powerful declarations of the prophetic Word. Can you imagine what these gates and bars are there for? They are there to stop you entering your prophetic destiny. They will literally stop you in your tracks if you do not stand up to them and pronounce their destruction.

And when you have done with the declaration and destroyed the gates and bars, see what follows next. God says, 'I will give you the treasures of darkness and the hidden riches of secret places.' That is your God-ordained destiny unfolding right before your eyes. This could mean anything from wealth and finances, your marriage and children, your ministry and profession, or whatever the Lord has called you to accomplish on earth for him.

Apparently, in Psalm 24:7–10, it is believed that these ancient doors were speaking back at Jesus and would not open to him for him to enter his glory after his triumphant redemption mission on earth until they were commanded. If the ancient doors would not open for Jesus without being commanded, well, what makes us think they are going to flung open just because we showed up!

In 1 Samuel 17:45–47, David made some rather bold declarations that got the heavens stirred up for battle.

> Then David said to the Philistine, 'You come to me with a sword, with a spear, and with a javelin. But I come to you in the name of the LORD of hosts, the God of the armies of Israel, whom you have defied. This day the LORD will deliver you into my hand, and I will strike you and take your head from you. And this day I will give the carcasses of the camp of the Philistines to the birds of the air and the wild beasts of the earth, that all the earth may know that there is a God in Israel. Then all this assembly shall know that the LORD does not save with sword and spear; for the battle is the LORD's, and He will give you into our hands.'

Our God loves a good scrap with his enemies, and when David made that bold declaration of faith, saying, 'I will take your head from you,' when he did not even have a sword, God knew he was calling for him to get involved, and get involved he did, and the rest, they say, is history. No wonder David became the most successful king of Israel of all time. Yes, he was a great warrior and a brave soldier in his own right, but, above all else, he knew how to get God on his side in all his battles through his powerful faith declarations. His total reliance on God always gave him total victory.

Our declaration invokes angelic intervention in the battles we fight. Angels are assigned to help believers in the battles they have to fight against demonic opposition to our lives and destinies, but they are only activated by the positive declaration of the Word of God. Angels recognise and respond only to the declarations we make in faith based on the Word of God. If you are not declaring the Word of God over your life, your angels have nothing to work with and no invitation to intervene in your life, according to Psalm 103:20–21.

> Bless the LORD, you His angels,
> Who excel in strength, who do His word,
> Heeding the voice of His word.
> Bless the LORD, all you His hosts,
> You [a]ministers of His, who do His pleasure.

God's angels are very powerful, much more powerful than the devil's demonic agents who are sent to harass and block the fulfilment of our destinies. But the angels only hearken to or heed the voice of God's Word.

There is a declaration for every reality or manifestation in your life. Your words create the desired environment and atmosphere around you. You can use your declarations like a thermostat to set the atmosphere around you. It is the atmosphere or the environment around you that actually determines your state of life.

In Isaiah 54:17, he says that you have power to condemn every tongue that speaks condemnation against you. Literally, you can command the contrary voices of witches and the demonic over your destiny, ministry, finances, marriage, family, and health to shut up, and they will have to obey you.

You see, declaration is destiny changing. There are different types of prayers and different times to pray. All prayers are good and will bring benefits to your life, but the most far-reaching, destiny-changing prayers are the bold declarations you make at midnight, when destinies are determined or changed for the ensuing day. The midnight is not for sleeping but for destiny-changing prayers. God reckons the day from evening to morning, according to the Genesis creation account. So by the time you wake up at five or six o'clock in the morning, the course of your day has already been determined the night before. So most of the prayers we pray are playing catch up. Noted author and Bible teacher Dr. Cindy Trimm teaches in her landmark book *Commanding Your Morning* that you can set the course of your day, and hence your life, the night before with powerful declarations, and I could not agree with her more, as I have belatedly discovered.

In Job 38:12–13, we learn this vital truth.

> Have you commanded the morning since your days
> began,
> And caused the dawn to know its place,
> That it might take hold of the ends of the earth,
> And the wicked be shaken out of it?

God is asking you to set the course of your day by commanding your morning and shaking the wicked out of it. Your miracle already exists in the secret unseen realm, and you have to command its manifestation. The book of Job actually says God opens the mind of man and gives him inspirational thoughts so he can keep man from pursuing his own limited way. He wants you to speak these inspirational thoughts into existence. He wants you to mature in wisdom, authority, and supernatural ability so you can bear witness to the splendour of his kingdom. Like the donkey Jesus needed for his triumphal entry into Jerusalem, you may be tied up until Jesus gave the command for it to be loosed and brought to him. In the same way, the things that must happen in your life need your express permission to manifest and exist in your life. Throughout the Bible, God is calling his people to take command of their destinies by learning to command their mornings. To command is to order with authority, take charge, exercise direct authority, to lead, to dominate by position, to guard, and to overlook. Don't just let life happen to you. Take charge of your thoughts, words, and time, and wrestle your destiny from defeat. Keep awake, alert, and watchful. Do not be a victim of circumstances. Be a victor, call the shots, and change your destiny. In Job 33:5, God says, 'Set your words in order and take your stand before me.' 'Let me know that you like what I want for you. Agree with Me and expect what you are declaring to come to pass by commanding with conviction and speaking with expectation,' according to Mark 11:23-24 and Job 22:38. ''For assuredly I say to you, whoever says to this mountain, 'Be removed and be cast into the sea,' and does not doubt in his heart, but believes that those things he says will be done, he will have whatever he says. Therefore I say to you whatever things you ask when you pray, believe that you receive them, and you will have them.''

''You will also declare a thing, and it will be established for you; So light will shine on your ways.''

Proverbs 10:11 says, 'The mouth of the righteous is a well of life,' so use your mouth to water your life unto fruitfulness. Yes, fools may destroy their lives with their own mouths, but be wise and use your mouth to draw life to your life. Declare your own greatness as the Lord reveals to you, and so shall it be unto you according to your words.

What have you got to lose by trying this for yourself? Jesus did most of his praying at night or just before the break of day and then ministered to the multitudes in the day. Could that be the key to his extraordinary success in ministry? I know you would be thinking that, yeah, but he is the son of God. But hear me good. Jesus did not minister as God; otherwise, he would not need anyone to anoint him as he was in Acts 10:38. He ministered as a man, anointed by the Holy Spirit, to show us what is possible with all of us in the ministry.

You exercise your dominion by your declarations. According to Job 22:28, you must have what you declare.

> You will also declare a thing, And it will be established for you;
> So light will shine on your ways.

In the name of Jesus, I have dominion, authority, control, and rulership over all things. Therefore, whatever I command, declare, or decree must come to pass. I command supernatural doors of favour and blessings to open to me for favour, wealth, finances, healing, etc.

I command sickness, disease, failure, and lack to leave my life. Father, give me eyes to see beyond every obstacle this year. May the God of my fathers make me a thousand times more numerous than I am now. May every blessing and opportunity that passed me by last year come back to me this year. May God bring me help from unusual circles. I command every iron gate to my city of wealth, financial blessing, favour, and increase be open to me in Jesus's name.

By the power of the blood of Jesus, I command every evil blood covenant and curse working against my life to be broken now.

In the name of Jesus, I inherit the anointing and wealth of my fathers Abraham, Isaac, and Jacob. Father, thank you for qualifying me to share in your financial abundance, favour, wisdom, blessing, health, and good marriage, according to Genesis 12:1–4; 24:35–36; 26:12–14; 30:43; 41:38–44.

Because of the Abrahamic blessing, may God make people favour you and bless you.

It was by a declaration that someone put you in bondage, so it is by a declaration that you are going to break that bondage and be free. I declare that, according to Isaiah 44:18, I have been redeemed by the Lord, therefore I am free.

According to Galatians 5:1 'It is for freedom that Christ has set us free. Stand firm, then, and do not let yourself be burdened again by a yoke of slavery.'(NIV)

It is not a matter of time but a matter of truth. Not where you are but what you can see. It is the seeing that brings the possession. Father, open my eyes so I can see beyond every obstacle and problem in my life, and to see my purpose and destiny in life. My purpose is greater than every obstacle, and I am unstoppable. Let God's ordained greatness in me begin to manifest now in the name of Jesus. I command every dead vision and dream in my life to receive resurrection power and come back to life, in Jesus's name. Let the call of God upon my life receive power and live again. I call my destiny, my greatness, my wealth, my anointing, and the gifts of the Spirit in my life to receive life and live again. Father, accelerate my destiny, O Lord.

According to Micah 5:12 (NIV), he says, 'I will destroy your witchcraft and you will no longer cast spells.'

May the consuming fire of God destroy every witchcraft power that seeks to destroy destinies and bring disasters, curses, sicknesses, fruitlessness, barrenness, failure, and accidents in my family. I command all the works of witchcraft powers in my family to be destroyed by fire in the mighty name of Jesus.

I declare boldly that the Lord is my Helper, I shall not fear what shall man do to me.

Declaration is what creates your future. Your dominion is only expressed when you speak. Careless words produce a careless life. So speak with deliberate purpose and calculated intent. You are born again a sheep, but you grow to become a lion, just like the Lion of the tribe of Judah. A lion does not whisper; it roars. It may not be the biggest and the strongest animal in the jungle but it won't be bullied or intimidated by any, irrespective of size. That is why it is called the king of the jungle. And when it roars, all creatures in the jungle take notice. As he is so are we in this world. He is not weak, timid, or indecisive. On the contrary, he is strong, bold, and decisive in every move he makes.

We are commanded to war with the prophecy declared over our lives, according to Genesis 24:14, 50; 25:20–21; and 1 Timothy 1:18.

> Now let it be that the young woman to whom I say, 'Please let down your pitcher that I may drink,' and she says, 'Drink, and I will also give your camels a drink'—let her be the one You have appointed for Your servant Isaac. And by this I will know that You have shown kindness to my master.

Then Laban and Bethuel answered and said, 'The thing comes from the LORD; we cannot speak to you either bad or good.'

Isaac was forty years old when he took Rebekah as wife, the daughter of Bethuel the Syrian of Padan Aram, the sister of Laban the Syrian. Now Isaac pleaded with the LORD for his wife, because she was barren; and the LORD granted his plea, and Rebekah his wife conceived.

This charge I commit to you, son Timothy, according to the prophecies previously made concerning you, that by them you may wage the good warfare.

As we approach the end of the age, there is no more time to waste. Everything is accelerated, and the days seem shorter and faster. It has to happen now or it may never happen. We cannot wait until we figure everything out before we make a move. It is time to operate out of our imagination and see the limitless possibilities that may be too much for the rational mind to comprehend. Like a popular author once wrote, 'Life is too short to play it safe.'

Let's make some ripples before the curtain comes down. This is a lifetime opportunity we cannot afford to miss. You will not have the opportunities you have to make a real difference apart from those you have on earth right now.

Whatever you accomplish in this life, good or bad, will stay with you for all eternity, so do not be casual about life and end up a casualty. This life is your unique opportunity to decide what kind of life you are going to have in the next. Lay hold of all the opportunities God deliberately orchestrates your way to shape the course of history and make a difference. You can do all things through the Anointed One and his anointing. He is able to do exceedingly, abundantly, above all that you ask or imagine, according to the power that works in you. This is another way of saying your possibilities are limitless, so tell yourself that failure is not an option, and no excuse is good enough. See all opposition and obstacles as training to help you build the necessary spiritual muscle and stamina.

Whatever you do, make your life count because all of heaven is watching with baited breath and excited anticipation.

Make it count.

ACTIVATING THE PROPHETIC WORD FOR YOUR LIFE

The following will be our key scriptures for this message: Psalm 119:89; Hebrews 11:3; and Joshua 1:8–9.

There is a spiritual law that we must know and understand.

'Forever O Lord, Your word is settled in heaven,' declares Psalm 119:89. The Word of God is settled, established, done, perfected, and fulfilled in heaven. Heaven is complete in every respect; peaceful, perfect, with no lack, no pain, no sickness, no sorrow, no death, but full of joy. It means that all the things we pray for to be fulfilled on earth are the norm in heaven. Heaven is the kingdom of God, and over there, the will of God is the prevailing law. That is why we were instructed in Matthew 6:10 to pray for his kingdom to come and his will to be done on earth as it is in heaven. In that prayer, we are literally seeking to pull heaven's atmosphere down to the earth.

How, then, do we get his Word established on earth, in our lives, in our families, in our bodies, in our marriages, and in our situations and circumstances, whatever they happen to be? According to Ephesians 1:3; Colossians 1:12; and Romans 8:17,

> Blessed be the God and Father of our Lord Jesus Christ, who has blessed us with every spiritual blessing in the heavenly places in Christ,

> Giving thanks to the Father who has qualified us to be partakers of the inheritance of the saints in the light.
>
> And if children, then heirs—heirs of God and joint heirs with Christ, if indeed we suffer with Him, that we may also be glorified together.

All the above scriptures are clearly declaring that God has already blessed his children immensely with all kinds of blessings. But these are in the unseen spiritual realm, as that is where all of God's transactions and provisions originate. Really not much comfort for humans who are earth dwellers and need to have all their provisions in tangible physical form for their benefit.

According to 1 Corinthians 13:1b, 'By the mouth of two or three witnesses every word shall be established.' God is the first one to utter his Word in the Logos, or his declared will in his written Word. The Logos is the expression of God's general will on any particular issue. It is general and not particularly targeted or personalised. He says he needs a second witness to agree with him and say what he has already said. This is the general meaning of 'confess'; it is to agree with God by saying what he has already said in his Word. That is why after the death of Moses, God literally took Joshua, Moses's assistant, to school to teach him how to succeed in his assigned role of leading the Jewish nation into their God-given inheritance. In Joshua 1:1–9, God personally instructs Joshua, saying,

> After the death of Moses the servant of the LORD, it came to pass that the LORD spoke to Joshua the son of Nun, Moses' assistant, saying: 'Moses My servant is dead. Now therefore, arise, go over this Jordan, you and all this people, to the land which I am giving to them—the children of Israel. Every place that the sole of your foot will tread upon I have given you, as I said to Moses. From the wilderness and this Lebanon as far as the great river, the River Euphrates, all the

land of the Hittites, and to the Great Sea toward the going down of the sun, shall be your territory. No man shall be able to stand before you all the days of your life; as I was with Moses, so I will be with you. I will not leave you nor forsake you. Be strong and of good courage, for to this people you shall divide as an inheritance the land which I swore to their fathers to give them. Only be strong and very courageous, that you may observe to do according to all the law which Moses My servant commanded you; do not turn from it to the right hand or to the left, that you may prosper wherever you go. This Book of the Law shall not depart from your mouth, but you shall meditate in it day and night, that you may observe to do according to all that is written in it. For then you will make your way prosperous, and then you will have good success. Have I not commanded you? Be strong and of good courage; do not be afraid, nor be dismayed, for the LORD your God is with you wherever you go.'

God is literally saying to Joshua, 'I have done my part in blessing you and this people. I have given you the land of Canaan. I have given you victory over the present inhabitants whom I want to dispossess of the land. But your possession of the land and achievement of the victory and success I have already given you depends on you. First, decide whether you want what I want for you. Decide whether you are going to trust in me and the words I have spoken to you, assuring you of victory. I have made you a success, now prove that you want to be a success. You do all these by meditating on my Word day and night as if it were your medical prescription for success. Take my Word a minimum of twice a day. Remind yourself of what I have said to you constantly so you don't forget. This way, your success and the realisation of what I have provided you and the children of Israel will really be up to you. I have given you the power to make what I have provided come to pass for you and this people.' God is literally saying, 'Joshua, I have made you a success, now go and make yourself a success.' He is saying the same to every one of His children, 'Take my Word for you and make yourself a success.'

In Luke 8:11, the Bible says that God's seed is his Word. Seed is no good unless it is sown. But when it is sown, it yields a harvest. We sow God's seed, his Word, with our mouths to produce the necessary fruit or manifestation or the desired blessing in the form of healing, deliverance, prosperity, favour, and increase.

The same thought of sowing God's Word with our mouths is reiterated in Proverbs 4:20–23.

> My son, give attention to my words;
> Incline your ear to my sayings.
> Do not let them depart from your eyes;
> Keep them in the midst of your heart;
> For they are life to those who find them,
> And health to all their flesh.
> Keep your heart with all diligence,
> For out of it spring the issues of life.

Like God's success instructions to Joshua, he is saying in Proverbs we should take his Word to heart and focus on them continually and meditate on them and keep them in our hearts, and when we do, it will be life and health to our whole life. God says when we store his Word in our hearts, it will bring refreshing benefits to our whole life in every desirable way.

WHAT HAPPENS WHEN WE SPEAK THE WORD OF GOD?

The book of Hebrews gives a pathway of what happens when we speak God's Word back to him. In Hebrews 3:1,

> Therefore, holy brethren, partakers of the heavenly
> calling, consider the Apostle and High Priest of our
> confession, Christ Jesus.

When we confess God's Word back to him, we are literally invoking the high priestly ministry of the Lord Jesus for him to appear in God's presence on our behalf with our desired petition. Jesus, the Living Word, takes our confession, the spoken Word, or the rhema and goes before God on our behalf. It is important to realise that the written Word, which we normally call the Logos, expresses God's general will or intention on any particular issue. The Logos can be said to be inert and not activated until someone takes it and confesses it, thereby activating it and giving it power to transmute into reality in the person's life. That is what God meant when he told Joshua, 'You shall make your way prosperous and you shall have good success.' God is saying the general intention of 'My will, will do you no good until you give wind to it by agreeing with me and saying the same thing I have said to you with your own mouth.' So the success and the victory and the realisation of the promise are in your own mouth.

In Hebrews 4:14, God continues to teach that when you begin to say what I have said. Do not waver or do it once and stop.

> Seeing then that we have a great High Priest who has passed through the heavens, Jesus the Son of God, let us hold fast our confession.

God is saying, do not yield to discouragement because you do not see the manifestation of what you are saying immediately. Remember that God says that his Word is really a seed, the seed of the desired miracle. The life-giving power to bring forth the promise is within the seed itself. But you don't sow a seed today and harvest the fruit tomorrow. There is a process involved, as the seasoned farmer will teach us; we need patience, careful tending, and watering for the seed to germinate and grow and bud and bring forth the fruit ready for the harvest. In addition, after sowing the seed, the enemy of our souls, who does not want God's children to receive any of his promised blessings so he can malign our good God, will do everything to stop us receiving the intended blessing. He will do this with discouragement, unbelief, distractions, and direct attacks such as accidents, sickness, debt, and disruptions in relationships intended to destabilise us. That is why we are encouraged to hold fast our confession. Keep at it no matter what. He is warning us to expect all manner of upheavals in our lives and relationships to erupt from nowhere the moment we begin to confess the Word of God. In Mark 11:14, when Jesus cursed the fig tree for failing to produce fruit, it did not wither there and then, and they only saw the evidence of the effect of the curse the following morning, in Mark 11:20, when they saw it withered from the roots up. It must be understood that the words Jesus spoke over the fig tree took effect the very moment he spoke in the unseen part, the root system, of the tree. In the same way, when you begin to confess the Word of God, it goes straight to work in the unseen supernatural realm where most of our problems originate. It is only a matter of time that the results begin to manifest in the seen natural realm.

He goes on in Hebrews 10:23 to say to us, hold on, no matter what. He actually puts his reputation on the line saying know whom you are trusting in all of this, God, the faithful God. The book of Hebrews declares that it is through faith and patience that we inherit God's promises.

> Let us hold fast the confession of our hope without wavering, for He who promised is faithful.

This reminds us of God's promise to us in Hebrews 6:17, saying his Word is further backed by his oath, thus making his promise to you and me unchangeable.

> Thus God, determining to show more abundantly to the heirs of promise the immutability of His counsel, confirmed it by an oath.

ANGELS DO HIS WORD

Hebrews 1:14

> Are they not all ministering spirits sent forth to minister for those who will inherit salvation?

Matthew 18:10

> Take heed that you do not despise one of these little ones, for I say to you that in heaven their angels always see the face of My Father who is in heaven.

Psalm 91:11

> For He shall give His angels charge over you,
> To keep you in all your ways.

The above scriptures attest to the fact that God's angels are his servants he uses to help his children. It teaches that every one of God's children has angels assigned to them to help them in life. Some people may have more angels assigned by God to help them because of the kind of assignment they have been entrusted. When a believer confesses the Word of God or prays for God's help with any situation, God releases his angels to assist his children. Prayer and confession activate the angels of God to assist believers on earth. When we, instead, complain or neglect to pray or confess God's Word, or fight in the natural realm by attacking or blaming other people, the angels assigned to God's children are generally powerless to do anything to help them. Very frequently, God also releases his angels to minister to his children in church meetings and services in response to prayer and worship. There are all kinds of specialist angels that God may send to assist his children, who may include messengers, doctors and surgeons, nurses and midwives, financial experts, and warriors, depending on the need.

It is even believed, and with some scriptural support according to Matthew 1:10, that children have angels allotted to them for protection. But if they grow up and do not accept Jesus as their Lord and Saviour, then the angel goes back to heaven. If they accept the Lord, then the angel stays.

According to Psalm 103:20, not only are God's angels strong and powerful but also they are the enforcers of the Word of God. That is why it is important to speak God's Word back to him. They only do the Word of God, not their own will or desire and certainly not ours apart from that based on the word of God.

> Bless the LORD, you His angels,
> Who excel in strength, who do His word,
> Heeding the voice of His word.

And as if that is not enough, the voice of God's Word could be spoken by our own voice. The angels do not distinguish between the voice of God and our voice. The only thing that activates them is the Word of God the voice speaks, whether it is by God or any of his children. It does not always have to be the exact quote of the Bible even though that is best; they will respond to any word that is spoken in faith, reflecting the spirit of God's Word. The principle is that no Word, no angelic assistance. Your guardian angel may just stand by passively if you don't speak the activating Word in faith.

When the Word of God is spoken, on this side, we do not exactly know what happens in the spirit realm, but, occasionally, God gives us glimpses of what is going on in the spirit realm. However, the Bible says that the Word of God is fire, a sword, a hammer, or any required weapon to destroy the enemies of God and their devices in his children's lives. We can also do the Word in acts and deeds as well in addition to the spoken Word.

Ephesians 6:17

> And take the helmet of salvation, and the sword of the
> Spirit, which is the word of God.

Hebrews 4:12

> For the word of God is living and powerful, and sharper than any two-edged sword, piercing even to the division of soul and spirit, and of joints and marrow, and is a discerner of the thoughts and intents of the heart.

Revelation 1:6; 19:15

> He had in His right hand seven stars, out of His mouth went a sharp two-edged sword, and His countenance was like the sun shining in its strength.

> Now out of His mouth goes a sharp sword, that with it He should strike the nations. And He Himself will rule them with a rod of iron. He Himself treads the winepress of the fierceness and wrath of Almighty God.

Jeremiah 5:14; 23:29

> Therefore thus says the LORD God of hosts:
> 'Because you speak this word,
> Behold, I will make My words in your mouth fire,
> And this people wood,
> And it shall devour them.'

> 'Is not My word like a fire?' says the LORD,
> 'And like a hammer that breaks the rock in pieces?'

I believe, based on all the above scriptures, that when we pray or declare the Word of God, it sets in action any of the above weapons on our behalf to do serious damage to the kingdom of darkness and undo many of their evil works.

So Shall My Word Be

God says in Isaiah 55:11, his Word that goes out of his mouth never returns to him void or empty.

> So shall My word be that goes forth from My mouth;
> It shall not return to Me void,
> But it shall accomplish what I please,
> And it shall prosper in the thing for which I sent it.

God is the first to speak his Word. We are the second. God's spoken Word returns to him when we confess it back to him in faith. And God says such a declaration of his Word back to him will always produce what that particular Word is designed to accomplish. This means we can look disease straight in the face and declare God's covenant promise of long life over it and see the situation reversed, according to Psalm 118:17. The power to fulfil the promise is in the Word itself. The Word has inherent power to destroy sickness and disease, break curses, weaknesses, and untimely death, and in their place produce health and healing, blessing, prosperity, and peace.

God says, 'I call heaven and earth as witness today against you, that I have set before you life and death, blessing and cursing, therefore choose life that both you and your descendants may live,' according to Deuteronomy 30:19.

Notice that we do the choosing. We are the ones to choose. God does not force any choice on anyone, even though he gives a good advice as the choice to make, but the decision is freely ours. Because if we do not choose life, the curse and the death are already in operation on earth, and we don't have to do anything to experience them, just spurn God's advice to make a conscious choice of life.

How do we choose life?

According to Proverbs 18:21, death and life are in the power of the tongue, and those who indulge in it shall eat the fruit of it. God's promises are not automatic, but they must be acquired by faith and patience, and both are equally important in receiving from God.

In Genesis 17:19 and Romans 9:7, God promised Abraham that through his son, Isaac, the promised seed will come.

> Then God said: 'No, Sarah your wife shall bear you a son, and you shall call his name Isaac; I will establish My covenant with him for an everlasting covenant, and with his descendants after him.'

> Nor are they all children because they are the seed of Abraham; but, 'In Isaac your seed shall be called.'

God picked a wife for Isaac, according to Genesis 24:12–14, 50, 56. Abraham sent his servant to go back to Mesopotamia to look for a wife for Isaac. The servant prayed, and the Lord graciously answered his prayer and prospered his journey, according to the following account in the Bible:

> Then he said, 'O LORD God of my master Abraham, please give me success this day, and show kindness to my master Abraham. Behold, here I stand by the well of water, and the daughters of the men of the city are coming out to draw water. Now let it be that the young woman to whom I say, "Please let down your pitcher that I may drink," and she says, "Drink, and I will also give your camels a drink"—let her be the one You have appointed for Your servant Isaac. And by this I will know that You have shown kindness to my master.'

> Then Laban and Bethuel answered and said, 'The thing comes from the LORD; we cannot speak to you either bad or good.'

> And he said to them, 'Do not hinder me, since the LORD has prospered my way; send me away so that I may go to my master.'

God miraculously picked Rebecca to be Isaac's wife. However, after marrying her, Rebecca was found to be barren and could not have children. How could God choose a barren wife for Isaac when he himself has said that the promised seed would come through Isaac?

There is a rather profound lesson in all this. The promises of God are not automatic. They have to be acquired and received by faith. The reception of God's promises and their fulfilment more often than not will entail much testing and warfare before they come into fruition. This is highlighted in several places in the Bible, including Paul's letter to his young protégé Timothy in chapter 1 verse 18.

> This charge I commit to you, son Timothy, according
> to the prophecies previously made concerning you,
> that by them you may wage the good warfare.

Paul is advising his young understudy Timothy that if you want to see God's prophetic Word over your life come to pass, you may have to do some warfare with the same Word. He is telling Timothy that there is going to be opposition and resistance to the very prophetic Word you carry and you will have to fight all kinds of opposition to see the Word come to pass. Opposition could well come from the people closest to you who do not believe that you, of all people, could be God's choice or his instrument for anything worthwhile. These could be your friends and family who not only don't believe in you but also prefer you to stay as you are, the one they know and are comfortable with. Breaking free into your greatness will not only make them feel and look bad, it is an indictment on their sloth and a graphic reminder of their tardiness. The other source of opposition comes from the evil and demonic powers that are determined to stop, thwart, or delay God's agenda on earth and more so through you. Their motive is to stop you having any reason to give God thanks by experiencing his goodness in your life.

But always remember that God's purpose for your life is greater than any obstacle you encounter on earth and is unstoppable. There is a book written about every person who lands on planet Earth, according to Psalm 139:16. This document on your earthly assignment is stronger than any negative environmental circumstance, physical or spiritual, you may encounter. The environment cannot negate the document and, hence, the destiny or prophetic Word you carry. It is even not a matter of time; it is a matter of truth. If you believe that you have received a true promise from God, see it as done. Stand on the unstoppable, immutable Word of God and begin to see it as done because if you can see it with the eyes of faith, you sure will have it, because the confession of faith brings possession. Faith sees the invisible and calls those things that are not as though they were. There is no impossibility in God's vocabulary because with him, all things are possible, and all things are possible to him that believes. Where there is no hope, create your own hope based on the Word of God you carry in your heart. Make your own environment or atmosphere.

Psalm 105:19 declares that the very Word of God you carry in your heart will try you to prove your motives, to develop your character, and to see how badly you really want to see the promise fulfilled. All that Joseph went through at the hands of his brothers, in the house of Potiphar, in the prison, and thereafter was the testing of the Word of promise he carried. That godly saint had so much understanding of spiritual things as to look his wicked brothers in their faces and literally say, 'It was not you but God who brought me here and took me through all that happened,' and forgave his brothers. What a lesson he teaches all of us.

> Until the time that his word came to pass,
> The word of the LORD tested him.

Now coming back to God's choice of a wife for Isaac, Rebecca, who was found to be barren, Isaac did not complain how that could possibly happen after all the prayer and fasting that went into this search for a wife but went to God in prayer in Genesis 25:21.

Now Isaac pleaded with the LORD for his wife, because
she was barren; and the LORD granted his plea, and
Rebekah his wife conceived.

God will always grant the plea of his children who take his
promises back to him in prayer. As said earlier, God's promises
have to be possessed by faith and patience. Faith fights and patience
endures, persists, and never gives up.

Hebrews 6:11–12

And we desire that each one of you show the same
diligence to the full assurance of hope until the end,
that you do not become sluggish, but imitate those
who through faith and patience inherit the promises.

Between the reception of God's promise and its ultimate
fulfilment is the time of preparation and growth, which may involve
building a life of closeness and intimacy with God, learning to
depend solely on him, and character building, which may involve
humility, stewardship, integrity, and perseverance. He tests our faith
with the prophetic Word and our character with the written Word.
When all hell breaks loose and friends desert you and you feel like
you are lost in the midst of a desert and God seems nowhere to be
found, remember that your confession is working. It is a time to draw
closer to God even though he seems to have deserted you. It is a time
to stay in the Word of God and work it till it begins to work for you.
After you have been through all this, your elevation is just around the
corner, and, suddenly, he will appear and the waiting will be over.

WHO IS THIS JESUS?

The following are key scriptures detailing the person of Jesus: John 1:1–5; Hebrews 1:2; and Colossians 1:15–16, 17, 19, 20. Together, they declare the deity of Christ, his eternity of being, his coequality with the Father and the Spirit, and his ministry as the principal agent of creation and the source and sustainer of all life. He is also the self-expression of the Father as the Word and as the embodiment of the triune Godhead. He is the only legitimate access to the Father and the owner and possessor of all the created order. In addition, he is the founder and head of the church, which is an expression of himself on earth. It is apparent that we are talking of no mean person here. He is the be it and end it all. We are talking about the Lord Jesus Christ, the Jewish Messiah and King.

> In the beginning was the Word, and the Word was with God, and the Word was God. He was with God in the beginning. Through him all things were made; without him nothing was made that has been made. In him was life, and that life was the light of all mankind. The light shines in the darkness, and the darkness has not overcome it. (John 1:1–5, NIV)

> But in these last days he has spoken to us by his Son, whom he appointed heir of all things, and through whom also he made the universe. (Hebrews 1:2, NIV)

> The Son is the image of the invisible God, the firstborn
> over all creation. For in him all things were created:
> things in heaven and on earth, visible and invisible,
> whether thrones or powers or rulers or authorities; all
> things have been created through him and for him. He
> is before all things, and in him all things hold together.
> And he is the head of the body, the church; he is the
> beginning and the firstborn from among the dead,
> so that in everything he might have the supremacy.
> For God was pleased to have all his fullness dwell
> in him, and through him to reconcile to himself all
> things, whether things on earth or things in heaven,
> by making peace through his blood, shed on the cross.
> (Colossians 1:15–20, NIV)

He is the second person of the Trinity, coequal with the Father
and with the Spirit. He is coeternal, which means he has always
existed and he has no beginning and predates the beginning.

The Bible teaches that all things were made through him and for
him. Acts 17:28 says that 'in Him we live and move and have our
being'. In him was life, both physical life and spiritual or eternal life.
This is how 1 John 5:11 puts it:

> And this is the testimony: God has given us eternal
> life, and this life is in his Son. (NIV)

John 17:3 picks it up and adds that 'now this is eternal life: that
they may know you, the only true God, and Jesus Christ, whom you
have sent'.

You are not living until you pluck into his life, the life source.
According to John 15:5, he is the vine and we are the branches, and
unless we abide in the vine, we cannot bear any fruit, the same way
a detached branch cannot bear any fruit, but it is doomed to wither
and die.

According to 1 John 5:20, he came to give us understanding. You do not how to do life until you get an understanding of what this life is all about from him. This explains why many people go through life majoring on the minors. They climb to the top of their profession, their careers, and achieve their cherished goals only to realise their ladder is leaning against the wrong wall. This is the lot of the majority of people in the world who come to the end of their lives and at the last irretrievable moment realise they have been pursuing the wrong goals all their lives and that nothing they have achieved has any significance for eternity. Not only have they sacrificed their health, vital relationships with family including spouse and children, but vitally their eternal destiny as well to achieve earthly wealth, riches and position. It is crucial to find out what Jesus will have you do with your life and pursue that with singleness of purpose and focused determination.

The psalmist, in recognition of the futility of human effort apart from God, asked the pointed question, 'What shall it profit a man, if he gains the whole world and loses his own soul . . . ?'

'In Him was life and the life is the light of men.' Life lived in the presence of Jesus is the light of men. And the light shines in the darkness, and the darkness did not comprehend it. There is darkness in this world and in this life. This darkness manifests as ignorance, wickedness, evil, trouble, sickness, and all kinds of pain, but none of these can snuff out the life of a believer, the one who has the light of Christ in themselves. Psalm 91:10 puts it this way: 'No evil shall befall you nor shall any plague come near your dwelling.' This is because 'your Word is a lamp to my feet and a light to my path'.

In John 12:46, Jesus himself declares, 'I am the light of the world, he who follows me shall not abide in darkness.'

Colossians 1:16 says, 'For by Him all things were created, that are in heaven—the spirit realm—and that are on earth—the natural, physical realm, visible and invisible, whether thrones or dominions or principalities or powers. All things were created through Him and for Him.' This tells you that Jesus is of no ordinary order of being.

He is the Omnipotent Creator God himself and Master and Owner of the universe of worlds.

Colossians 1:20 says he has reconciled all things to himself through the blood of his cross. His blood is the only reconciling agent between God and man and between man and his fellow man. Outside of the blood of Jesus, there is no reconciliation but rather hatred and estrangement. This reconciling power of his blood is very evident in the reconciliation between Jew and Gentile and between former Muslims who come to Christ and Jews. It melts all hatred in an instant from the heart of Muslims towards Jews as if they never existed. This is a demonstration of the reconciling power of his blood. It does the same for true Christians in their attitudes towards the unbelieving world.

2 Corinthians 5:18–19

> Now all things are of God, who has reconciled us to Himself through Jesus Christ, and has given us the ministry of reconciliation, that is, that God was in Christ reconciling the world to Himself, not imputing their trespasses to them, and has committed to us the word of reconciliation.

It is important to understand that to receive Jesus's offer of salvation, you have to come personally to him. His righteousness is a gift to all who come to him in repentance. The good news is that it is readily available to everyone who asks him in faith, no matter what they had done previously or their present condition. However, to live a successful Christian life, you have to learn the principles of Christ, which is the Word of God, and apply these to your life. When these principles of Christ or principles of the kingdom are incorporated into your life and applied, they have power to transform the believer's body and health, their attitude and relationships, their minds, their accomplishments in life, their family life including marriage and children, and, of course, their finances.

To be a successful Christian, you must keep your focus on the person of Christ because he is the author and finisher of your faith. The cross of Jesus must be your object of faith. The cross is a symbol of his love for you and the manifestation of his power on your behalf. The cross led to his death, burial, and victorious resurrection on your behalf. It is the power of God in your life. It is also crucial you know and focus on the person of the Holy Spirit, who is your divine helper in all that you do as a Christian. The Holy Spirit is the power source of the believer, and it is important you always go to him for his help in everything you do as a Christian. These are the ingredients of successful Christian living. It is important that you receive the baptism of the spirit and cultivate the habit of always praying in tongues. Jude 20 says that this is the way to build spiritual muscle:

> But you, beloved, building yourselves up on your most holy faith, praying in the Holy Spirit.

2 Corinthians 2:9 says, 'Eye has not seen, nor ear heard, nor has entered the heart of man the things which God has prepared for those who love Him.'

Ephesians 2:10 says, 'For we are His workmanship, created in Christ Jesus for good works, that we should work in them.'

This is saying that Jesus made each one of us with a unique and distinct personality and wired and equipped each of us differently for a specific assignment before he released us into this earth realm to discover and fulfil that assignment. Anything else one pursues and even accomplishes on this earth apart from this God-ordained assignment will not bring fulfilment and satisfaction to the human soul.

Psalm 139:13–17

> For You formed my inward parts;
> You covered me in my mother's womb.

I will praise You, for I am fearfully and wonderfully
made;
Marvelous are Your works,
And that my soul knows very well.
My frame was not hidden from You,
When I was made in secret,
And skilfully wrought in the lowest parts of the earth.
Your eyes saw my substance, being yet unformed.
And in Your book they all were written,
The days fashioned for me,
When as yet there were none of them.
How precious also are Your thoughts to me, O God!
How great is the sum of them!

This psalm is a great eye-opener about the great care God took in fashioning each of us in the secrets of our mothers' wombs and wrote each one's life assignment in their personal individual book for us to discover and fulfil on earth. For some, their gifts and talents, and hence their life's assignment, are obvious, but for others, this may take some searching and prayers to discover, but discover they will if they invest the time to wait and pray. There is nothing more life enhancing and exhilarating than discovering and living your dream. It is like getting paid on your favourite holiday or for a hobby. This would be our individual contribution to his great purpose and plan for the earth and the peoples thereof.

I AM THE ALPHA AND THE OMEGA

Revelation 1:8 declares, "'I am the Alpha and the Omega, the Beginning and the End," says the Lord, "who is and who was and who is to come, the Almighty.'" The apostle John was on the island of Patmos, the Island of Death, but Jesus reached him there and gave him an awesome revelation contained in the book of Revelation. By this, he is saying, 'There is nowhere you can be that I cannot reach you.' No matter where you are in your life today, understand that

God can reach you. Psalm 139:7–12 declares that there is nowhere in the cosmos that you can hide from his presence because he is omnipresent. Not even death removes you from his all-pervading reach. Also he will want you to understand that there is nothing happening to you that is outside his power and reach to deliver you, according to Isaiah 59:1.

> Behold, the LORD's hand is not shortened,
> That it cannot save;
> Nor His ear heavy,
> That it cannot hear.

There is no person strong enough in the universe to hold you that He cannot deliver you from, according to Isaiah 49:24–26.

> Shall the prey be taken from the mighty,
> Or the captives of the righteous be delivered?
>
> But thus says the LORD:
>
> 'Even the captives of the mighty shall be taken away,
> And the prey of the terrible be delivered;
> For I will contend with him who contends with you,
> And I will save your children.
> I will feed those who oppress you with their own flesh,
> And they shall be drunk with their own blood as with sweet wine.
> All flesh shall know
> That I, the LORD, am your Savior,
> And your Redeemer, the Mighty One of Jacob.'

No circumstance of your life is too complex for him to resolve, and he asks, in Genesis 18:14, 'Is anything too hard for Me?'

'I am the Alpha and the Omega, the First and the Last. No matter the chapter of your life playing right now, your life cannot end without me having the last word. I write the last chapter of your life. Whatever I purposed for your life in eternity, before you were conceived, I am here to guarantee it, if you will let me. Do not fear the future because I am able to make it all work according to my original plan for your life.' Jesus is the future. He is the friend that jumped into the pit to rescue the trapped; the fourth man in the fiery furnace to quench the fires against Meshach, Shadrach, and Abednego; the angel that muzzled the lions' mouths so they could not hurt Daniel; and the pillar of fire and of cloud that followed the children of Israel in their wilderness journey. He is the salvage expert extraordinaire. When you need him, your God will appear with healing in his wings, to wipe away every tear, to restore whatever was eaten, broken, destroyed, or lost, and to make you complete in him.

IN THE LIGHT OF THIS WONDERFUL TRUTH, WHY DO SOME PEOPLE NOT WANT TO COME TO CHRIST?

According to 2 Corinthians 4:4, Satan, the god of this world, has blinded the minds of some people to believe wrong things about Jesus and his saving mission for mankind.

This calls for prayer by Christians to break the power of these deceiving agents of Satan off the minds of unbelievers to enable the light and truth of the gospel of grace to have access to their minds. If you want unbelieving relatives or friends saved, it is not just trying to reason with them or persuade them but tell them the truth of the gospel and back it with prayer. Continue praying till they give their lives to Jesus.

2 Corinthians 4:3–4

But even if our gospel is veiled, it is veiled to those who are perishing, whose minds the god of this age has blinded, who do not believe, lest the light of the

> gospel of the glory of Christ, who is the image of God,
> should shine on them.

Others may not want to come to Jesus because, according to John 3:19, 'Men loved darkness because their deeds were evil.'

Simply put, they love their sinful ways and sinful habits and sinful lifestyles. They know that a commitment to Jesus might require that they cease from certain habits and lifestyles, but they are not prepared to make that trade-off. This is also a satanic deception to believe that commitment to Christ would mean a loss on their part, not realising that it is freedom to make life enhancing choices, freedom to say no to the things that will ultimately harm you and bring you to tears. The Bible says the thief does not come except to steal, to kill, and to destroy. He will steal your peace, kill your destiny, and ultimately destroy your soul in hell.

1 Corinthians 1:18 says, 'For the message of the cross is foolishness to those who are perishing, but to us who are being saved it is the power of God.'

The devil in his deceptive schemes makes God's generous offer of forgiveness all seem like foolishness to unbelieving men and women.

But Romans 1:16 says the gospel of Christ is 'the power of God unto salvation to everyone who believes'. Our task is to tell people about the love and saving grace of Jesus and back it with prayer, and the Bible says, God will do the saving of souls.

INSTEAD

When it comes to the person of Jesus, many people, instead of finding out the truth for themselves, only believe and regurgitate what they have heard from others. But on 'the question of Jesus', God wants everyone to speak for themselves alone. In Matthew 16:13–16, we have this episode between Jesus and his disciples:

When Jesus came into the region of Caesarea Philippi, he asked his disciples, saying, 'Who do men say that I, the Son of Man, am?'

So they said, 'Some say John the Baptist, some Elijah, and others Jeremiah or one of the prophets.'

He said to them, 'But who do you say that I am?'

Simon Peter answered and said, 'You are the Christ, the Son of the living God.'

You see, it was not enough for the disciples to say what others said about Jesus. He brought the question down to every individual. Yes, others may say what they think and know, and they may be right or wrong, but who do you say Jesus is? This is the central question everyone has to answer for themselves in this life. How you answer this question and what you do with that answer will determine the eternity that awaits you. Is he Christ, the Son of the Living God to you, the only one you are trusting for your salvation, or just a mere historical figure, perhaps even a great prophet and a miracle worker?

In his interrogation, Pilate asked him, 'What have you done?' not realising that Jesus did not come into the world because of what he had done but rather because of what *we* have done. That is why in the end, Pilate had to concede. 'I find no fault in Him at all.' No wonder the apostle Paul said in 2 Timothy:12, 'For this reason I also suffer these things; nevertheless I am not ashamed, for I know whom I have believed and am persuaded that He is able to keep what I have committed to Him until that Day.'

If you have already believed in him, do you really know him? How sure are you that he is the one? We all need role models, godly examples, and trailblazers to look up to, but Jesus is the only perfect role model for men, women, husbands, wives, leaders, fathers, sons, daughters, teachers, ministers, and simply human beings (Rom. 5:14–15). According to Hebrews1:1, Jesus is God's final Word to us. God spoke His final Word to man through his Son, Jesus Christ. He was and is the very image of the Father, according to Hebrews 1:3.

> Who being the brightness of His glory and the express image of His person, and upholding all things by the word of His power, when He had by Himself purged

our sins, sat down at the right hand of the Majesty on high.

Jesus represents God in every respect. He is fully God and fully man, one of a kind in the universe. He came down to us because we could not go up to him. Colossians 1:15–16, 19 says,

> He is the image of the invisible God, the firstborn over all creation. For by Him all things were created that are in heaven and that are on earth, visible and invisible, whether thrones or dominions or principalities or powers. All things were created through Him and for Him.

> For it pleased the Father that in Him all the fullness should dwell, and by Him to reconcile all things to Himself, by Him, whether things on earth or things in heaven, having made peace through the blood of His cross.

1 Timothy 1:17 puts it beautifully,

> Now to the King eternal, immortal, invisible, to God who alone is wise, be honor and glory forever and ever. Amen.

When Pilate replied, 'You are a king then,' he did not deny it but replied, 'You say rightly that I am a King, for this cause I was born, and for this cause I came into the world to show you what a king is like, and, which standard you have lost, and to restore your lost dominion on earth. All of you are supposed to be kings like Me.' That is why he is the King of kings and the Lord of lords.

WHOEVER BELIEVES IN HIM

Whoever believes in him shall not perish but have eternal life. People are encouraged in today's world to believe in themselves. There is nothing wrong to have the right estimation of yourself, but there is a limit beyond which this cannot be taken. Self-reliance, DIY, and all such philosophies have their rightful place to a limit. Do not believe in yourself because you cannot save yourself; neither can others. But when it comes to your eternal destiny, you need someone who knows what lies yonder, beyond the veil, that is Jesus Christ. But one might ask, why in him? Don't all roads lead to heaven? Can all roads lead to heaven, really, seeing they are headed in different directions and often have conflicting and contradictory messages? How could the same God give contradictory messages often on the same issue? Who is he trying to deceive? What about Islam, Hinduism, Buddhism, humanism, and all the rest of them? Doesn't salvation come in different forms and in many ways? But Jesus says no, they don't. Salvation is not found in them but in him alone. With Jesus, we bring nothing to the table because our morality, our good works, and our charitable endeavours count for nothing. All other religions say you can save you by being a good person, but Jesus says, 'It does not work that way at all. Only My death on the cross saves you.' This is beautifully espoused in Acts 2:12.

> Nor is there salvation in any other, for there is no other name under heaven given among men by which we must be saved.

Jesus himself declared in John 14:6,

> Jesus said to him, 'I am the way, the truth, and the life. No one comes to the Father except through Me.'

Apart from Jesus, there is no access to the Father. He is the only authorised dealer in town when it comes to our salvation.

When we come to Jesus, Romans 4:5 says, 'To the one who does not work, but believes in Him who justifies the ungodly, his faith is credited as righteousness. Salvation is not worked for, but received by faith alone.'

In John 10:28, he says, 'I give them eternal life, and they shall never perish, no one can snatch them out of my hands.' As children of God, no one can take us out of his hands. We may be disciplined or chastised, but we are now family with him, according to Romans 8:15–17.

> For you did not receive the spirit of bondage again to fear, but you received the Spirit of adoption by whom we cry out, 'Abba, Father.' The Spirit Himself bears witness with our spirit that we are children of God, and if children, then heirs—heirs of God and joint heirs with Christ, if indeed we suffer with Him, that we may also be glorified together.

We have his DNA and are eternally connected by blood and sealed and secured in him with the Holy Spirit.

It is no longer waiting for salvation based on his decision on the Judgment Day, based on our conduct. Or doing more good deeds and earning our way to heaven that way as Islam and other work-based religions teach.

JESUS IS NOT ASHAMED OF ANYONE WHO COMES TO HIM

He declared in Hebrews 11:16; John 6:37; and Matthew 11:28 that all are welcome to him and that he is not ashamed to be associated with any of us no matter our reputation and history.

> But now they desire a better, that is, a heavenly country. Therefore God is not ashamed to be called their God, for He has prepared a city for them.

All that the Father gives Me will come to Me, and the one who comes to Me I will by no means cast out.

Come to Me, all you who labor and are heavy laden, and I will give you rest.

As if to demonstrate his readiness to accept the lowest of the low and the meanest of the mean, he chose to enter the world as a baby via a young and simple country girl, even 'fatherless' (with the stigma that entailed in ancient Jewish culture), and chose to be born in a manger, the feeding trough of lowly sheep. Amongst his maternal lineage was an adulterer, a prostitute, an idol worshipper, and one that had the double dishonour of having a baby by her father-in-law. He begged for a drop of water to quench his thirst in his final moments on the cross and was buried in a borrowed tomb. And yet he owns the whole universe. What manner of man is this Jesus! He understands where each one of us is coming from. He did all these to make a statement: 'You are all welcome. I have been where you are before. I understand what you are going through because I have had a firsthand experience of your situation.' That is why he is able to save to the uttermost those who come to God through him.

He has factored your special circumstance in, so do not count yourself out.

CHRIST, OUR HOPE OF GLORY

Our study will be based on the following key Bible references in our attempt to understand the hope that we have as believers in the person and redemptive career of the Lord Jesus Christ: Luke 1:46–56; John 1:14; 2 Kings 20:3; and Hebrews 2:11.

We have a God who came down to our level, who took our humanity upon himself at a time that it was not popular to be human, to be born as a child, and to live with us in the 'occupied neighbourhood'. In today's language, he lived with us in the projects or on a housing estate. Our God is the personally knowable God. The Christian God came and lived right in the midst of his people, reminiscent of the Garden of Eden where he often visited Adam and Eve in the cool of the day. According to Romans 8:3,

> For what the law could not do in that it was weak
> through the flesh, God did by sending His own Son
> in the likeness of sinful flesh, on account of sin: He
> condemned sin in the flesh.

Some religions serve a vindictive God they cannot see, they do not know, who does not speak to them, and of whom they are certainly scared, as was the case with the gods of Ancient Greece in Acts 17:22–23.

Then Paul stood in the midst of the Areopagus and said, 'Men of Athens, I perceive that in all things you are very religious; for as I was passing through and considering the objects of your worship, I even found an altar with this inscription.'

TO THE UNKNOWN GOD

Therefore, the One whom you worship without knowing, Him I proclaim to you.

Our God became flesh and dwelt with us and in us. He loved all people but had special compassion for the poor and weak and the outcasts in society. Poor could also mean having a humble and teachable spirit, ready to admit your need for his saving grace. He was approachable, and today, all can come to him in simple repentance without any complicated formalities whatsoever.

He came to cancel your debt, deserved or undeserved, and offered forgiveness to all who respond to his invitation. His mercy is on those who fear him, according to Colossians 2:13.

And you, being dead in your trespasses and the uncircumcision of your flesh, He has made alive together with Him, having forgiven you all trespasses.

He offered a fresh start to everyone who comes to him to begin again on a fresh sheet of paper to write their life's story afresh.

2 Corinthians 5:17, 21

Therefore, if anyone is in Christ, he is a new creation; old things have passed away; behold, all things have become new.

For He made Him who knew no sin to be sin for us, that we might become the righteousness of God in Him.

Romans 8:1–4 (NIV)

Therefore, there is now no condemnation for those who are in Christ Jesus, because through Christ Jesus the law of the Spirit who gives life has set you free from the law of sin and death. For what the law was powerless to do because it was weakened by the flesh, God did by sending his own Son in the likeness of sinful flesh to be a sin offering. And so he condemned sin in the flesh, in order that the righteous requirement of the law might be fully met in us, who do not live according to the flesh but according to the Spirit.

His offer of a pardon and forgiveness is total and unconditional to all who come with a penitent heart to him. Do not believe the lies of the accuser of the brethren who would like you to look over your shoulder every second, thinking God is looking for the opportunity to clobber you every second.

Psalm 103:1–3

Bless the LORD, O my soul; And all that is within me, bless His holy name!
Bless the LORD, O my soul, And forget not all His benefits:
Who forgives all your iniquities, Who heals all your diseases.

The psalmist declares above that God's forgiveness is total and complete, and it is freely given to us but on his account.

John 8:10–11

> When Jesus had raised Himself up and saw no one but the woman, He said to her, 'Woman, where are those accusers of yours? Has no one condemned you?'
>
> She said, 'No one, Lord.'
>
> And Jesus said to her, 'Neither do I condemn you; go and sin no more.'

'Do not be afraid, Mary, you have found favour with God.' He came to be a friend to the poor and the underdog, the vulnerable and the disadvantaged, the sick and the invalid, and all who are humble enough to come to him and fall into his mighty arms for refuge. He declares to all, 'Call on me, and I will answer you,' according to Romans 10:11–13.

> For the Scripture says, 'Whoever believes on Him will not be put to shame.' For there is no distinction between Jew and Greek, for the same Lord over all is rich to all who call upon Him. For whoever calls on the name of the LORD shall be saved.

He is Emmanuel, God with us. He reconnected with us after our sin separated us from him. He did not wait for us to get right, because that would never have happened. He knew we could not come to him, so He came to us, in person. When Harold, the Edomite king, was troubled, all Israel was troubled with him. He has scattered the proud in the imagination of their hearts. Some vindictive gods mete out the cruellest of punishments to their devotees. Our God is not only merciful and compassionate but also caring and forgiving, not once or twice but as many times as we may need his forgiveness. This is so because unlike other gods, he is not angry at his children, but he is loving, kind, and forgiving. He came to be with us so that he will experience what we experience and understand our plight. He literally put his feet in our shoes. As if it was not enough to be for us and be with us, he decided to complete the circle by being in us so he can experience us firsthand.

It is only the proud, the rich, the self-confident, the self-reliant, the self-made, the independent, the humanly noble, and the powerful that he casts away. But once you renounce self and come poor and needy, he has made provision for you at his banqueting table.

Hebrews 2:11

> For both He who sanctifies and those who are being sanctified are all of one, for which reason He is not ashamed to call them brethren.

And wretched as we are, he is still proud to be associated with us and share his inheritance and kingdom with us, calling us his brothers.

He is a God that remembers. When he pronounced in the Garden of Eden all those primal years ago that the seed of the woman would crush the head of the serpent, it seemed nothing was happening for a long time. But he remembers. He never forgets. He did not forget his promise to Adam and Eve and their generations. Neither will he forget his promise to you; even though it tarries, wait for it, it will not tarry (forever). In 2 Kings 20, King Hezekiah prayed to God to remember; he sure did remember the good the king had done over the years.

> Then he turned his face toward the wall, and prayed to the LORD, saying, 'Remember now, O LORD, I pray, how I have walked before You in truth and with a loyal heart, and have done what was good in Your sight.' And Hezekiah wept bitterly.

And it happened, before Isaiah had gone out into the middle court, that the word of the LORD came to him, saying, 'Return and tell Hezekiah the leader of My people, "Thus says the LORD, the God of David your father: 'I have heard your prayer, I have seen your tears; surely I will heal you. On the third day you shall go up to the house of the LORD. And I will add to your days fifteen years. I will deliver you and this city from the hand of the king of Assyria; and I will defend this city for My own sake, and for the sake of My servant David.'"'

He is a God that remembers because he neither sleeps nor slumbers. He extended Hezekiah's life fifteen more years. Is it your vision that seems dead and buried? Let me assure you, God's vision for your life never dies. It may be buried and even forgotten, but never dead. Yours will come back to life, as I have discovered mine in my twilight years. Yours will blossom again, and no matter how dry they may be, your dry bones will come back to life with his resurrection life. If he has to reverse your biological clock like Abraham and Sarah, well, he has done it before, so we can count on him to do it again so that you can give birth to your life dream, whatever it happens to be.

Exodus 2:23–25

Now it happened in the process of time that the king of Egypt died. Then the children of Israel groaned because of the bondage, and they cried out; and their cry came up to God because of the bondage. So God heard their groaning, and God remembered His covenant with Abraham, with Isaac, and with Jacob. And God looked upon the children of Israel, and God acknowledged them.

Israel had no hope of coming out of Egyptian slavery, and I believe many of them had given up hope of ever being free, but the God of their fathers remembered them in their hour of need. This is written to reassure you that he never forgets, not even you, because you are his dearly beloved.

Just don't give up, give in, or give out. Just be steadfast and unmoving in your resolve, as we are all advised in 1 Corinthians 15:58.

> Therefore, my beloved brethren, be steadfast, immovable, always abounding in the work of the Lord, knowing that your labor is not in vain in the Lord.

He did not plan for you *because* you got here; he planned for you *before* you got here. What he recorded about your life in your book before you got here is more powerful than any obstacles in your environment, be they human, physical, or demonic.

KEEP YOUR EYES ON JESUS AT ALL TIMES

It is important not to base your Christian walk on someone's experience because we are all fallible and have the potential to disappoint. He preached on marriage, but his marriage failed! What will you do? Or his children are into all kinds of illicit lifestyles. He was a great preacher and teacher on integrity but was jailed for financial embezzlement. Because these things do happen in life, it is important that we all keep our gaze on the Lord Jesus Christ, the only Perfect Man to walk the earth. Oh yeah, we are free to learn and even imitate godly things we observe about other believers, mentors, and leaders, as Paul once rightly said, 'Follow me as I follow Christ.'

Even a great man of God like Moses failed God and was not allowed to enter the Promised Land, according to Hebrews 12:2; 1 Corinthians 10:1–7; Exodus 17:1–6; and Numbers 20:11–12.

> Looking unto Jesus, the author and finisher of our faith, who for the joy that was set before Him endured

the cross, despising the shame, and has sat down at the right hand of the throne of God.

Moreover, brethren, I do not want you to be unaware that all our fathers were under the cloud, all passed through the sea, all were baptized into Moses in the cloud and in the sea, all ate the same spiritual food, and all drank the same spiritual drink. For they drank of that spiritual Rock that followed them, and that Rock was Christ. But with most of them God was not well pleased, for their bodies were scattered in the wilderness.

Now these things became our examples, to the intent that we should not lust after evil things as they also lusted. And do not become idolaters as were some of them. As it is written, 'The people sat down to eat and drink, and rose up to play.'

Then Moses lifted his hand and struck the rock twice with his rod; and water came out abundantly, and the congregation and their animals drank.

Then the LORD spoke to Moses and Aaron, 'Because you did not believe Me, to hallow Me in the eyes of the children of Israel, therefore you shall not bring this assembly into the land which I have given them.'

Moses was not allowed to enter the Promised Land because he got angry with the people and disobeyed God, striking the rock twice when God had asked him to speak to the rock. You see, that rock is Jesus, and Jesus was to suffer (be struck) once, thus he misrepresented God and our salvation and redemption. This is why it was such a big deal with God. If you have noticed at all, God is very exact with his word and instructions. God expects us to obey with exactitude and precision. A lot of Christians have the deceptive notion that God will overlook certain failures and maybe what they regard as little sins and failures. Please be warned that God cannot let you into his presence in heaven if you do not fully avail yourself with his provision for your redemption. He is not asking for perfection, but we cannot be presumptuous and overlook issues we very well know he wants us to deal with.

That is why our gaze should be on the Lord alone as our example and model, according to 2 Corinthians 3:18.

> But we all, with unveiled face, beholding as in a mirror the glory of the Lord, are being transformed into the same image from glory to glory, just as by the Spirit of the Lord.

As he instructed Joshua at the beginning of his ministry, you have to be strong and of good courage to serve God, especially in these crucial times we live in. It is going to take *sheer grit* to obey God and not be a people pleaser. Our preaching can no longer be intellectual suggestions and 'take it if you feel comfortable with it'. That is not the gospel of Christ. God gives commands and prohibitions. We have to be bold in our declarations and proclamations if we want to change this world and people's lives. We have to meditate in the Word if we want to experience its life-transforming power.

Jesus told Martha, who was burdened with many good but peripheral things, that 'one thing is needful', and Mary has chosen that. That needful one thing is waiting in the presence of the Lord and spending time in his Word. That one thing is even more needful today as the end of the age approaches. It is only by meditation that we are going to transform our head knowledge and information into revelation and his power.

We are told to meditate on three things in the scripture, which are the following:

The Word of God: It is meditation in the Word of God that brings the blessing and prosperity and fruitfulness into our lives. It is also what gives the power of consecration to stay away from the world in their fleshly pursuits. If we do not meditate in the Word, the fear to please man will draw us like magnetic cobwebs into their counsel and dilute our profession.

According to Psalm 1:1–3,

> Blessed is the man Who walks not in the counsel of the ungodly,
> Nor stands in the path of sinners, Nor sits in the seat of the scornful;
> But his delight is in the law of the LORD, And in His law he meditates day and night.
> He shall be like a tree. Planted by the rivers of water, That brings forth its fruit in its season, Whose leaf also shall not wither;
> And whatever he does shall prosper.

This meditation is to be day and night as God instructed Joshua at the beginning of his daunting ministry, following on the heels of Moses.

The person of Jesus Christ: We are to meditate on God, his character, his nature, his goodness, his love, and his compassion, according to Psalm 63:6.

> When I remember You on my bed, I meditate on You in the night watches.

Things of a good report, according to Philippians 4:8

> Finally, brethren, whatever things are true, whatever things are noble, whatever things are just, whatever things are pure, whatever things are lovely, whatever things are of good report, if there is any virtue and if there is anything praiseworthy—meditate on these things.

Meditation on his Word is what will bring his promised blessing to the believer, according to Psalm 92:12–14; Jeremiah 17:7–8; and Psalm 37:4.

> The righteous shall flourish like a palm tree, He shall grow like a cedar in Lebanon. Those who are planted in the house of the LORD

> Shall flourish in the courts of our God. They shall still bear fruit in old age;

> They shall be fresh and flourishing.

> Blessed is the man who trusts in the LORD, And whose hope is the LORD.

> For he shall be like a tree planted by the waters, Which spreads out its roots by the river, And will not fear when heat comes; But its leaf will be green,

> And will not be anxious in the year of drought, Nor will cease from yielding fruit.

> Delight yourself also in the LORD, And He shall give you the desires of your heart.

When we meditate in his Word, he watches upon his Word to perform it. He exalts his Word and makes it living and active and a sharp sword in our mouth. His Word that is faithful, sure, powerful, and settled in heaven begins to come to pass on earth, bringing the atmosphere of heaven to the earth. When we meditate on the Word, we begin to see and experience his person, in his majesty, glory, beauty, love, and fatherly compassion.

Look unto Jesus!

BEHOLD THE LAMB OF GOD WHO TAKES AWAY THE SIN OF THE WORLD

Our key scriptures on this topic will include John 1:29 and Revelation 5:6, 12, 13.

> And I looked, and behold in the midst of the throne and of the four living creatures, and in the midst of the elders, stood a Lamb as though it had been slain, having seven horns and seven eyes, which are the seven Spirits of God sent out into all the earth.
>
> Saying with a loud voice: 'Worthy is the Lamb who was slain to receive power and riches and wisdom, And strength and honor and glory and blessing!'
>
> And every creature which is in heaven and on the earth and under the earth and such as are in the sea, and all that are in them, I heard saying:
>
> 'Blessing and honor and glory and power Be to Him who sits on the throne, And to the Lamb, forever and ever!'

God's eternal purpose is wholly centred in the person of the Lord Jesus Christ. We can only access God's purpose and be involved in it through the Lord Jesus. Jesus himself is God's eternal purpose, and apart from him, God has no eternal purpose. God's purpose is not in the plural 'purposes' but in the singular 'purpose' because God has only one purpose, and that purpose is centred in the person of Jesus Christ. It is all 'in him', 'in Christ', as highlighted in the lofty book of Ephesians.

See it all in Christ in Ephesians 1:1–13.

Paul, an apostle of Jesus Christ by the will of God,

To the saints who are in Ephesus, and faithful in Christ Jesus:

Grace to you and peace from God our Father and the Lord Jesus Christ.

Redemption in Christ

Blessed be the God and Father of our Lord Jesus Christ, who has blessed us with every spiritual blessing in the heavenly places in Christ, just as He chose us in Him before the foundation of the world, that we should be holy and without blame before Him in love, having predestined us to adoption as sons by Jesus Christ to Himself, according to the good pleasure of His will, to the praise of the glory of His grace, by which He made us accepted in the Beloved.

In Him we have redemption through His blood, the forgiveness of sins, according to the riches of His grace which He made to abound toward us in all wisdom and prudence, having made known to us the mystery of His will, according to His good pleasure which He purposed in Himself, that in the dispensation of the fullness of the times He might gather together in one all things in Christ, both which are in heaven and which are on earth—in Him. In Him also we have obtained an inheritance, being predestined according to the purpose of Him who works all things according to the counsel of His will, that we who first trusted in Christ should be to the praise of His glory.

In Him you also trusted, after you heard the word of truth, the gospel of your salvation; in whom also, having believed, you were sealed with the Holy Spirit of promise.

This is taken up in Ephesians 2:4–13, 18.

But God, who is rich in mercy, because of His great love with which He loved us, even when we were dead in trespasses, made us alive together with Christ (by grace you have been saved), and raised us up together, and made us sit together in the heavenly places in Christ Jesus, that in the ages to come He might show the exceeding riches of His grace in His kindness toward us in Christ Jesus. For by grace you have been saved through faith, and that not of yourselves; it is the gift of God, not of works, lest anyone should boast. For we are His workmanship, created in Christ Jesus for good works, which God prepared beforehand that we should walk in them.

Brought Near by His Blood

Therefore remember that you, once Gentiles in the flesh—who are called Uncircumcision by what is called the Circumcision made in the flesh by hands— that at that time you were without Christ, being aliens from the commonwealth of Israel and strangers from the covenants of promise, having no hope and without God in the world. But now in Christ Jesus you who once were far off have been brought near by the blood of Christ.

For through Him we both have access by one Spirit to the Father.

It is all 'in him' and in Christ alone; our whole salvation, all the blessings, the supply of all our needs, the fullness of God, eternal life, healing, and deliverance, and our completeness are all 'in him'. The following are additional 'in him scriptures' worth perusing: Colossians 1:18–19; 2:9; 3:3–4; Ephesians 4:15–16; 2 Timothy 2:10; Philippians 4:19; and 1 Corinthians 12:12.

In John 14:6, it says,

Jesus said to him, 'I am the way, the truth, and the life. No one comes to the Father except through Me.'

In 1 John 5:10–13, God declares that his whole salvation package is centred in the person of his Son and that whoever rejects the Son has no portion in him.

He who believes in the Son of God has the witness in himself; he who does not believe God has made Him a liar, because he has not believed the testimony that God has given of His Son. And this is the testimony: that God has given us eternal life, and this life is in His Son. He who has the Son has life; he who does not have the Son of God does not have life. These things I have written to you who believe in the name of the Son of God, that you may know that you have eternal life, and that you may continue to believe in the name of the Son of God.

God the Father can only be known and experienced in and through his Son. No Son, no access to God. This was the object lesson the Lord was trying to teach his disciples in John 14:7–11 below.

'If you had known Me, you would have known My Father also; and from now on you know Him and have seen Him.'

Philip said to Him, 'Lord, show us the Father, and it is sufficient for us.'

Jesus said to him, 'Have I been with you so long, and yet you have not known Me, Philip? He who has seen Me has seen the Father; so how can you say, "Show us the Father"? Do you not believe that I am in the Father, and the Father in Me? The words that I speak to you I do not speak on My own authority; but the Father who dwells in Me does the works. Believe Me that I am in the Father and the Father in Me, or else believe Me for the sake of the works themselves.'

And the whole canon of scripture is to reveal Christ in his person, his deity, and his redemption career. The end purpose of studying the scriptures is to get to know Jesus. Everything else is tangential or secondary. That is why any preaching or teaching, though from the Bible, that does not have Christ at its centre and focus becomes a motivational speech at best and potentially deceptive.

Jesus, through his substitutionary sacrifice, provided complete atonement for mankind to be received by grace through faith alone. Unlike the Old Testament, animal sacrifices, where the blood of those animals only covered the sin of the worshipper temporarily, the blood of Jesus takes man's sin away completely, once and for all. That is why it did not have to be repeated.

This is the chief theme of the book of Hebrews.

Hebrews 9:11–14, 17; 10:12–14

> But Christ came as High Priest of the good things to come, with the greater and more perfect tabernacle not made with hands, that is, not of this creation. Not with the blood of goats and calves, but with His own blood He entered the Most Holy Place once for all, having obtained eternal redemption. For if the blood of bulls and goats and the ashes of a heifer, sprinkling the unclean, sanctifies for the purifying of the flesh, how much more shall the blood of Christ, who through the eternal Spirit offered Himself without spot to God, cleanse your conscience from dead works to serve the living God?

> For a testament is in force after men are dead, since it has no power at all while the testator lives.

> But this Man, after He had offered one sacrifice for sins forever, sat down at the right hand of God, from that time waiting till His enemies are made His footstool. For by one offering He has perfected forever those who are being sanctified.

So Jesus, through the offer of his perfect sinless life and blood, provided the means not only for our sin to be forgiven but also for us to be perfected in the sight of God. His was the perfect redemption providing atonement for the whole man, spirit, soul, and body.

SO WHAT ABOUT MARY, THE MOTHER OF JESUS?

Mary was a virgin when she conceived Jesus by the Holy Spirit and never knew a man until after the birth of Jesus. That is why the Bible attests to the virgin birth. The following scriptures attest to the virgin birth:

Matthew 1:16, 18–23

And Jacob begot Joseph the husband of Mary, of whom was born Jesus who is called Christ.

Now the birth of Jesus Christ was as follows: After His mother Mary was betrothed to Joseph, before they came together, she was found with child of the Holy Spirit. Then Joseph her husband, being a just man, and not wanting to make her a public example, was minded to put her away secretly. But while he thought about these things, behold, an angel of the Lord appeared to him in a dream, saying, 'Joseph, son of David, do not be afraid to take to you Mary your wife, for that which is conceived in her is of the Holy Spirit. And she will bring forth a Son, and you shall call His name JESUS, for He will save His people from their sins.'

So all this was done that it might be fulfilled which was spoken by the Lord through the prophet, saying: 'Behold, the virgin shall be with child, and bear a Son, and they shall call His name Immanuel,' which is translated, 'God with us.'

Luke 1:27, 34, 35

To a virgin betrothed to a man whose name was Joseph, of the house of David. The virgin's name was Mary.

Then Mary said to the angel, 'How can this be, since I do not know a man?'

And the angel answered and said to her, 'The Holy Spirit will come upon you, and the power of the Highest will overshadow you; therefore, also, that Holy One who is to be born will be called the Son of God.'

Mary was no more a virgin after giving birth to Jesus. She went on to have normal marital relationship with her husband, Joseph, according to Matthew 1:18, 25.

Now the birth of Jesus Christ was as follows: After His mother Mary was betrothed to Joseph, before they came together, she was found with child of the Holy Spirit.

And did not know her till she had brought forth her firstborn Son. And he called His name JESUS.

Mary and Joseph actually got married and became husband and wife, according to Matthew 1:19–24.

Then Joseph her husband, being a just man, and not wanting to make her a public example, was minded to put her away secretly. But while he thought about these things, behold, an angel of the Lord appeared to him in a dream, saying, 'Joseph, son of David, do not be afraid to take to you Mary your wife, for that which is conceived in her is of the Holy Spirit. And she will bring forth a Son, and you shall call His name JESUS, for He will save His people from their sins.'

So all this was done that it might be fulfilled which was spoken by the Lord through the prophet, saying: 'Behold, the virgin shall be with child, and bear a

Son, and they shall call His name Immanuel,' which is translated, 'God with us.'

Then Joseph, being aroused from sleep, did as the angel of the Lord commanded him and took to him his wife.

Joseph and Mary actually went on to have more children, at least five sons and two daughters. They were a large family, according to Matthew 12:46–47; John 7:3; Mark 6:3; and Jude 1. Matthew 13:55 reports thus,

Is this not the carpenter's son? Is not His mother called Mary? And His brothers James, Joses, Simon, and Judas? And His sisters, are they not all with us? Where then did this Man get all these things.

'Is this not the carpenter, the Son of Mary, and brother of James, Joses, Judas, and Simon? And are not His sisters here with us?' So they were offended at Him.

While He was still talking to the multitudes, behold, His mother and brothers stood outside, seeking to speak with Him. Then one said to Him, 'Look, Your mother and Your brothers are standing outside, seeking to speak with You.'

Jesus never called Mary his mother. He did not want attention on her, according to Luke 2:48; 8:19–21; 11:27–28; John 2:4; 19:26.

Then His mother and brothers came to Him, and could not approach Him because of the crowd. And it was told Him by some, who said, 'Your mother and Your brothers are standing outside, desiring to see You.'

> But He answered and said to them, 'My mother and
> My brothers are these who hear the word of God and
> do it.'

Jesus was obedient to his parents at all times and was subject to them, according to Luke 2:51.

> Then He went down with them and came to Nazareth,
> and was subject to them, but His mother kept all these
> things in her heart.

Mary was blessed of God, according to Luke 1:28–30, 42, 48.

> And having come in, the angel said to her, 'Rejoice,
> highly favoured one, the Lord is with you; blessed are
> you among women!'

> But when she saw him, she was troubled at his saying,
> and considered what manner of greeting this was.
> Then the angel said to her, 'Do not be afraid, Mary,
> for you have found favor with God.'

> Then she spoke out with a loud voice and said,
> 'Blessed are you among women, and blessed is the
> fruit of your womb!'

> For He has regarded the lowly state of His maidservant;

> For behold, henceforth all generations will call me
> blessed.

So what about the Immaculate Conception?

The simple answer is that it is not in the Bible. Mary was a sinner just like any other human and needed a saviour like us all. In Luke 1:47, she declared, 'And my spirit has rejoiced in God my

Saviour.' She offered the sin offering on having her son, according to the Law of Moses in Luke 2:22–24, 27.

> Now when the days of her purification according to the law of Moses were completed, they brought Him to Jerusalem to present Him to the Lord (as it is written in the law of the Lord, 'Every male who opens the womb shall be called holy to the LORD'), and to offer a sacrifice according to what is said in the law of the Lord, 'A pair of turtledoves or two young pigeons.'

> So he came by the Spirit into the temple. And when the parents brought in the Child Jesus, to do for Him according to the custom of the law.

Leviticus 12:2–8

> Speak to the children of Israel, saying: 'If a woman has conceived, and borne a male child, then she shall be unclean seven days; as in the days of her customary impurity she shall be unclean. And on the eighth day the flesh of his foreskin shall be circumcised. She shall then continue in the blood of her purification thirty-three days. She shall not touch any hallowed thing, nor come into the sanctuary until the days of her purification are fulfilled.

> 'But if she bears a female child, then she shall be unclean two weeks, as in her customary impurity, and she shall continue in the blood of her purification sixty-six days.

> 'When the days of her purification are fulfilled, whether for a son or a daughter, she shall bring to the priest a lamb of the first year as a burnt offering, and

a young pigeon or a turtledove as a sin offering, to the door of the tabernacle of meeting. Then he shall offer it before the LORD, and make atonement for her. And she shall be clean from the flow of her blood. This is the law for her who has borne a male or a female.

'And if she is not able to bring a lamb, then she may bring two turtledoves or two young pigeons—one as a burnt offering and the other as a sin offering. So the priest shall make atonement for her, and she will be clean.'

If Mary was sinless, then her parents had to be sinless, and her parents' parents had to be sinless, and so on and on. By offering these sacrifices for her purification, Mary was acknowledging her sinfulness and her need for a saviour just like any human.

JESUS IS THE ONLY MEDIATOR BETWEEN GOD AND MAN

According to 1 Timothy 2:5–6,

For there is one God and one Mediator between God and men, the Man Christ Jesus, who gave Himself a ransom for all, to be testified in due time.

This is further reiterated in Hebrews 8:6; 12:24; John 14:6; and Acts 4:12.

But now He has obtained a more excellent ministry, inasmuch as He is also Mediator of a better covenant, which was established on better promises.

To Jesus the Mediator of the new covenant, and to the blood of sprinkling that speaks better things than that of Abel.

Jesus said to him, 'I am the way, the truth, and the life. No one comes to the Father except through Me.

'Nor is there salvation in any other, for there is no other name under heaven given among men by which we must be saved.'

It is not Jesus and Mary. He alone is our high priest and Prophet before the throne of God.

According to Hebrews 7:24–28, Jesus is our eternal high priest before God's throne, interceding for us.

But He, because He continues forever, has an unchangeable priesthood. Therefore He is also able to save to the uttermost those who come to God through Him, since He always lives to make intercession for them.

For such a High Priest was fitting for us, who is holy, harmless, undefiled, separate from sinners, and has become higher than the heavens; who does not need daily, as those high priests, to offer up sacrifices, first for His own sins and then for the people's, for this He did once for all when He offered up Himself. For the law appoints as high priests men who have weakness, but the word of the oath, which came after the law, appoints the Son who has been perfected forever.

It is worth noting that the cross is now empty, Jesus having provided a once-for-all salvation for mankind. He is no more on the cross, but he is seated at the right hand of the Father, denoting a place of absolute authority and rest from his work. This is highlighted in Hebrews 10:12; Colossians 3:1; Ephesians 1:20; and Psalm 110:1.

But this Man, after He had offered one sacrifice for sins forever, sat down at the right hand of God.

If then you were raised with Christ, seek those things which are above, where Christ is, sitting at the right hand of God.

Which He worked in Christ when He raised Him from the dead and seated Him at His right hand in the heavenly places.

The LORD said to my Lord,
'Sit at My right hand,
Till I make Your enemies Your footstool.'

The Bible does not teach that Jesus is still on the cross dying for our sins. He is not still on the cross providing salvation for mankind. He died once and for all and rose again from the dead, never to die again. He suffered once for our sins and is now exalted and glorified and seated in the place of supreme power and absolute authority. Anything you add to what Jesus has done will destroy it. Neither should anything be taken from it. According to Galatians 2:21; 5:4,

I do not set aside the grace of God; for if righteousness comes through the law, then Christ died in vain.

You have become estranged from Christ, you who attempt to be justified by law; you have fallen from grace.

We cannot repeat it enough that he has offered a once-for-all sacrifice for our sin, and it is now done, finished, and sealed. This is highlighted in the book of Hebrews 9:26–28; 10:10–14.

He then would have had to suffer often since the foundation of the world; but now, once at the end of the ages, He has appeared to put away sin by the sacrifice of Himself. And as it is appointed for men to die once, but after this the judgment, so Christ was offered once to bear the sins of many. To those who eagerly wait for Him He will appear a second time, apart from sin, for salvation.

By that will we have been sanctified through the offering of the body of Jesus Christ once for all.

Christ's Death Perfects the Sanctified

And every priest stands ministering daily and offering repeatedly the same sacrifices, which can never take away sins. But this Man, after He had offered one sacrifice for sins forever, sat down at the right hand of God, from that time waiting till His enemies are made His footstool. For by one offering He has perfected forever those who are being sanctified.

Jesus is still the lamb of God in heaven, according to Revelation 5:6, 9, 12, 13.

And I looked, and behold, in the midst of the throne and of the four living creatures, and in the midst of the elders, stood a Lamb as though it had been slain, having seven horns and seven eyes, which are the seven Spirits of God sent out into all the earth.

And they sang a new song, saying:

'You are worthy to take the scroll,
And to open its seals;
For You were slain,
And have redeemed us to God by Your blood

Out of every tribe and tongue and people and nation,
saying with a loud voice:
'Worthy is the Lamb who was slain
To receive power and riches and wisdom,
And strength and honor and glory and blessing!'

And every creature which is in heaven and on the
earth and under the earth and such as are in the sea,
and all that are in them, I heard saying:

'Blessing and honor and glory and power
Be to Him who sits on the throne,
And to the Lamb, forever and ever!'

He achieved his greatest exploit as the Lamb of God. It is in his humiliation that he received his greatest honour and exaltation. Jesus is remembered best as the sacrificial Lamb of God who gave his life as a ransom for mankind. Yes, he is a king in his own right. He is the Almighty Creator of the universe, the head of all principality and power, the owner and possessor of the heavens and the earth, to whom belong all authority in heaven and on earth, but it is in his humiliation and substitutionary role as the lamb of God that he received the highest honour. This is what puts him in a class of his own as the very definition of love, according to Romans 5:8 and John 15:13.

But God demonstrates His own love toward us, in that
while we were still sinners, Christ died for us.

Greater love has no one than this, than to lay down
one's life for his friends.

This is the greatest love story of all time. What Jesus did on the cross for mankind cannot and will never be repeated in the history of the universe.

This is what sets him apart from all pretenders.

Now, because we are in the very end of time, this message has taken on added significance. Jesus says to you, 'If you are in the wrong Church, come out of it.' This is the warning he gave his people in the harlot Babylonian church that will sweep the world during the tribulation period, but it has relevance for believers of all time, especially in these days of a plethora of Christian beliefs and churches of all shapes and colours.

Revelation 18:4

> And I heard another voice from heaven saying, 'Come out of her, my people, lest you share in her sins, and lest you receive of her plagues.'

HOW DO YOU GET TO KNOW CHRIST?

See the last chapter of this book under "How to Get Saved."

WHAT THINK YE OF CHRIST?

Our key scriptures for this topic would be Matthew 22:42 and 1 Timothy 3:16.

In Matthew 27:22, Pilate said to them, 'What then shall I do with Jesus who is called Christ?' This was his answer and question to the multitudes after they asked him to release Barabbas, the murderer to them. The multitudes responded, 'Let Him be crucified.' There is no ambiguity here, as they made their choice crystal clear. They chose the murderer over Jesus, whom the governor affirmed to be innocent of the false charges levied against him. In Matthew 16:13–16, Jesus asked the disciples who the people said he was.

> When Jesus came into the region of Caesarea Philippi,
> He asked His disciples, saying, 'Who do men say that
> I, the Son of Man, am?'
>
> So they said, 'Some say John the Baptist, some Elijah,
> and others Jeremiah or one of the prophets.'
>
> He said to them, 'But who do you say that I am?'
>
> Simon Peter answered and said, 'You are the Christ,
> the Son of the living God.'

The disciples responded by telling him what they had heard people say about him. It is good to hear what others say about Jesus. At the end of the day, that may be our only starting point in getting to hear about Jesus. Others may tell us all kinds of things about Jesus, and we are all commanded to tell others about him. However, whatever we hear others say about him should not be our final word. We need to make our own opinion about him for ourselves.

That is why after hearing the disciples recount what others say about him, Jesus went on to ask further, 'But who do you say that I am?' Because what you think and say about him personally is your personal individual million-dollar question you will have to answer for yourself one way or the other whilst you are alive in this world. Not making a decision is taken as a 'no' decision or a rejection of who he is and thus making God a liar. This is crucial because what you believe about Jesus will determine how you relate to him, which will in turn determine your eternal state or where and with whom you will spend all eternity.

In the story of Jesus and the Samaritan woman at the well, reported in the gospel of John chapter 4, the Bible reveals some interesting truths for our instruction. In John 4:29, 39–42,

> Come, see a Man who told me all things that I ever did. Could this be the Christ?
>
> And many of the Samaritans of that city believed in Him because of the word of the woman who testified, 'He told me all that I ever did.' So when the Samaritans had come to Him, they urged Him to stay with them; and He stayed there two days. And many more believed because of His own word.

Then they said to the woman, 'Now we believe, not because of what you said, for we ourselves have heard Him and we know that this is indeed the Christ, the Savior of the world.'

The witness that the woman bore about Jesus to her was a good starter as she reported pretty accurately her personal experience with Jesus, and the people pretty much believed her testimony of Jesus. But after they had had a personal, experiential knowledge of Jesus, they were now in a position to say, 'Now we know the truth about Jesus for ourselves. We have experienced him for ourselves. Your initial evidence was good for us, but now we have a personal experience of the man for ourselves, so now our faith in him is not just based on your hearsay, which may have been good as introductory information, but now we know better, based on our personal experience of the man.'

In Acts 17:11, God bears witness to the fair-minded attitude of the Berean Christians, because after hearing the truth about Jesus taught to them by Paul and his ministry team, which must have been as good as any that God has ever assembled in the entire history of the church, they received the Word with all readiness, but they went on to verify what they have been taught from the scriptures.

> These were more fair-minded than those in Thessalonica, in that they received the word with all readiness, and searched the Scriptures daily to find out whether these things were so.

God sees this experiential exploration of the truth about the person of Jesus as everyone's individual and personal responsibility they owe themselves. In the same way, God gave the story of the woman with a flow of blood for twelve years as another object lesson for believers for all time. In Mark 5:27, the Bible reports,

> When she heard about Jesus, she came behind Him in the crowd and touched His garment.

It was obvious that this woman was not going to stop at hearing about Jesus, good or bad as it may be. She needed to find out for herself to experience what she had heard for herself. And upon taking the necessary difficult steps, even at some risk to her life, she got to know the truth about all that she had heard, thus immortalising her place in the scriptures.

In Matthew 2:1–2, we read the immortalised story of the wise men from the east who heard about the birth of Jesus. Obviously, they were told about the birth of the new king by others who were, in turn, told by others. But they will not be content with hearing. They made the trip of several hundreds of miles, perhaps for several weeks and possibly months, to come and see the Messiah for themselves, and I guess they were not disappointed by their decision.

> Now after Jesus was born in Bethlehem of Judea in the days of Herod the king, behold, wise men from the East came to Jerusalem, saying, 'Where is He who has been born King of the Jews? For we have seen His star in the East and have come to worship Him.'

They were amongst the few of their day who had the opportunity to worship and bless the infant Messiah. I cannot begin to imagine what this gesture will mean to the Lord in his kingdom when these wise men crossed over to meet him in eternity.

Of course, King Herod had also sought to go and see him but with a murderous intent, and God made sure he did not live long enough to realise his desire.

How does the world see Jesus?

To most of the world, Jesus is another founder and leader of a religious movement just like Mohammad, the prophet of Islam, or Rev Moon or Buddha or one of the old Hebrew prophets like Elijah who had come back to life.

Many see him as a prophet of God amongst other prophets such as Adam, Abraham, Moses, David, and Mohammed.

To others, he was a great teacher and thinker like Plato, Socrates, and the Greek philosophers of old.

To others, he was a freedom fighter seeking the freedom of the oppressed like Mahatma Gandhi or even Pres. Nelson Mandela of recent memory.

He was a teacher and a healer, a worker of miracles.

But what does the Bible say about him?

The Bible declares that Jesus Christ is the eternal Son of God, according to Romans 1:3–4. In addition to that, his humanity was of the seed of David.

> Concerning His Son Jesus Christ our Lord, who was born of the seed of David according to the flesh, and declared to be the Son of God with power according to the Spirit of holiness, by the resurrection from the dead.

That he was born of a virgin, according to Matthew 1:18, 20.

> Now the birth of Jesus Christ was as follows: After His mother Mary was betrothed to Joseph, before they came together, she was found with child of the Holy Spirit. But while he thought about these things, behold, an angel of the Lord appeared to him in a dream, saying, 'Joseph, son of David, do not be afraid to take to you Mary your wife, for that which is conceived in her is of the Holy Spirit.'

That he lived a sinless life, according to John 1:1–5.

> In the beginning was the Word, and the Word was with God, and the Word was God. He was in the beginning with God. All things were made through Him, and without Him nothing was made that was made. In Him was life, and the life was the light of men. And the light shines in the darkness, and the darkness did not comprehend it.

That he died a vicarious death, was buried, but rose again from the dead on the third day, according to 1 Corinthians 15:1–4.

Moreover, brethren, I declare to you the gospel which I preached to you, which also you received and in which you stand, by which also you are saved, if you hold fast that word which I preached to you—unless you believed in vain.

For I delivered to you first of all that which I also received: that Christ died for our sins according to the Scriptures, and that He was buried, and that He rose again the third day according to the Scriptures.

That by his death, he made a perfect sacrifice for sin, thereby making redemption available for fallen man, according to Hebrews 9:22.

And according to the law almost all things are purified with blood, and without shedding of blood there is no remission.

And that apart from who he is and what he has done, there is absolutely no way of approach to the Father God, according to John 14:6; Acts 4:12; and 1 John 5:10–12.

Jesus said to him, 'I am the way, the truth, and the life. No one comes to the Father except through Me.'

'Nor is there salvation in any other, for there is no other name under heaven given among men by which we must be saved.'

He who believes in the Son of God has the witness in himself; he who does not believe God has made Him a liar, because he has not believed the testimony that God has given of His Son. And this is the testimony: that God has given us eternal life, and this life is in

His Son. He who has the Son has life; he who does not have the Son of God does not have life.

The Old Testament prophecies addressed the two streams of thought regarding the deity and the humanity of Christ. The following is a sample of the scriptures addressing the deity and the humanity of Christ.

Isaiah 7:14

Therefore the Lord Himself will give you a sign: Behold, the virgin shall conceive and bear a Son, and shall call His name Immanuel.

Isaiah 9:6

For unto us a Child is born,
Unto us a Son is given;
And the government will be upon His shoulder.
And His name will be called
Wonderful, Counselor, Mighty God,
Everlasting Father, Prince of Peace.

The child that is born is Jesus, the man, but the Son, not born but given, is Christ, the eternal God, the second person in the triune Godhead.

Luke 1:35

And the angel answered and said to her, 'The Holy Spirit will come upon you, and the power of the Highest will overshadow you; therefore, also, that Holy One who is to be born will be called the Son of God.'

1 Timothy 3:16

> And without controversy great is the mystery of
> godliness:
> God was manifested in the flesh, Justified in the Spirit,
> Seen by angels,
> Preached among the Gentiles, Believed on in the
> world,
> Received up in glory.

These show how God singled out a man (Abraham) and then a nation from that man (Israel) and then a tribe from that nation (the tribe of Judah) and then a house from that tribe (the house of David) and then a virgin from that house (the Virgin Mary) and thus preserved the genealogy of the Messiah as to his humanity. Thus, the virgin birth and the incarnation are God's unique way of reconciling both streams of Messianic prophecy, as foretold in Genesis 3:15; Isaiah 7:14; 9:6; and elsewhere in the Bible. Come to think of it this way: If Jesus was not virgin born, then he was not sinless, and if he was not sinless, then he needs a saviour himself. If he needed a saviour himself, then he could not be our saviour, and God's whole plan of redemption falls apart. But Jesus was virgin born, and, hence, he was sinless and needed no saviour himself. This qualified him to be the Saviour of all mankind. He is the Lord and King of the universe. It is he and he alone that saves from sin and sickness, from death and the grave, from the curse of eternal death, from poverty and pain, and from rejection and separation.

1 John 5:10

> He who believes in the Son of God has the witness in
> himself; he who does not believe God has made Him
> a liar, because he has not believed the testimony that
> God has given of His Son.

That is why when cults attack the virgin birth and the humanity of Jesus, when they attack the death, burial, and triumphant resurrection of the Lord from the grave, they are not just criticising Christianity and the Christian faith. They are seeking to undermine the very foundation and roots of the Christian faith as a whole. Without the virgin birth and the death and the resurrection of Jesus, there would be no Christianity, or at best, we would not be any different from any of the myriads of world religions on the planet today. Somehow, the devil knows that bloodless Christianity is powerless Christianity. And this is the very reason Christianity and Christians are hated, vilified, persecuted, even murdered all over the world. But James has a word of encouragement for us all in James 1:2–4.

> My brethren, count it all joy when you fall into various trials, knowing that the testing of your faith produces patience. But let patience have its perfect work, that you may be perfect and complete, lacking nothing.

Someone has asked, and rightly so, 'How can one man's blood atone for the sins of all mankind for all time?' Perhaps it is better in all matters of argument and dispute to let the Bible speak for itself because nobody can defend God better than God. Let us establish the fact that all sin is against God in the first place because it is his law that sin breaks. And remember that when we sin against God, we are sinning against a holy and eternal God so it is of more serious and eternal consequence than sinning against our fellow man.

Let's see how God answers that question from his own Word, according to 1 Timothy 3:16; Colossians 1:15–18, 20; and Acts 20:28.

> And without controversy great is the mystery of godliness:
>
> God was manifested in the flesh, Justified in the Spirit, Seen by angels, Preached among the Gentiles, Believed on in the world, Received up in glory.

He is the image of the invisible God, the firstborn over all creation. For by Him all things were created that are in heaven and that are on earth, visible and invisible, whether thrones or dominions or principalities or powers. All things were created through Him and for Him. And He is before all things, and in Him all things consist. And He is the head of the body, the church, who is the beginning, the firstborn from the dead, that in all things He may have the preeminence . . . and by Him to reconcile all things to Himself, by Him, whether things on earth or things in heaven, having made peace through the blood of His cross.

Therefore take heed to yourselves and to all the flock, among which the Holy Spirit has made you overseers, to shepherd the church of God which He purchased with His own blood.

Jesus's blood can atone for the whole world because it is the blood of God. According to Leviticus 17:11, God says,

For the life of the flesh is in the blood, and I have given it to you upon the altar to make atonement for your souls; for it is the blood that makes atonement for the soul.

God has established his principle that it is blood that is to provide atonement for the soul. He reaffirms this in the New Testament, according to Hebrews 9:22, so that no one can say this was an Old Testament doctrine relevant only to Israel.

And according to the law almost all things are purified with blood, and without shedding of blood there is no remission.

So blood was necessary to provide atonement for man's sin. In the spirit, and especially the cultic realm, it is widely known that blood not only has power but has a voice as well according to Genesis 4:10; Hebrews 12:24. The higher the life form sacrificed, the more powerful the blood to appease 'spirit deities'. Hence, the blood of a dog will be more powerful than that of a cat, and that of a goat more powerful than a dog, and a sheep's blood more powerful than that of a goat. That of a cow would be infinitely more powerful in its appeasing power than that of the lesser animals mentioned earlier. But the ultimate sacrifice and blood is human sacrifice and human blood. In historical narratives, kingdoms have been known to sacrifice high-ranking princes to save the entire kingdoms from being overrun and for victory in battle. In many primitive societies, the ritualistic murder and sacrifice of pregnant women has been known to be practiced, the logic being the offer of two humans in one and that of the innocent foetus making it even more powerful. Well, because Jesus was sinless, his blood was infinitely more powerful than any possible human blood. And above all, it is God's blood, eternal and therefore able to atone for time and eternity. Because all sin is against an eternal and infinitely holy God, only an eternal, infinitely holy blood could atone for man's sin, hence the blood of Jesus. That is why the blood of Jesus speaks better things than the blood of Abel. The blood of Jesus is sinless, so it does not have to plead for itself but to plead for man's forgiveness and blessing. It has no need for vengeance or retribution because it was offered willingly according to John 10:11, 15, 17, 18. The blood of Jesus has not lost any of its potency since the day it was shed on the hills of Golgotha, some two thousand years ago, and never will because it is eternal blood. That is the whole essence of the incarnation, so Jesus will have blood to shed for mankind, and the virgin birth, so his blood will be sinless and therefore acceptable unto God. This is eloquently declared in Hebrews 10:5–7.

Therefore, when He came into the world, He said:

'Sacrifice and offering You did not desire,
But a body You have prepared for Me.
In burnt offerings and sacrifices for sin
You had no pleasure.
Then I said, "Behold, I have come—
In the volume of the book it is written of Me—
To do Your will, O God."'

If you want to go to heaven and be with God, would you not rather trust someone who came from heaven and returned thereto and told us how to get there? If you are concerned about what will happen to you after you die, does it not make sense to trust in someone who died and rose again and declared that he has power over death and the grave, and that if you trust him, his resurrection experience will be your resurrection experience as well? It may be a coincidence, but as I am writing this very chapter, my computer is singing, 'Yedawase a ensa da efise wayi yen afi owuo mu na wama yen nkwa a enni awiei,' in the Akan language of Ghana, meaning, 'We thank you endlessly for delivering us from death and giving us eternal life.'

It makes every sense to trust in Jesus because Christianity is far from being a speculative faith. It all stands up to the most critical scrutiny. It is all based on solid, verifiable, historical evidence. Don't be fooled by the little glimmers of truth here and there found in almost every religion on earth. They have all borrowed snippets of truth from Christianity. Don't be fooled by the fact that some people in every religion do some good works and some worthwhile charitable deeds. That does not make them true. Jesus is the embodiment of all truth and anything that does not have him at its source and core cannot be true. He made his person and being the essence of all truth when he declared in John 14:6 'I am the way, the truth and the life.' I have always maintained that in rightly judging spiritual phenomena, you don't just have to consider whether something looks good and beautiful. Consider the source from where that thing is coming. If you wanted a counterfeit to deceive people, you will do everything to make it resemble the original as much as you possibly can. Herein lies the power of the counterfeit to deceive, its close resemblance to the original. The devil often sugarcoats his wares to make them look good and attractive and desirable. He is the master deceiver of all time. He and his ministers often pose as angels of light, but whatever they offer is poison at its core, and like the capsule, you will not know how bitter and poisonous it is by looking at it or even by swallowing it. The damage is only done after you have swallowed it, and then the poison begins to destroy you from the inside, by which time it may be too late. He only comes to steal and kill and destroy, and his final destruction of your soul would be in the lake of fire when he and his cruel demons will begin to mock and jeer you for being so stupid and gullible not to see through their deceptions.

Jesus was not exaggerating when he declared in John 14:6,

> I am the way, the truth, and the life. No one comes to
> the Father except through Me.

Almost every religion attempts to claim a belief and a respect of some sort for the person of Jesus, hailing him as one of their many prophets or a great teacher, but come to mention the definitive aspects of his being, his deity, virgin birth, sinless life, and death and resurrection, and then you will notice which kind of Jesus they claim to believe: a Jesus who is a figment of their religious imagination, not the one of the bible. Only the scarred Jesus of the bible is the true Jesus.

JESUS WAS BORN UNDER THE LAW TO REDEEM THOSE UNDER THE LAW

Jesus said in John 5:17, 'Do not think that I came to destroy the Law or the Prophets. I did not come to destroy but to fulfil.'

He came not to abolish the Law of Moses but to fulfil it. He was the only person ever to meet all the requirements of the Law completely. He had to fulfil the Law because he was born under the Law for the specific purpose of meeting its requirement for all mankind, since no one was capable of fulfilling it.

Before the advent of Christianity, the Jews practiced baptism, according to Matthew 3:5–6, 11. They were baptised confessing their sins. Christian baptism is done in the name of the Lord Jesus.

John's baptism, which preceded Christ, was not Christian baptism.

> Then Jerusalem, all Judea, and all the region around the Jordan went out to him and were baptized by him in the Jordan, confessing their sins.

> I indeed baptize you with water unto repentance, but He who is coming after me is mightier than I, whose sandals I am not worthy to carry. He will baptize you with the Holy Spirit and fire.

John was drawing the distinction between the baptism he practiced and the one Jesus was to bring. Those who were baptised by John would have had to be baptised again when they later accepted Jesus as Lord and Saviour. This means John's baptism was temporary and was superseded by Christian baptism, as we learn in Acts 19:3–5.

> And he said to them, 'Into what then were you baptized?'

> So they said, 'Into John's baptism.'

> Then Paul said, 'John indeed baptized with a baptism of repentance, saying to the people that they should believe on Him who would come after him, that is, on Christ Jesus.'

> When they heard this, they were baptized in the name of the Lord Jesus.

Here we see the apostle Paul rebaptising the Ephesian believers who had only been baptised with John's baptism.

Other references on John's baptism include Mark 1:48; Luke 3:16; John1:26; Acts 1:5; and Matthew 3:16.

Fasting was also regularly practiced by the Jews before the advent of Christianity, as we learn in several passages including Matthew 9:14; Luke 5:33; 18:12; and Isaiah 58:3–8.

> Then the disciples of John came to Him, saying, 'Why do we and the Pharisees fast often, but Your disciples do not fast?'

> I fast twice a week; I give tithes of all that I possess.

Jesus held his meetings in the synagogue, according to Matthew 4:23; 9:35; Mark 1:21; 6:2; 10:1; and Luke 4:15; 66:6.

> And Jesus went about all Galilee, teaching in their synagogues, preaching the gospel of the kingdom, and healing all kinds of sickness and all kinds of disease among the people. (Matthew 4:23)

This means that Jesus himself regularly worshipped in the synagogue and observed the Sabbath, according to Mark 3:1–5.

Jesus wore rabbinical clothes, the prayer shawl, or tallith, according to Mark 5:28, 30 and Matthew 14:36.

> For she said, 'If only I may touch His clothes, I shall be made well.'

> Immediately the fountain of her blood was dried up, and she felt in her body that she was healed of the affliction. And Jesus, immediately knowing in Himself that power had gone out of Him, turned

around in the crowd and said, 'Who touched My clothes?' (Mark 5:28–30)

The Law of Moses is a point of separation between Jew and Gentile. That is why the Roman centurion answered, 'Lord I am not worthy that you should come under my roof' (Why? Because I am a Gentile). And the same reason why the Samaritan woman said, 'Jews have no dealings with Samaritans.'
Matthew 10:5–6; 15:24; John 4:9; Acts 10:28; 11:2–3

> Then he said to them, 'You know how unlawful it is for a Jewish man to keep company with or go to one of another nation. But God has shown me that I should not call any man common or unclean.'

> And when Peter came up to Jerusalem, those of the circumcision contended with him, saying, 'You went in to uncircumcised men and ate with them!'

He observed the Passover, according to Matthew 26:17–18.

> Now on the first day of the Feast of Unleavened Bread the disciples came to Jesus, saying to Him, 'Where do You want us to prepare for You to eat the Passover?'

> And He said, 'Go into the city to a certain man, and say to him, "The Teacher says, 'My time is at hand; I will keep the Passover at your house with My disciples.'"'

After healing the leper, he asked him to go show himself to the priest to be certified clean and offer those things commanded by Moses, according to Mark 1:44; Leviticus14:1–32; and Luke 5:14; 17:14.
When the rich young ruler came to enquire about salvation, he gave him the Law of Moses, according to Luke 18:18–20.

> Now a certain ruler asked Him, saying, 'Good
> Teacher, what shall I do to inherit eternal life?'
>
> So Jesus said to him, 'Why do you call Me good?
> No one is good but One, that is, God. You know the
> commandments: "Do not commit adultery," "Do not
> murder," "Do not steal," "Do not bear false witness,"
> "Honor your father and your mother."'

Other scriptures showing that he observed the Law of Moses include Leviticus 12:2–8 and Luke 2:21. He was circumcised the eighth day, according to the Law of Moses, and was presented to the Lord, and his parents offered a sacrifice to the Lord according to the Law. His parents, Joseph and Mary, were observant Jews and celebrated the Passover yearly, according to Luke 2:41 and Exodus 23:15, 17.

Jesus raised the bar on the Law.

He did not come to tag the New Covenant of grace upon the Old Testament Law. He came to fulfil the Law so that the New Covenant of grace could be ushered in. The two could not be mixed because they are two different dispensations, given for different purposes, according Luke 5:36–38 and Matthew 9:16–17; 5:17.

He interpreted the Law of Moses and showed how impossible it was for any man to meet the requirements of the Law. He greatly raised the bar, according to Matthew 5:20.

> For I say to you, that unless your righteousness exceeds
> the righteousness of the scribes and Pharisees, you
> will by no means enter the kingdom of heaven.

Now when it came to outward righteousness, remember that these people were blameless. They kept the Law to the letter, tithing even their garden herbs in the process. Paul was a law observant Pharisee before his Damascus road conversion and recounts his standing in Philippians 3:6 as 'concerning the righteousness which is of the law, blameless'. This is the standard of righteousness we are called to exceed as New Covenant believers. Are you not grateful for God's grace? In the average New Covenant Church, over 90 percent of the members do not pay their tithes regularly, if at all, and many give minimal offering of any kind. How many of us enlightened new Covenant believers can honestly say like the Rich Young Ruler, 'All these things I have kept from my youth?' or like the apostle Paul, 'as concerning the righteousness which is of the law, blameless?'

He went on to declare that even if you are angry with your brother without a cause, or you say 'Raca' or 'you fool' to your brother, you are in danger of hellfire.

You do not have to physically commit adultery to be guilty of the act, but just look lustfully at a woman, and you are guilty of it, thus telling men, there is no hope for any of you. Which man out there is not guilty raise your hand.

He said if your right eye causes you to sin, pluck it out. If your right hand causes you to sin, cut it off.

In Matthew 5:48, he said, 'Therefor be perfect as your Heavenly Father is Perfect.'

In all of these, Jesus was describing the impossibility of self-righteousness or righteousness by works. In Romans 2, Paul seems to be suggesting that some would earn their way into heaven by their good deeds. But a much closer examination reveals that he is talking about rewards or punishment as the case may be after we have found ourselves in our respective destinations as believers or unbelievers. That subsequent judgment for rewards or punishment will be based on our works, good or bad deeds. The truth of the matter is that without Christ in your life, your whole life is one hell of a bad deed because your good deeds will not count for much anyway. Paul continues to answer his own question to say that neither Gentiles without the Law nor Jews with their written law and circumcision have met God's righteous standard of righteousness. In Romans 9:9–19, he says Jews and Gentiles are equally guilty; there is none righteous, no, not one. He continues in Romans 3:19, 20 that all mankind stands condemned, with none justified by their works. (There is not a single 'good' person in heaven and never ever will be. However, heaven is full of grace-saved saints who made it there because of his goodness).

However, you will notice that the New Testament apostles did not preach these seemingly harsh truths. They understood that the dispensation of the Law was over and that Jesus was illustrating the impossibility of man to meet these conditions by himself, no matter who they were. Yes, in Matthew 28:20, he commanded his disciples to make disciples in all nations.

> Teaching them to observe all things that I have commanded you; and lo, I am with you always, even to the end of the age. Amen

But in every one of the epistles, their massage was all *grace, grace, and more grace.* They clearly understood that it was a new dispensation, a new day where man did not have to work for his righteousness anymore but believe for it as a gift from God, according to 2 Corinthians 5:21 and Romans 5:17–20, became our reality.

> For He made Him who knew no sin to be sin for us, that we might become the righteousness of God in Him.

> For if by the one man's offense death reigned through the one, much more those who receive abundance of grace and of the gift of righteousness will reign in life through the One, Jesus Christ.

> Therefore, as through one man's offense judgment came to all men, resulting in condemnation, even so through one Man's righteous act the free gift came to all men, resulting in justification of life. For as by one man's disobedience many were made sinners, so also by one Man's obedience many will be made righteous.

Moreover the law entered that the offense might abound. But where sin abounded, grace abounded much more.

It is clear that the times have changed under the new dispensation. In the Old Testament, in 1 Kings 1:12, it was OK for the prophet Elijah to call fire to devour the wayward kids, but when his disciples showed a similar intemperance in Luke 9:54, Jesus sharply rebuked them, saying, 'You do not know what manner of spirit you are of.'

Job bemoaned his lack of a mediator between him and God, to answer God back for him in Job 9:32–33,

> For He is not a man, as I am,
> That I may answer Him,
> And that we should go to court together.
> Nor is there any mediator between us,
> Who may lay his hand on us both.

But Jesus became our mediator on the cross, according to 1 Timothy 2:5 and Hebrews 8:6; 12:24.

> For there is one God and one Mediator between God and men, the Man Christ Jesus.

> But now He has obtained a more excellent ministry, inasmuch as He is also Mediator of a better covenant, which was established on better promises.

> To Jesus the Mediator of the new covenant, and to the blood of sprinkling that speaks better things than that of Abel.

We now have a mediator in the person of the man Christ Jesus who became a ransom for our sins.

There was no provision for forgiveness under the Law, and whoever was guilty of transgression had to pay the full penalty, often with their lives.

This was true, whether your name was Moses or David or Achan. In Joshua 7:23–26, when Achan sinned by stealing the accursed things of Jericho, it was not a matter of if we confess our sins. He is faithful and just to forgive our sins and to cleanse us of all unrighteousness. No, that did not apply then. He and his entire family had to be stoned to death by God's express instructions. In Numbers 15:32–36, a man was stoned to death for gathering sticks (firewood) on the Sabbath. In the same way, in Numbers 13, nearly the entire nation of Israel perished in the wilderness for their unbelief when they refused to believe the report of Joshua and Caleb. Moses himself, the human author of the Law, was forbidden to enter the Promised Land for his frustration at the people and for disobeying God's instructions. (In 70 AD the entire Jewish nation was destroyed and millions killed and countless others sold into slavery as a result of their unbelief in rejecting their Promised Messiah under the law).

But all these were to belong to history and a distant age in Matthew 27:51.

> Then, behold, the veil of the temple was torn in two from top to bottom; and the earth quaked, and the rocks were split.

Hereby giving us an open invitation into his very presence, according to Hebrews 4:16; 10:19; and Ephesians 2:18.

> Let us therefore come boldly to the throne of grace, that we may obtain mercy and find grace to help in time of need.

> Therefore, brethren, having boldness to enter the Holiest by the blood of Jesus.

For through Him we both have access by one Spirit
to the Father.

Jesus's death and resurrection has not only brought us forgiveness and righteousness but also given us access to the very presence of our Heavenly Father. What his love has provided, his grace has made available to us. We have a commission to let the whole world know of God's amazing love and his generous provision in Christ, as explained in 2 Corinthians 5:18–20.

Now all things are of God, who has reconciled us to Himself through Jesus Christ, and has given us the ministry of reconciliation, that is, that God was in Christ reconciling the world to Himself, not imputing their trespasses to them, and has committed to us the word of reconciliation.

Now then, we are ambassadors for Christ, as though God were pleading through us: we implore you on Christ's behalf, be reconciled to God.

Who desires all men to be saved and to come to the knowledge of the truth, according to 1 Timothy 2:4.

The coming of Jesus changed the whole dynamic of man's relationship with God. It has become personal, relational, and intimate. We are now sons and daughters and treated as royalty and priests. What was once the preserve of the few clergy is now available to all, and everyone can have as much God in their lives as they desire. Jesus, the trailblazer, he is truly the way. Outside of him, there is absolutely no access to the Father.

Thank God for his grace. Thank God for his Son, the Lord Jesus Christ.

WHAT IS TRUTH? JESUS, THE EMBODIMENT OF TRUTH

This is our key reference text for our discussion: John 18:33–38.

This is a scene at the infamous trial of Jesus. Pontius Pilate, the Roman governor of Judea, sits imposing in his regal clothes and poses series of questions to the prisoner shackled between two soldiers. He asks his bloodied prisoner, 'Are you the king of the Jews?'

Unbemused and unperturbed and unlike many other prisoners facing imminent condemnation and eventual crucifixion, he stands straight and looks at the governor turned judge straight in the eyes and answers, 'I am not an earthly King, My Kingdom is not of this world.'

'You are a King then?' the governor answers back.

The prisoner replies, 'You say that I am a King.' The prisoner answers back, fully aware that his interrogator is in a prickly political position, 'And you are right.' The prisoner looks at the politician with piercing eyes that seem to read not only the expression on his face but his soul as well. 'I was born for that purpose,' he continues, 'and I came to bring truth to the world. All who love the truth recognise that what I am saying is the truth.'

And Pilate responds, 'What is truth?'

WHAT IS TRUTH?

Imagine yourself in the hall with Pilate and his prisoner. Imagine the expression on Pilate's face as he poses the question (scornful, serious, disturbed, perplexed, bemused?). Take a glimpse into Pilate's thoughts for a second; who is this man? Why does he gaze at me so? And the prisoner's 'Have I not just told you? I came to bring truth to the world. Pilate, you could be looking at the very answer to your own question. I am the truth.' Pilate was not just discussing the truth in his Jerusalem palace the day he met Jesus. He was literally looking at truth. Truth was standing before him, clothed in human flesh. Jesus Christ, who came from the Father, full of grace and truth, is the very embodiment and essence of absolute, moral, and spiritual truth itself.

John 1:14

You see, moral and spiritual truth is not so much a concept as it is a person. It is not so much something we believe as it is someone we come to know and relate to. Moral and spiritual truth has flesh. It is a person, or rather he is a person. And so truth is not just a concept or an idea but intrinsically relational. This was something Pilate could not grasp. It is not something the world can understand and embrace in their human wisdom and instruction, even today, with all our sophistication.

One of *Webster's* definitions of truth is 'fidelity to an original or standard'. For example, when a carpenter says that a floor or a table is 'true', he is saying it is faithful to the original blueprint or measurements. But what is the original or standard for transcendent truth for the kind of truth Jesus talked about when he said, 'I came to bring truth into the world'? (John 18:37)

The standard is Jesus himself. 'For by Jesus Christ, all things were created that are in heaven and that are on earth, visible and invisible, whether thrones or dominions, or principalities or powers. All things were created through Him and for Him' (Col. 1:16–17).

No wonder God looked at his creation and said, 'It is good.' God is the original. He is the origin of all things that are in existence, and if we wish to know if anything is right or wrong, good or bad/evil, we must measure it against the person who is true. He is the Rock, as Moses said. 'His work is perfect, a God of truth and without injustice or iniquity, just and right is He' (Deut. 32:4). You see, it is the very person and nature of God that defines truth. It is something he is.

This means that moral and spiritual truth is not simply abstract or philosophical; it is innately concrete, because truth is a person, best understood as a *who* and not as a *what.* The apostle James was not talking about abstractions when he wrote,

> Whatever is good and perfect comes to us from God above who created all heavens lights. Unlike them He never changes or cast shifting shadows. In His goodness He chose to make us His own children by giving us His true Word. (James 1:17–18)

As the apostle John also declared in John 1:14, 'The Word became flesh and made His dwelling amongst us. We have seen His glory, the glory of the One and only, who came from the Father, full of grace and truth.' In John 8:32, Jesus told his disciples, 'You will know the truth, and the truth will set you free.' The Law came through Moses, but grace and truth came by Jesus Christ (John 1:17).

In just a few moments later, in John 8:36, Jesus made it clear that the truth he had in mind was not only a concept but also a person when he said, 'So if the Son sets you free you will be free indeed.' He was neither confused nor contradicting himself when he said, 'the truth' sets you free, and then a few verses later, he said it is 'the Son' who sets you free. It was he who boldly said, 'I AM the way, the truth and the life,' in John 14:6. See what you believe in the context of *whom* you believe. Christianity is not just believing in a set of concepts or principles, but believing in *a person,* the person of *Christ Jesus.* It is not even just believing the Bible, as noble and necessary as that is. It is believing the Bible's witness about the person of Christ. In John 5:39, Jesus told his Jewish audience, 'You search the scriptures for in them you think you have eternal life: and these are they which testify of Me.' He was saying that the primary purpose and benefit of searching the scriptures is to come to know the God of the Bible, the Lord Jesus Christ. The scriptures per se do not save; it is Christ who does. Eternal life is in the person of Christ alone, for his is the only name given for the salvation of man as eloquently declared by the apostle Peter to the Jerusalem crowd in Acts 4:12.

> Nor is there salvation in any other, for there is no other name under heaven given among men by which we must be saved.

And 1 John 5:11 adds,

> And this is the testimony: that God has given us eternal life, and this life is in His Son.

John 17:3 highlights the same truth by declaring,

> And this is eternal life, that they may know You, the only true God, and Jesus Christ whom You have sent.

LOVING GOD

Jesus is saying that the secret to really loving him is to come to know him, for to know him is to love him. 'Learn of my mercy and faithfulness, and you will come to love me. Get to know my goodness and my holiness, and you will love me. Learn of my justice, tempered with my patience, and you will love me. Know what I love and what I hate, and you will love me. Know what saddens my heart and what gives me pleasure, and you will love me. This is the way to eternal life; to know me, the only true God. And the more you know me the more you will become like me.'

Hebrews 12:2

> Looking unto Jesus, the author and finisher of our faith, who for the joy that was set before Him endured the cross, despising the shame, and has sat down at the right hand of the throne of God.

This is further amplified in 2 Corinthians 3:18, which says,

> But we all, with unveiled face, beholding as in a mirror the glory of the Lord, are being transformed into the same image from glory to glory, just as by the Spirit of the Lord.

The more you know Jesus, the more you will praise and thank him and honour His name. 'For the more you know Me, the more you can glorify Me . . . and the more I will know your love. And the way to know Me is through the written revelation of Myself, the Word of God, the collection of My love letters to you.' Luke 24:27 clearly explains that both the Law and the Prophets, the Old Testament scriptures, and the New Testament were written to us so we will know the person and Ministry of the Lord Jesus Christ. Everything else is secondary.

> And beginning at Moses and all the Prophets, He expounded to them in all the Scriptures the things concerning Himself.

As Revelation 19:19 also highlights, 'For the testimony of Jesus is the spirit of prophecy.'

He adds, 'Read My Words, hide them in your heart, and know Me for who I AM, your friend—the one and only true God.'

CONTEND FOR THE FAITH

Guard against people who creep in quietly and smooth-talk their way in, appearing humble and even anointed. They may use the lingo, wear the right clothes, and talk the talk. They can only steal because we lowered our guard, caught up in the fanfare of religion, the glitz, the excitement, the noise, and the razzmatazz (and we forgot to 'watch). Whenever we take our eyes off the Lord, we are very vulnerable. Jude, in his epistle, admonishes us to make sure we come to know the right Jesus, the King of kings and the Lord of lords, the glorified Son of God, not just the Jesus of the figment of someone's imagination. After coming to know the true Jesus, make sure you come to know the principle of Christ as espoused in the Word of God. Get to know the Word of God and live in the power of the Holy Spirit. Build yourself up by praying in the Holy Spirit daily. Do not let go of the supernatural by continuing to believe in Jesus as healer, deliverer, and miracle worker by making yourself available for the Holy Spirit to use you to do all of these through you. Like he told the church in Philadelphia, in Revelation 3:11, 'Hold fast what you have, that no one may take your crown.' Don't let go of the supernatural and do not let anyone talk you out of what you believe. Remember that without us, he won't, and without him, we can't. God has chosen to work in partnership with us, and his primary vehicle is through our prayers, as he declared in Philippians 4:6, 'Everything by prayer,' meaning God does nothing on earth without us inviting and entreating him through our prayers. It also means we do not have to assume that because God knows about a need in our lives, he will automatically step in and intervene.

Rely on the Holy Spirit to spot false teachers. Know that you are anointed to recognise error and falsehood, according to 1 John 2:20, 27.

> But you have an anointing from the Holy One, and you know all things.
>
> But the anointing which you have received from Him abides in you, and you do not need that anyone teach you; but as the same anointing teaches you concerning all things, and is true, and is not a lie, and just as it has taught you, you will abide in Him.

He is saying to us that he has put his anointing in every one of his children to help them discern truth and deception. Whenever you come into a new environment such as a new church or ministry or any new place, listen carefully to your heart and conscience, and you will know what is going on spiritually.

In 2 Timothy 3:5, we are advised to stay clear of people who profess a form of religion but deny God's power by not believing in the supernatural. God is a spirit and therefore a supernatural being. Everything he does originate in the supernatural, spirit realm first before it eventually manifests on our natural senses in this physical realm. So do not discount the supernatural.

> Having a form of godliness but denying its power.
> And from such people turn away!

Believe in and wait for the rapture with keen anticipation. Look for his appearance daily and live accordingly, with the requisite sense of urgency, as Acts 1:11 admonishes.

> Who also said, 'Men of Galilee, why do you stand gazing up into heaven? This same Jesus, who was taken up from you into heaven, will so come in like manner as you saw Him go into heaven.'

When he appears, will you recognise him? Have you enough of his Word in you? His Word in you is he in you.

Believe all the Bible or none of it.

IN DEFENCE OF THE RESURRECTION OF JESUS CHRIST

The following will be our key reference texts, and the reader is encouraged to read them all: Matthew 16:21; 17:22, 23; 20:18–19; Luke 24:44–48; Romans 1:44; Luke 22:44; Hebrews 1:8, 10; Psalm 45:6–10; and John2:19–22.

Of course, we cannot prove the resurrection of Jesus scientifically, since that would require observation-(seeing it happen) and experimentation (repeating the event and recording it). But other ways of proving an event is by eyewitness account, which is the most reliable to prove, and evidence or circumstantial evidence, which is the trail of events one can follow to a logical conclusion that an event did take place. This is admissible in any court of law. Of the latter two, there are loads to support our conclusion that Jesus did die on the cross, was buried, but rose again on the third day and was seen by numerous eyewitnesses.

The death, burial, and resurrection of Jesus Christ is the foundation of the Christian faith. Christianity is the religion of the empty tomb. The whole work of redemption of Jesus stands or falls with the resurrection from the dead, as noted in 1 Corinthians 15:12–19.

> Now if Christ is preached that He has been raised from the dead, how do some among you say that there is no resurrection of the dead? But if there is no resurrection of the dead, then Christ is not risen.

And if Christ is not risen, then our preaching is empty and your faith is also empty. Yes, and we are found false witnesses of God, because we have testified of God that He raised up Christ, whom He did not raise up—if in fact the dead do not rise. For if the dead do not rise, then Christ is not risen. And if Christ is not risen, your faith is futile; you are still in your sins! Then also those who have fallen asleep in Christ have perished. If in this life only we have hope in Christ, we are of all men the most pitiable.

So essentially, Paul is saying Christianity stands or falls with the resurrection of Jesus Christ from the dead. If Christ did not rise from the dead, then we are all deceived and are deceivers. In this teaching, we want to prove the truth of the resurrection of Jesus from the dead, according to the scriptures.

JESUS PROPHESIED HIS OWN DEATH LONG BEFORE IT HAPPENED

Matthew 16:21; 17:22–23; 20:18–19

From that time Jesus began to show to His disciples that He must go to Jerusalem, and suffer many things from the elders and chief priests and scribes, and be killed, and be raised the third day.

Now while they were staying in Galilee, Jesus said to them, 'The Son of Man is about to be betrayed into the hands of men, and they will kill Him, and the third day He will be raised up.' And they were exceedingly sorrowful.

Behold, we are going up to Jerusalem, and the Son of Man will be betrayed to the chief priests and to the scribes; and they will condemn Him to death, and deliver Him to the Gentiles to mock and to scourge and to crucify. And the third day He will rise again.

Mark 8:31–32

And He began to teach them that the Son of Man must suffer many things, and be rejected by the elders and chief priests and scribes, and be killed, and after three days rise again. He spoke this word openly.

Luke 24:44–46

Then He said to them, 'These are the words which I spoke to you while I was still with you, that all things must be fulfilled which were written in the Law of Moses and the Prophets and the Psalms concerning Me.' And He opened their understanding, that they might comprehend the Scriptures.

Then He said to them, 'Thus it is written, and thus it was necessary for the Christ to suffer and to rise from the dead the third day.

John 2:19–22

Jesus answered and said to them, 'Destroy this temple, and in three days I will raise it up.'

Then the Jews said, 'It has taken forty-six years to build this temple, and will You raise it up in three days?'

But He was speaking of the temple of His body. Therefore, when He had risen from the dead, His disciples remembered that He had said this to them;

and they believed the Scripture and the word which
Jesus had said.

In John 10:11, he said, 'I am the good shepherd. The good shepherd
gives His life for the sheep.'

In all the scriptures above, Jesus made his resurrection from
the dead the litmus test of the authenticity of his claims and, more
importantly, his entire redemption career. He prophesied it ahead of
the event, and did so in several different places and settings. He often
prophesied it to his disciples but did it also in public, in the presence
of his enemies, as they themselves recalled in Matthew 27:63.

Saying, 'Sir, we remember, while He was still alive,
how that deceiver said, "After three days I will rise."'

Thus, this is reported in all four gospels that record the accounts
of his life, ministry, death, and resurrection.

HE WAS ADJUDGED TO BE INNOCENT AT HIS TRIAL

If Jesus was found guilty and died for his wrongdoing, that would
be another story altogether. But he was found innocent by friend and
foe alike and declared not guilty but was still put to death. According
to Isaiah 53:4–5,

Surely He has borne our griefs, And carried our
sorrows; Yet we esteemed Him stricken, Smitten by
God, and afflicted.

But He was wounded for our transgressions, He was
bruised for our iniquities; The chastisement for our
peace was upon Him, And by His stripes we are
healed.

Isaiah had prophesied thousands of years earlier that he would
come and die for all our emotional problems, whether they be

physical, chemical, hormonal, or relational. This would include all our sicknesses, anxieties, afflictions, weaknesses, and pains.

Pilate, the prosecuting judge, said, 'I find no fault in him.' But the religious authorities said, 'He ought to die because He makes Himself the Son of God.' Let's look at the testimony of scripture on his innocence: John 19:4, 6, 7; Matthew 26:59, 63–66; 27:18; and Luke 23:14–15.

> Pilate then went out again, and said to them, 'Behold, I am bringing Him out to you, that you may know that I find no fault in Him.'

Pilate's Decision

> Then Jesus came out, wearing the crown of thorns and the purple robe. And Pilate said to them, 'Behold the Man!'

> Therefore, when the chief priests and officers saw Him, they cried out, saying, 'Crucify Him, crucify Him!'

> Pilate said to them, 'You take Him and crucify Him, for I find no fault in Him.'

> The Jews answered him, 'We have a law, and according to our law He ought to die, because He made Himself the Son of God.'

> Now the chief priests, the elders, and all the council sought false testimony against Jesus to put Him to death.

> But Jesus kept silent. And the high priest answered and said to Him, 'I put You under oath by the living God: Tell us if You are the Christ, the Son of God!'

Jesus said to him, 'It is as you said. Nevertheless, I say to you, hereafter you will see the Son of Man sitting at the right hand of the Power, and coming on the clouds of heaven.'

Then the high priest tore his clothes, saying, 'He has spoken blasphemy! What further need do we have of witnesses? Look, now you have heard His blasphemy! What do you think?'

They answered and said, 'He is deserving of death.'

According to Matthew 27:18 and Mark 15:10,

Pilate, for he knew that they had handed Him over because of envy, said to them, 'You have brought this Man to me, as one who misleads the people. And indeed, having examined Him in your presence, I have found no fault in this Man concerning those things of which you accuse Him; no, neither did Herod, for I sent you back to him; and indeed nothing deserving of death has been done by Him.'

Both Herod and Pilate examined the accusations against Jesus, and both concluded that he was not guilty of any of the charges levelled against him.

THE CHARGE AGAINST JESUS

The charge was that he being a man makes himself the Son of God, according to Matthew 26:63–66. In the Jewish mindset, calling yourself the Son of God and sitting at the right hand of the Power is making yourself equal to God, which is blasphemy, punishable by death. So to them, Jesus was calling himself God and therefore blaspheming and therefore had to die. The Jewish religious authorities were basing their decision on Leviticus 24:16, which says, whoever blasphemes the name of God shall be put to death.

Yes, Jesus called himself God and made himself equal to God. But listen to the Father's testimony about his Son in Hebrews 1:8, which is quoted from Psalm 45:6, 7.

> But to the Son He says:
>
> 'Your throne, O God, is forever and ever;
> A scepter of righteousness is the scepter of Your kingdom.

God the Father is calling his Son God and King and says he is higher than all the angels. He continues and calls Jesus Lord, the Creator who predates the beginning because he is eternal. Not only that, Thomas, one of Jesus's disciples who must have known him well, called him God and worshipped him after his resurrection, in John 20:28.

> And Thomas answered and said to Him, 'My Lord and my God!'

Not only did both Pilate and Herod find him not guilty, but also Judas Iscariot, who betrayed him, testified in Matthew 27:4, saying,

> I have sinned by betraying the innocent blood. (KJV)

The King James Version translates it accurately with the adjective 'the' preceding 'innocent blood'. Jesus is the only man with the innocent blood because his blood is the blood of God, untainted and undefiled by sin. That is the whole essence of the virgin birth. Acts 20:28 declares it by saying,

> Therefore take heed to yourselves and to all the flock, among which the Holy Spirit has made you overseers,

to shepherd the church of God which He purchased with His own blood.

This further proves that Jesus is God Almighty.

Pilate's wife, who was believed to be a believer in Jesus, came to her husband during the trial to tell him about a troubling dream she had about Jesus the night before and advised her husband not to have anything to do with the trial of Jesus.

Matthew 27:19

> While he was sitting on the judgment seat, his wife sent to him, saying, 'Have nothing to do with that just Man, for I have suffered many things today in a dream because of Him.'

She actually called Jesus a just man, believing in his innocence. That might explain that when Pilate saw he was making no headway in his efforts to set Jesus free, he actually took water and washed his hands off the whole trial, as reported in Matthew 27:23–24, saying, 'I am innocent of the blood of this just person.'

Even the thief on the cross, crucified alongside Jesus, put in a word for him to declare his innocence in Luke 23:39–41.

> Then one of the criminals who were hanged blasphemed Him, saying, 'If You are the Christ, save Yourself and us.'

> But the other, answering, rebuked him, saying, 'Do you not even fear God, seeing you are under the same condemnation? And we indeed justly, for we receive the due reward of our deeds; but this Man has done nothing wrong.'

The Roman centurion guarding Jesus, after observing all that had happened on the momentous day, concluded that Jesus was innocent and righteous, according to Luke 23:47.

> So when the centurion saw what had happened, he glorified God, saying, 'Certainly this was a righteous Man!'

In any trial, eyewitness testimony is the most reliable evidence for a decision. When you have the opposition testifying for you, this carries even more weight. Here were find both Herod and Pilate affirming Jesus's innocence, as does Pilate's wife, the thief on the cross, the Roman soldier, and, crucially, Judas Iscariot. There was an obvious rift between Pilate, who wanted to release Jesus because he did not deserve any punishment, let alone death by crucifixion, and the Jewish religious establishment, who were hell bent on crucifying Jesus at all cost irrespective of the evidence to the contrary, because of their own envy of him. That may explain why when the chief priests protested at the inscription,

> Jesus of Nazareth,
> The King of the Jews

Pilate sarcastically replied to them, 'What I have written, I have written,' in John 19:21–22.

JESUS ACTUALLY DIED ON THE CROSS

Many are those who have all kinds of theories about the death and resurrection of Jesus. Some believe that he did not die at all, but at the last minute, God made a look-alike, possibly one of the disciples, take the place of Jesus on the cross and crucified him (the substitute) instead and whisked Jesus to heaven alive. Now, where they get this fanciful idea from is only known to them. These spurious claims should be compared with the accounts of the believers who wrote from eyewitness accounts, as Paul reports in 1 Corinthians 15:3.

For I delivered to you first of all that which I also received: that Christ died for our sins according to the Scriptures.

Mark 15:37–45 gives a vivid description of the account of Jesus's death we may do well to examine.

And Jesus cried out with a loud voice, and breathed His last.

Then the veil of the temple was torn in two from top to bottom. So when the centurion, who stood opposite Him, saw that He cried out like this and breathed His last he said, 'Truly this Man was the Son of God!'

There were also women looking on from afar, among whom were Mary Magdalene, Mary the mother of James the Less and of Joses, and Salome, who also followed Him and ministered to Him when He was in Galilee, and many other women who came up with Him to Jerusalem.

Jesus Buried in Joseph's Tomb

Now when evening had come, because it was the Preparation Day, that is, the day before the Sabbath, Joseph of Arimathea, a prominent council member, who was himself waiting for the kingdom of God, coming and taking courage, went in to Pilate and asked for the body of Jesus. Pilate marveled that He was already dead; and summoning the centurion, he asked him if He had been dead for some time. So when he found out from the centurion, he granted the body to Joseph.

The Bible says Jesus cried out and breathed his last. The Roman soldier guarding him saw that he was dead. The women who came on Sunday morning were all part of the onlooking crowd the Friday before when he was crucified. They returned with their embalming spices the Sunday morning to embalm the body properly because of the lateness of the time that Friday. They came expecting a corpse in the tomb. Joseph of Arimathea came to Pilate to ask for the body of Jesus, having witnessed his death earlier on. Pilate certified that he was dead by checking with the centurion who affirmed that it was so. If anybody could tell a dead body, certainly the Roman soldier should be the one because death is their business. When they came to break the legs of the prisoners to hasten their deaths, they did not break Jesus's legs because they found he was already dead, according to John 19:33–35.

> But when they came to Jesus and saw that He was already dead, they did not break His legs. But one of the soldiers pierced His side with a spear, and immediately blood and water came out. And he who has seen has testified, and his testimony is true; and he knows that he is telling the truth, so that you may believe.

Rather, the text says when they found that he was already dead, one of the soldiers pierced his side with a spear, and blood and water came out. The spear was more than enough to kill him if by any miracle he had survived the horrendous ordeal he had been through. The outpour of water and blood was further indication he was already dead, as the spear must have ruptured his heart.

When Joseph of Arimathea took the body down and prepared it for burial, had there been any trace of life in him, he would have known, as recounted in Matthew 27:57–60 and John 19:38–40.

> Now when evening had come, there came a rich man from Arimathea, named Joseph, who himself had

also become a disciple of Jesus. This man went to Pilate and asked for the body of Jesus. Then Pilate commanded the body to be given to him. When Joseph had taken the body, he wrapped it in a clean linen cloth, and laid it in his new tomb which he had hewn out of the rock; and he rolled a large stone against the door of the tomb, and departed.

As we have said previously, the women returned the Sunday morning with spices expecting to anoint the body after the Sabbath because they expected to see the body in the tomb, according to Luke 24:1 and Mark 16:1–3.

The Bible is now referring to the body of Jesus as 'it', and rightly so because he is dead, a corpse. The Roman centurion, after witnessing what had transpired, referred to Jesus in the past tense, believing he was dead by declaring, 'This was truly the Son of God,' in Matthew 27:54.

HIS DISCIPLES DID NOT BELIEVE IN THE RESURRECTION

Before he rose from the dead, Jesus had told his disciples on numerous occasions that he would rise from the dead, but the disciples neither understood nor believed in it.

Mark 16:10–14; Luke 24:1–11, 19–43

She went and told those who had been with Him, as they mourned and wept. And when they heard that He was alive and had been seen by her, they did not believe.

Jesus Appears to Two Disciples

After that, He appeared in another form to two of them as they walked and went into the country. And they went and told it to the rest, but they did not believe them either.

The Great Commission

Later He appeared to the eleven as they sat at the table; and He rebuked their unbelief and hardness of heart, because they did not believe those who had seen Him after He had risen.

Now on the first day of the week, very early in the morning, they, and certain other women with them, came to the tomb bringing the spices which they had prepared. But they found the stone rolled away from the tomb. Then they went in and did not find the body of the Lord Jesus. And it happened, as they were greatly perplexed about this, that behold, two men stood by them in shining garments. Then, as they were afraid and bowed their faces to the earth, they said to them, 'Why do you seek the living among the dead? He is not here, but is risen! Remember how He spoke to you when He was still in Galilee, saying, "The Son of Man must be delivered into the hands of sinful men, and be crucified, and the third day rise again."'

And they remembered His words. Then they returned from the tomb and told all these things to the eleven and to all the rest. It was Mary Magdalene, Joanna, Mary the mother of James, and the other women with them, who told these things to the apostles. And their words seemed to them like idle tales, and they did not believe them.

And He said to them, 'What things?'

So they said to Him, 'The things concerning Jesus of Nazareth, who was a Prophet mighty in deed and word before God and all the people, and how the chief priests and our rulers delivered Him to be condemned to death, and crucified Him. But we were hoping that it was He who was going to redeem Israel. Indeed, besides all this, today is the third day since these things happened. Yes, and certain women of our company, who arrived at the tomb early, astonished us. When they did not find His body, they came saying that they had also seen a vision of angels who said He was alive. And certain of those who were with us went to the tomb and found it just as the women had said; but Him they did not see.'

Now as they said these things, Jesus Himself stood in the midst of them, and said to them, 'Peace to you.' But they were terrified and frightened, and supposed they had seen a spirit. And He said to them, 'Why are you troubled? And why do doubts arise in your hearts? Behold My hands and My feet, that it is I Myself. Handle Me and see, for a spirit does not have flesh and bones as you see I have.'

When He had said this, He showed them His hands and His feet. But while they still did not believe for joy, and marveled, He said to them, 'Have you any food here?' So they gave Him a piece of a broiled fish and some honeycomb. And He took it and ate in their presence.

However, the chief priests and Pharisees expected him to come out of the tomb physically and were not taking any undue risks. That explains why they demanded that the tomb be sealed and guarded, according to Matthew 27:62–66.

On the next day, which followed the Day of Preparation, the chief priests and Pharisees gathered together to Pilate, saying, 'Sir, we remember, while He was still alive, how that deceiver said, "After three days I will rise." Therefore command that the tomb be made secure until the third day, lest His disciples come by night and steal Him away, and say to the people, "He has risen from the dead." So the last deception will be worse than the first.'

Pilate said to them, 'You have a guard; go your way, make it as secure as you know how.' So they went and made the tomb secure, sealing the stone and setting the guard.

Consequently, Pilate asked them to seal the tomb the best way they knew how, and he supplied the Roman guard. They therefore rolled a large stone to seal the tomb. Thus, the tomb was sealed with Caesar's authority, and anybody who tampered with it did so at the risk of death, according to Matthew 27:59–60 and Mark 15:46.

When Joseph had taken the body, he wrapped it in a clean linen cloth and laid it in his new tomb, which he had hewn out of the rock, and he rolled a large stone against the door of the tomb and departed.

MANIFESTATIONS AT HIS DEATH

The awesome manifestations that took place at the death of Jesus are further proof of his divine credentials. According to Matthew 27:45, there was darkness for three hours following Jesus's death.

Now from the sixth hour until the ninth hour there was darkness over all the land.

This is proof indeed that Jesus is the One who upholds all things by the Word of his power, as Hebrews 1:3 declares. It is said of him in John 1:4–9.

In Him was life, and the life was the light of men. And the light shines in the darkness, and the darkness did not comprehend it.

John's Witness: The True Light

There was a man sent from God, whose name was John. This man came for a witness, to bear witness of the Light, that all through him might believe. He was not that Light, but was sent to bear witness of that Light. That was the true Light which gives light to every man coming into the world.

Was it any wonder that the sun refused to shine and the moon went into hiding at his death? How could they shine when their power source was shut down! It was a moment of gloom indeed for the world because the author of life itself had ceased to be.

According to Matthew 27:51–53 (Mark 15:39; Luke 23:47; Matt. 27:54; 14:33; John 20:28),

Then, behold, the veil of the temple was torn in two from top to bottom; and the earth quaked, and the rocks were split, and the graves were opened; and many bodies of the saints who had fallen asleep were raised; and coming out of the graves after His resurrection, they went into the holy city and appeared to many.

The veil of the temple that separated the Holy of Holies where God's presence dwelt, and which was visited once a year by the high priest with the blood of an innocent animal, from the rest of the temple, was torn in two from top to bottom. This signified a 'new and living way which He consecrated for us, through the veil, that is his flesh', thereby giving everyone access into the very presence of God, according to Hebrews 10:20. It is written that no one has seen

God at any time, but now the only begotten Son who is in the intimate presence of the Father has come to reveal the Father to all mankind and to open the access into his presence by his blood. So we can now approach God in boldness, confident assurance, and with conviction. His throne is the throne of grace to which we are invited in time of need to obtain mercy and find grace. Now, by this, he had become our high priest, representing us in the presence of God the Father. This heralded the coming of a new dispensation where all believers in Christ would be called into the priesthood, according to 1 Peter 2:9.

The other manifestations at his death included an earthquake, the rocks were split, the graves in the vicinity were opened, and the bodies of dead saints buried in the vicinity were raised back to life and appeared to many in Jerusalem. This means that this resurrection of the dead saints was a physical rather than a spiritual manifestation.

His death also meant he who upholds all things by his power had exited the world, according to Hebrews 1:6. Consequently, there was impalpable chaos in the whole created universe because the pillar on which it all rested was broken.

The Old Testament saints raised from the grave were those buried in the field of Machpelah, which was before Mamre in Hebron, which Abraham bought from the sons of Hamor, according to Genesis 23:16–20.

> And Abraham listened to Ephron; and Abraham weighed out the silver for Ephron which he had named in the hearing of the sons of Heth, four hundred shekels of silver, currency of the merchants.

> So the field of Ephron which was in Machpelah, which was before Mamre, the field and the cave which was in it, and all the trees that were in the field, which were within all the surrounding borders, were deeded to Abraham as a possession in the presence of the sons of Heth, before all who went in at the gate of his city.

> And after this, Abraham buried Sarah his wife in the
> cave of the field of Machpelah, before Mamre (that is,
> Hebron) in the land of Canaan. So the field and the
> cave that is in it were deeded to Abraham by the sons
> of Heth as property for a burial place.

These Old Testament Patriarchs, being prophets themselves, knew that Jesus was going to die for mankind on the same spot and hill and that he will raise those buried there on his death, hence their insistence to be buried within that locality.

This was where Sarah, the matriarch, was buried, that was where Abraham, her husband, was buried, that was where Jacob, who died in Egypt, insisted and was brought back to be buried, according to Genesis 49:29–32.

> Then he charged them and said to them: 'I am to be
> gathered to my people; bury me with my fathers in
> the cave that is in the field of Ephron the Hittite, in the
> cave that is in the field of Machpelah, which is before
> Mamre in the land of Canaan, which Abraham bought
> with the field of Ephron the Hittite as a possession for
> a burial place. There they buried Abraham and Sarah
> his wife, there they buried Isaac and Rebekah his
> wife, and there I buried Leah. The field and the cave
> that is there were purchased from the sons of Heth.'

No wonder Joseph instructed the Jewish leaders to keep his embalmed body in Egypt till the day of their deliverance from servitude several hundreds of years later, which happened in the Exodus under Moses's leadership, and bring his body with them for burial in that square mile, according to Genesis 50:24–26. From the account in Acts 7:15–16, the bodies all the fathers of the Jewish people who died in Egypt were carried back to Canaan and buried on this patch of land.

> So Jacob went down to Egypt; and he died, he and our
> fathers. And they were carried back to Shechem and
> laid in the tomb that Abraham bought for a sum of
> money from the sons of Hamor, the father of Shechem.

It should be pretty obvious that these people, the Jews, are no ordinary race, like any other. This should evoke awe and fascination, if not admiration, from any impartial observer who comes to know their history and the things they have experienced since the first day their first parents, Abraham and Sarah, set foot on the land of Canaan in obedience to God's call. Like them or hate them, but you cannot disagree that there is something about them that is far from ordinary or common. These were the people raised from the dead at Christ's death and appeared to many in Jerusalem, to bid them farewell before the Lord took them with him to heaven on his triumphant resurrection, according to Ephesians 4:8 (9–10).

> Therefore He says: 'When He ascended on high,
> He led captivity captive, And gave gifts to men.'

This limited resurrection of the Old Testament Patriarchs was a foretaste of what he was going to do for all those who put their trust in him. By raising these patriarchs from the dead and by his own subsequent resurrection, he was demonstrating the statement he made to Martha and her sister Mary in John 11:25–26, saying,

> I am the resurrection and the life. He who believes in
> Me, though he may die, he shall live. And whoever
> lives and believes in Me shall never die. Do you
> believe this?

He was by this act serving notice to all who will hear and take note that John 5:25–29 will come to pass for them as well.

> Most assuredly, I say to you, the hour is coming, and now is, when the dead will hear the voice of the Son of God; and those who hear will live. For as the Father has life in Himself, so He has granted the Son to have life in Himself, and has given Him authority to execute judgment also, because He is the Son of Man. Do not marvel at this; for the hour is coming in which all who are in the graves will hear His voice and come forth—those who have done good, to the resurrection of life, and those who have done evil, to the resurrection of condemnation.

Jesus is demonstrating his capacity as the author of all life and his power over death and the grave for all who would trust in him. The powerful phenomena serve to authenticate who he claimed to be, his entire message and career as Saviour Redeemer. We can all sing the refrain with the great apostle that we know whom we have believed, and we are persuaded that he is able to keep what we have entrusted to his care, our very souls and eternal destinies.

So we see that the strange phenomena that attended his death were not a vision or spiritual. The centurion and all those present saw and felt what happened and were no doubt terrified and said so. The Old Testament saints secured their eternity in death. You can secure yours in Christ whilst you are yet alive.

MANIFESTATIONS AT HIS RESURRECTION

There were equally powerful manifestations at his resurrection as attested his death, as reported in Matthew 28:1–4, 11, 15.

> Now after the Sabbath, as the first day of the week began to dawn, Mary Magdalene and the other Mary came to see the tomb. And behold, there was a great earthquake; for an angel of the Lord descended from heaven, and came and rolled back the stone from the

door, and sat on it. His countenance was like lightning, and his clothing as white as snow. And the guards shook for fear of him, and became like dead men.

These manifestations included a great earthquake that shook the guards, angels descending and rolling back the stone and sitting on it, the countenance of the risen Christ like lightning and his clothes white as snow, the guards shook for fear of Him and became like dead men.

According to Matthew 28:11, some of the soldiers deserted and disappeared; they literally went AWOL. Others came into the city and reported all that had happened. Then the soldiers were bribed to tell a lie that his disciples came at night and stole his body away 'while we slept'. The only problem is that Roman soldiers do not sleep on guard duty, as that would mean certain death. Besides, there were large numbers of soldiers guarding the tomb, and it is improbable they all could sleep at the same time. The disciples, at this time, were shattered, broken, devastated, as their hopes of a future kingdom for which most have sacrificed their lives and careers were in tatters. They were fearful, and in hiding for their own lives, what would they want to do with the corpse of a leader who had so seemingly led them to ruins? And if they had mustered the courage to come to the tomb, what are their chances of secretly extracting the body from the tomb, with its large stone door, without detection from the guards? And what would you do with a dead body apart from burying it again? If they stole the body, where is it? The Jewish religious authorities could have produced the corpse and put paid to this embryonic cult as they saw it. Who was that thief that had all the time in the world to fold the handkerchief that had been around his head, as John 20:7 recounts?

THE DISCIPLES GO TO SEE THE EMPTY TOMB

Luke 24:12; John 20:4–8

But Peter arose and ran to the tomb; and stooping down, he saw the linen cloths lying by themselves;

and he departed, marveling to himself at what had happened.

So they both ran together, and the other disciple outran Peter and came to the tomb first. And he, stooping down and looking in, saw the linen cloths lying there; yet he did not go in. Then Simon Peter came, following him, and went into the tomb; and he saw the linen cloths lying there, and the handkerchief that had been around His head, not lying with the linen cloths, but folded together in a place by itself. Then the other disciple, who came to the tomb first, went in also; and he saw and believed.

In the Luke 24 account above, Peter ran to the tomb, more in curiosity than expectation, following the women's reports of the resurrection, but he saw the empty tomb and linen cloths lying by themselves but did not really understand, so he departed, possibly more confused than when he first arrived at the tomb.

In the John account above, following the women's reports of the resurrection, both John and Peter ran to the tomb. John outruns Peter, being the younger of the two, and arrives at the tomb first, but he does not enter. Peter came later and ran straight into the open tomb, and then John followed him in. When John entered and saw the linen cloth that had been around Jesus's head neatly folded and lying by itself, the significance hit him. This is no break-in job. The occupant had time to fold the linen cloth before stepping out. This folded cloth also meant the occupant had still unfinished business to transact, pointing to the Lord's second coming. The balm of spices that held his body was not broken at any point, but like the cocoon, his resurrection body simply passed through the cast with the cast intact. This is what the writer meant by he saw and believed. John knew right away that something of cosmic proportions had taken place and that their Lord had risen from the dead. It was there and then that all the lessons Jesus had given them about his impending resurrection came flooding back into their minds. Now they believe he is risen from the dead as he has told them all along.

HIS POSTRESURRECTION APPEARANCES

The soldiers who were guarding the tomb were obviously the first to see the risen Christ and shook with fear, according to Matthew 28:4, 12, 15.

> And the guards shook for fear of him, and became like dead men.

The next person to see the risen Christ was Mary Magdalene, according to John 20:11–16 and Mark 16:9.
Mary Magdalene Sees the Risen Lord

> But Mary stood outside by the tomb weeping, and as she wept she stooped down and looked into the tomb. And she saw two angels in white sitting, one at the head and the other at the feet, where the body of Jesus had lain. Then they said to her, 'Woman, why are you weeping?'
>
> She said to them, 'Because they have taken away my Lord, and I do not know where they have laid Him.'
>
> Now when she had said this, she turned around and saw Jesus standing there, and did not know that it was Jesus. Jesus said to her, 'Woman, why are you weeping? Whom are you seeking?'
>
> She, supposing Him to be the gardener, said to Him, 'Sir, if You have carried Him away, tell me where You have laid Him, and I will take Him away.'

Jesus said to her, 'Mary!'

She turned and said to Him, 'Rabboni!' (which is to say, 'Teacher').

Now when He rose early on the first day of the week, He appeared first to Mary Magdalene, out of whom He had cast seven demons.

The Bible records that he appeared first to Mary Magdalene, she being the first believer or member of Jesus's 'ministry team' to see the risen Lord. The Lord was saying, 'In My Kingdom a woman's testimony is as valid as that of a man and by this singular act elevated the status of women to heights that were unknown in those days.' He accorded the woman at the well in John 4 the same privilege of going to tell the men in her city about Christ, thus making an evangelist of her.

He also appears to two disciples on the road to Emmaus, according to Mark 16:12 and Luke 24:13–16, 31, 33–34.

After that, He appeared in another form to two of them as they walked and went into the country.

Now behold, two of them were traveling that same day to a village called Emmaus, which was seven miles from Jerusalem. And they talked together of all these things which had happened. So it was, while they conversed and reasoned, that Jesus Himself drew near and went with them. But their eyes were restrained, so that they did not know Him.

Now it came to pass, as He sat at the table with them, that He took bread, blessed and broke it, and gave it to them. Then their eyes were opened and they knew Him; and He vanished from their sight.

So they rose up that very hour and returned to Jerusalem, and found the eleven and those who were with them gathered together, saying, 'The Lord is risen indeed, and has appeared to Simon!'

Now as they said these things, Jesus Himself stood in the midst of them, and said to them, 'Peace to you.' But they were terrified and frightened, and supposed they had seen a spirit. And He said to them, 'Why are you troubled? And why do doubts arise in your hearts? Behold My hands and My feet, that it is I Myself. Handle Me and see, for a spirit does not have flesh and bones as you see I have.'

According to 1 Corinthians 15:5–8, he appeared to several individuals and groups in the following order:

And that He was seen by Cephas, then by the twelve. After that He was seen by over five hundred brethren at once, of whom the greater part remain to the present, but some have fallen asleep. After that He was seen by James, then by all the apostles. Then last of all He was seen by me also, as by one born out of due time.

He was seen by Cephas, or Peter, and then by the twelve disciples and then by over five hundred disciples all at the same time and then to James, his half-brother, and then by all the apostles. All these were his pre-ascension appearances that happened in the first forty days after his resurrection. He appeared after his ascension to heaven to Paul on the road to Damascus, as reported in Acts 9.

At the time Paul was writing this account in 1 Corinthians 15, most of the five hundred brethren who had seen the Lord were still alive. This means his account could be verifiable by eyewitness accounts.

It was evident that after his resurrection, he would only appear to carefully selected believers so that unbelievers would have to accept him by faith, just as everyone else. The concluding verdict on all these is that it is true that Jesus died on the cross, was buried, and that the third day he rose again from the dead. This means you can put your trust in him. You can entrust your eternal destiny into his powerful hands and say with the apostle Paul in 2 Timothy 1:12, saying,

> For this reason I also suffer these things; nevertheless I am not ashamed, for I know whom I have believed and am persuaded that He is able to keep what I have committed to Him until that Day.

WHO KILLED JESUS?

This is a perennial question that would never go away, and it is worth exploring at every opportunity we get so that is what we are going to do here.

In the first place, people have blamed the Jewish people for their clear and definite role in the trial and subsequent crucifixion of Jesus, who claimed to be their long-awaited Messiah, in Matthew 26:1–5.

In the above account, we see the Jewish religious hierarchy scheming and plotting to arrest and kill Jesus by trickery, something they did throughout his public ministry.

When Jesus came before the Sanhedrin, the religious hierarchy sought false testimony against him so that they could have their wish to crucify him, but they found none, according to Matthew 26:59–60. When he answered their question as to whether he was the Son of God in the affirmative, all the people gathered responded that 'he is deserving of death', as reported in Matthew 26:63–68.

To add insult to injury, when Pilate had unsuccessfully sought to release him, the pressure from the Jewish 'mob' was so unbearable that Pilate might have thought his own life was in danger. At one point, he thought he could release Jesus under a long-standing tradition where one prisoner is always granted clemency and released. The Jewish mob chanted that they wanted Barabbas released and Jesus crucified. As if that was not enough, Pilate actually washed his hands of the trial, declaring that he had nothing to do with it any longer, and the whole multitudes of the Jews responded that his blood be on them and their children, according to the gospel account in Matthew 27:20–26.

> But the chief priests and elders persuaded the multitudes that they should ask for Barabbas and destroy Jesus. The governor answered and said to them, 'Which of the two do you want me to release to you?'
>
> They said, 'Barabbas!'
>
> Pilate said to them, 'What then shall I do with Jesus who is called Christ?'
>
> They all said to him, 'Let Him be crucified!'
>
> Then the governor said, 'Why, what evil has He done?'
>
> But they cried out all the more, saying, 'Let Him be crucified!'
>
> When Pilate saw that he could not prevail at all, but rather that a tumult was rising, he took water and washed his hands before the multitude, saying, 'I am innocent of the blood of this just Person. You see to it.'
>
> And all the people answered and said, 'His blood be on us and on our children.'

In the final analysis, the Sanhedrin could pass sentence, but this had to be ratified by the Roman authority before it could be carried out.

Then he released Barabbas to them; and when he had scourged Jesus, he delivered *him* to be crucified. So from all the above account, it is obvious the Jewish religious authorities had a big hand in the mock trial and subsequent crucifixion of Jesus because they feared for their own positions and were so envious of Jesus and his undoubted adulation by the common people. The Roman authorities had sought ways to release Jesus, knowing that he was innocent, but the Jews will not countenance that. In the end, they had their way, and Jesus was crucified.

It is equally valid to argue that as the occupying power, the Roman authorities had the final jurisdiction over life and death, and no matter what the Jewish authorities had wished, they had no power to put Jesus, or anyone for that matter, to death. In the end, the decision to crucify Jesus lay exclusively with Pilate, the Roman governor, and in John 19:16, it is reported, 'Then he delivered Him to them to be crucified.' So they took Jesus and led him away. The crucifixion was actually carried out by Roman soldiers, so, yes, the Romans crucified him. Without their consent, tacit or otherwise, it would not have taken place. They had to ratify whatever decision the Sanhedrin took, and ratify they did.

But the Bible teaches that Jesus died for the sin of all mankind, thus making all of us culpable for his death. This is the theme of the Old Testament Messianic chapter, Isaiah 53:4–5, which says his was a substitutionary death.

> Surely He has borne our griefs, And carried our sorrows;
> Yet we esteemed Him stricken, Smitten by God, and afflicted.
> But He was wounded for our transgressions, He was bruised for our iniquities;

> The chastisement for our peace was upon Him, And
> by His stripes we are healed.

Yes, he might have died for our sins all right, but doesn't the Bible also teach that it was his own Father that put him to death? Isaiah 53:5 above actually says he was smitten by God. It was God the Father who wounded and bruised his Son (Ps. 22:15–16).

Actually, 1 Corinthians 2:8 says the fallen hordes of the nether world, Satan and his demons, put Jesus to death, declaring,

> Which none of the rulers of this age knew; for had
> they known, they would not have crucified the Lord
> of glory.

So yes, the devil had a hand in Jesus's death, thinking that by his death, he was eliminating his archenemy for good, not realising that by his atoning sacrifice, Jesus was actually sowing his life as a seed to replicate many millions of little Jesuses all over the world.

Finally, it is crystal clear that Jesus gave his own life as an offering for the sins of all mankind. 1 Corinthians 15:3 says that 'Christ died for our sins according to the scriptures'. In John 10:11–18, he repeatedly declares that the decision to die was his own and that no one can take his life from him because he has power to lay it down and power to take it up again.

> I am the good shepherd. The good shepherd gives
> His life for the sheep. But a hireling, he who is not
> the shepherd, one who does not own the sheep, sees
> the wolf coming and leaves the sheep and flees; and
> the wolf catches the sheep and scatters them. The
> hireling flees because he is a hireling and does not
> care about the sheep. I am the good shepherd; and I
> know My sheep, and am known by My own. As the
> Father knows Me, even so I know the Father; and I lay
> down My life for the sheep. And other sheep I have

which are not of this fold; them also I must bring, and they will hear My voice; and there will be one flock and one shepherd.

Therefore My Father loves Me, because I lay down My life that I may take it again.

No one takes it from Me, but I lay it down of Myself. I have power to lay it down, and I have power to take it again. This command I have received. from My Father.

So the final verdict is that Jesus laid down his own life for the sins of the world. Whatever role anybody might have played was only possible because he allowed it to be so. As the onlookers taunted him to come down from the cross, he could have done so easily, but he chose, by an act of his will, to hang there and suffer and die so that the rest of mankind who will put their trust in him would not have to suffer a similar fate.

Most men will defend themselves in the face of danger, but not Jesus. Most will flee from death, at least what they consider as an undeserved death, but not Jesus. Whilst we were still without strength, in due time, Christ died for the ungodly, according to Romans 5:6. And why would anyone die for his enemies? But he answers in Romans 5:8, 'But God demonstrates His own love towards us, in that while we were still sinners, Christ died for us.' For 'greater love has no one than this, than to lay down one's life for his friends'.

So it is not so much as who killed Jesus as what killed him. He died for the sin of the world. If you need to get a life, or get your life back, Jesus said, 'I came that you may have life and have it more abundantly.' God made him to be sin for us so we might be made the righteousness of God. It is better to be a God-made man than a self-made man, because for the former, you simply trust him to do all the work, knowing what is best for you than you know yourself.

He died, yes, but he also rose from the dead and is alive forevermore. To demonstrate his loving heart towards his enemies, he asked his Father to forgive them, saying, 'Father forgive them, for they know not what they do.'

Following news of his resurrection, the multitudes flocked to the empty tomb in Jerusalem for the following several weeks to see for themselves what had taken place, and they saw and believed that something of cosmic proportions had indeed taken place. Thus, all the religious authorities' efforts to silence the new movement were futile because there was no other way to explain the empty tomb except that he who was buried there was not there anymore; he has risen from the dead, just as he said he would. And the new religion spread like wildfire throughout all the known world, even to the uttermost parts of the earth. Can you imagine Caiaphas's dread upon hearing about the resurrection? He surely must have mused to himself, 'Not again.'

HIS POSTRESURRECTION MINISTRY

After he rose from the dead, Jesus appeared and disappeared to his disciples and other believers over a period of forty days. These were carefully selected and timed appearances to select audiences, as he wanted all others to believe in him by faith, without necessarily having seen him first.

During this time, he taught them many things regarding the kingdom of God and the coming of the promised Holy Spirit, but he never cast out any demon or heal the sick, according to Acts 1:1--4. He did nothing that we will call 'ministry', as this has passed onto the disciples and all subsequent believers in his name. Then on the fortieth day, in Acts 1:9–10, he ascended to heaven in a cloud and was received up into glory while the disciples looked on. The disciples returned to Jerusalem, to the Upper Room where they have been instructed to await the coming Comforter, in the person of the Holy Spirit. They waited for ten days after his ascension to heaven, which is on the fiftieth day after his resurrection, on the day of Pentecost, when the Spirit came like a rushing mighty wind, like divided tongues of fire, and sat upon each of the 120 believers assembled and filled them. This is according to Acts 1:1–3, 12 and Acts 2:1–4.

KEY EVIDENCES OF THE RESURRECTION

The resurrection account is based exclusively on the authority of scripture as Paul repeatedly asserts in 1 Corinthians 15:3–4.

> For I delivered to you first of all that which I also received: that Christ died for our sins according to the Scriptures, and that He was buried, and that He rose again the third day according to the Scriptures.

The first is the disciples' eyewitness experiences of the postresurrection appearances of the risen Christ, as declared by 1 Corinthians 15:3–8 (Luke 24:28–35, 36–49; Mark 16:14–18; Matthew 28:16–20).

> For I delivered to you first of all that which I also received: that Christ died for our sins according to the Scriptures, and that He was buried, and that He rose again the third day according to the Scriptures, and that He was seen by Cephas, then by the twelve. After that He was seen by over five hundred brethren at once, of whom the greater part remain to the present, but some have fallen asleep. After that He was seen by James, then by all the apostles. Then last of all He was seen by me also, as by one born out of due time.

There is no better and more compelling evidence than eyewitness account.

The early proclamation of the resurrection by these eyewitnesses in all their apostolic preaching, according to Acts 1:1–11; 2:22–32; 3:14–15; 4:7–12; 5:28–32; 10:38; and Philippians 3:10.

Men of Israel, hear these words: Jesus of Nazareth, a Man attested by God to you by miracles, wonders, and signs which God did through Him in your midst, as you yourselves also know—Him, being delivered by the determined purpose and foreknowledge of God, you have taken[a]by lawless hands, have crucified, and put to death; whom God raised up, having loosed the pains of death, because it was not possible that He should be held by it.

The resurrection of Jesus was the centrepiece of all apostolic preaching, and it should be ours today as well. It became the key theme in the book of Acts, and the subsequent epistles were all aimed at interpreting the implications of the resurrection for believers of all times.

The transformation of the apostles into bold witnesses who were ready to die for their convictions is certain proof of the transforming power of the resurrection. These were people who were hiding for their lives following the crucifixion of their Master. They actually barricaded themselves behind doors and would not dare venture out the hours and days following the death of Jesus. How on earth could Peter and the rest of the disciples stand up on the day of Pentecost and declare as they did in Acts 3:36–38; 5:28–30, saying,

'Did we not strictly command you not to teach in this name? And look, you have filled Jerusalem with your doctrine, and intend to bring this Man's blood on us!'

But Peter and the other apostles answered and said, 'We ought to obey God rather than men. The God of our fathers raised up Jesus whom you murdered by hanging on a tree.'

Such bold transformation, to the degree that these disciples are prepared to defy ungodly religious and political authority and damn the consequences, could only have come as a result of the resurrection.

The empty tomb was a powerful and most eloquent witness in itself, according to John 20:8.

> Then the other disciple, who came to the tomb first,
> went in also; and he saw and believed.

The fact that the resurrection of Jesus was the centrepiece of apostolic messages, all of which required adequate explanations. This message they proclaimed loudly in Jerusalem, where it is actually reported that in numerous confrontations with the authorities, the Jewish leaders could not disprove their message, even though they had both the power and the political motivation to do so, as reported in Acts 2:22–24; 3:26; 10:40.

The emergence of the church, founded by monotheistic, law-abiding Jews, according to Acts 20:28 is further evidence of the power of his resurrection.

These law-abiding Jews not only founded the church but also were now prepared to worship on Sunday, instead of the Sabbath Saturday as their fathers handed down to them, according to Revelation 1:10.

The proof of the pudding, they say, is in the eating. A vital evidence of the truth of the resurrection is that when you invoke the name of Jesus or his Word or the blood of Jesus in prayer, they work. Manifestations follow as we witnessed in Acts 3:6–8.

> Then Peter said, 'Silver and gold I do not have, but
> what I do have I give you: In the name of Jesus Christ
> of Nazareth, rise up and walk.' And he took him by
> the right hand and lifted him up, and immediately his
> feet and ankle bones received strength. So he, leaping
> up, stood and walked and entered the temple with
> them—walking, leaping, and praising God.

The conversion of two powerful sceptics in the persons of James, the half-brother of Jesus, and Paul both of whom became great apostles and apologetics for the new faith, according to John 7:5;

Acts 20:7; 1 Corinthians 16:2; and Revelation 1:10. Both men became believers and apostles after having postresurrection appearances of the risen Christ. Paul, in recounting his former opposition to the church, was to record in 1 Timothy 1:12–13,

> And I thank Christ Jesus our Lord who has enabled me, because He counted me faithful, putting me into the ministry, although I was formerly a blasphemer, a persecutor, and an insolent man; but I obtained mercy because I did it ignorantly in unbelief.

ATTACKS ON THE RESURRECTION OF JESUS

Of course, the resurrection of Jesus would not be true if it had not met with the opposition and the vitriolic attacks it had been subject to for hundreds of years.

Judaism, past and present, swears that the resurrection never happened, as reported in Matthew 28:11–15.

> Now while they were going, behold, some of the guard came into the city and reported to the chief priests all the things that had happened. When they had assembled with the elders and consulted together, they gave a large sum of money to the soldiers, saying, 'Tell them, "His disciples came at night and stole Him away while we slept." And if this comes to the governor's ears, we will appease him and make you secure.' So they took the money and did as they were instructed; and this saying is commonly reported among the Jews until this day. How on earth a Roman soldier gets to sleep on guard duty is beyond comprehension. And if they were asleep, how did they know that the disciples came and stole the body?

This single lie has done more harm to Jewish acceptance of Christ than anything one can imagine. They were staring at the evidence in the face, but they chose to believe the lie concocted by the religious establishment who were more concerned about the preservation of their positions and reputations. Thank God Jewish conversions are gathering momentum as the Lord begins to turn his attention onto his chosen covenant people, the Jews, with the approach of the end of the church age.

Jehovah's witnesses suggest that Jesus's physical body was discarded, destroyed, or dissolved into gases, as if Charles Taze Russell was there as one of the eyewitnesses. What does he know that the eyewitness disciples did not know? And which is which, discarded, destroyed, or dissolved into gases? And more importantly, where did he get this information from?

The Jesus seminar fellows say that the resurrection is wishful thinking. This is a group set up by Robert Funk, ostensibly to discover the historical Jesus. Their real purpose was to attack what the Bible says about Jesus and what he taught. These are a bunch of scholars who do not believe in the deity of Christ, the resurrection of Christ, the miracles of Christ, or the substitutionary atonement death of Christ. They also deny that the Holy Spirit is the author of scripture. Their main agenda is essentially 'I do not believe that Jesus is God, so I am going to remove anything that records Jesus saying or teaching that He is God from the gospels.'

Well, we know better. Jesus is God. The resurrection is a historical fact. You can put your life and destiny in his hands. That is the only place of safety, really.

Muslims hold that Jesus was not crucified on the cross, but, rather, God made someone else look like Jesus, and this person was mistakenly crucified as Christ. They believe Jesus was taken up alive into heaven without dying. They believe this Jesus will come back again to kill all the Jews and Christians, except that the Christian Jesus that will come back is the one with scars in his feet and hands, the one that died, whom the disciples saw ascend into heaven after his resurrection. I need someone to explain the source of the scars on his hands, feet, and side if he was not crucified.

My problem is, how did they know, since Islam was founded about six hundred years after the death of Christ? Why should anyone believe their account instead of that of the eyewitnesses? And where did they get their information from? Oh, and more crucially, unlike the other gods, the God of the Bible cannot lie. In John 14:6, Jesus said to him, 'I am the way, the truth, and the life. No one comes to the Father except through Me.'

Everything about him is true because he is the truth, and any word or message that contradicts His Word is from another source, as he also declares in Hebrews 6:18, 'That by two immutable things, in which it is impossible for God to lie, we might have strong consolation, who have fled for refuge to lay hold of the hope set before us.'

God cannot lie in his Word, so why would he declare all over the place that Jesus was raised from the dead if that were not the case? They must be talking about another god, but not the God of the Bible, the God of Abraham, Isaac, and Jacob. See what he has to say about the resurrection of his Son in 1 Corinthians 15:3–4 (12–19).

> For I delivered to you first of all that which I also received: that Christ died for our sins according to the Scriptures, and that He was buried, and that He rose again the third day according to the Scriptures.

Believe that as the gospel truth and put your trust in Jesus to do for you what he has done for countless millions since that Sunday morning.

What you have to realise is that bloodless Christianity is powerless Christianity. The Jesus that escaped the cross is not the man Christ Jesus, who gave himself as ransom for all, to be testified in due time. The true Jesus came into the world expressly to die for man's sin, and, yes, he may have wrestled in the garden, but he stepped up unto the cross and gave his life for you and me.

Without the resurrection, there will be no Christianity. It is the one doctrine that elevates Christianity above all other world religions. Through his resurrection, Christ demonstrated that he is not at par with Abraham, Buddha, Confucius, Mohammed, or any other pretender. He has power, not only to lay down his life but also to take it up again, as he declared over and over in 1 Corinthians 15:12–20 and John 10:11, 15, 17, 18.

For four hundred years after the resurrection, the only explanation given by his enemies was that his body had been stolen by his disciples, according to the concocted account in Matthew 28. Thus, it took four hundred years for his enemies to come up with some other explanations. The reason was that there was no other explanation to the empty tomb apart from the fact that he rose from the dead. The disciples were forbidden to teach and preach in his name, and even though the entire environment in Jerusalem was hostile and antagonistic, they nevertheless turned the world upside down. Even in Jerusalem, it is recorded that a great many of the priests were obedient to the faith.

EFFECTS OF THE RESURRECTION

The following are some of the key scripture references on the effects of the resurrection of Jesus: Romans 1:4; 1 Corinthians 5:7; 11:23–26; Colossians 2:9; 1:19; and Hebrews 10:12, 14.

The Jews have kept the Sabbath for thousands of years as a celebration of God's creation, commanded them in the wilderness as part of the Ten Commandments in Exodus 20:8. This was expanded to incorporate the Passover celebrations following God's miraculous deliverance from Egyptian bondage and oppression in Exodus 12. But after the resurrection, all was to shift to a celebration of the rest we have in Christ for his deliverance from sin and the grave, according to Colossians 2:16–17.

> So let no one judge you in food or in drink, or regarding a festival or a new moon or Sabbaths, which

are a shadow of things to come, but the substance is
of Christ.

So essentially, all the earlier celebrations of the Sabbath and
the Passover were shadows pointing to the coming atonement
of Christ and his triumphant resurrection. These became the
Lord's Supper to commemorate the breaking of his body for our
healing and the shedding of his blood for our sin, as expounded in
1 Corinthians 11:23–26.

> For I received from the Lord that which I also delivered
> to you: that the Lord Jesus on the same night in which
> He was betrayed took bread; and when He had given
> thanks, He broke it and said, 'Take, eat; this is My
> body which is broken for you; do this in remembrance
> of Me.' In the same manner He also took the cup
> after supper, saying, 'This cup is the new covenant
> in My blood. This do, as often as you drink it, in
> remembrance of Me.'
>
> For as often as you eat this bread and drink this cup,
> you proclaim the Lord's death till He comes.

Thus, the observance of the Lord's Supper was to be a perpetual
re-enactment of the atonement and resurrection of the Lord and
the continuing appropriation of the blessings thereof (John 6:35–37,
48–51, 54–58). Even though Jesus taught his disciples at length about
the coming of the Lord's Supper to commemorate his atonement, it
was Paul who was to explain the meaning and significance of the
celebration, as he did many other New Testament doctrines.

Following the resurrection of Jesus, the Sabbath day worship, kept
on Saturday by the Jews since the days of the exodus, was changed to
Sunday, in commemoration of the resurrection. The apostles, elders,
and early believers noticed the speciality of this day and decided to
change the day of worship to Sunday. The resurrection took place

on Sunday, most of his postresurrection appearances took place on Sundays, and the Holy Spirit descended on the day of Pentecost, a Sunday. So they called Sunday the Lord's Day, according to Acts 20:7, Revelation 1:10; and 1 Corinthians 16:2.

> Now on the first day of the week, when the disciples came together to break bread, Paul, ready to depart the next day, spoke to them and continued his message until midnight.

> On the first day of the week let each one of you lay something aside, storing up as he may prosper, that there be no collections when I come.

> I was in the Spirit on the Lord's Day, and I heard behind me a loud voice, as of a trumpet.

Thus, Sunday worship evolved as a tradition of the church and stuck until this day because the early church deduced that the Lord was indicating his intention to set this day apart for worship.

Animal sacrifices for atonement for sin became a thing of the past as Christ gave his body and blood as the final sacrifice for man's sin, according to Hebrews 8:6, 10:5–7.

Hebrews 9:11–14 declares,

> But Christ came as High Priest of the good things to come, with the greater and more perfect tabernacle not made with hands, that is, not of this creation. Not with the blood of goats and calves, but with His own blood He entered the Most Holy Place once for all, having obtained eternal redemption. For if the blood of bulls and goats and the ashes of a heifer, sprinkling the unclean, sanctifies for the purifying of the flesh, how much more shall the blood of Christ, who through

the eternal Spirit offered Himself without spot to God,
cleanse your conscience from dead works to serve the
living God?

The new believers recognised that the blood of Jesus was the
final, ultimate sacrifice for sin, according to 1 Corinthians 5:7.

Therefore purge out the old leaven, that you may be a
new lump, since you truly are unleavened. For indeed
Christ, our Passover, was sacrificed for us.

That Jesus was the sacrificial Lamb of God who takes away the
sin of the world, something no animal blood could do, according to
John 1:29.

The next day John saw Jesus coming toward him, and
said, 'Behold! The Lamb of God who takes away the
sin of the world!'

The Holy Spirit descended on the day of Pentecost, which was
on a Sunday. So the only reason we have for celebrating the brutal
crucifixion of Christ was that it was followed by the triumphant
resurrection.

The ancient practice of baptism was also radically transformed
by the resurrection of Christ. After the resurrection, new converts
to Christianity were baptised in the name of the Lord Jesus Christ.
By this act, not only were they recognising Jesus as the God of
Israel, but also they were recognising the fact that Jesus Christ is the
embodiment of the entire Godhead, as declared in Philippians 2:5–11
and 1 Timothy 3:16.

Colossians 2:9 declares, 'For in Him dwells all the fullness of the
Godhead bodily.'

So following the resurrection of Christ from the dead, the early
church recognised that all the Old Testament celebrations and
sacrifices were but types and shadows pointing to Christ and his

atonement. All were done to point man to Christ in his awesome power in creation; the new life he gives us; his deliverance from sin, bondage, and oppression; baptism as his awesome legacy in his name as the highest authority in heaven, earth, and under the earth; the total freedom we have in him; and his empowering presence in our lives through the indwelling Holy Spirit; all these culminate in the person of the Lord Jesus Christ.

Now, Jesus Christ has become the focus and centre of our relationship with the triune God, and we are called to know him both evidentially and experientially, as the Bible declares in Revelation 19:10; John 5:39; John 6:28–29; and Luke 24:27.

> And I fell at his feet to worship him. But he said to me, 'See that you do not do that! I am your fellow servant, and of your brethren who have the testimony of Jesus. Worship God! For the testimony of Jesus is the spirit of prophecy.'

> You search the Scriptures, for in them you think you have eternal life; and these are they which testify of Me.

> Then they said to Him, 'What shall we do, that we may work the works of God?'

> Jesus answered and said to them, 'This is the work of God, that you believe in Him whom He sent.'

The resurrection confirmed Jesus's deity and divine credentials, his virgin birth and claim to be the Son of God. It confirmed his sinless life and that his vicarious death was accepted by God the Father. It sealed and legitimised all his works of miracles, healings, teaching, his entire mission and ours in his name. It is God's seal of approval on his Son that opened the way for all mankind to be reconciled to God upon believing in Jesus as Christ. It made the name and blood of Jesus the two most powerful things in the universe.

At the personal level, the believer in Christ is no more a sinner but a saint made righteous with his own righteousness, according to 2 Corinthians 5:17, 21.

> Therefore, if anyone is in Christ, he is a new creation; old things have passed away; behold, all things have become new.

As I have maintained elsewhere, knowing Jesus is knowing God. You cannot bypass Jesus and get to God. You cannot dishonour Jesus whilst you seek to please God. You will not find the way to heaven and to God if you do not come through Jesus, because he alone is the way to God.

> For He made Him who knew no sin to be sin for us, that we might become the righteousness of God in Him.

That the same power that raised Jesus from the dead dwells in you in the person of the Holy Spirit, according to Romans 8:11; 4:24–25.

> But if the Spirit of Him who raised Jesus from the dead dwells in you, He who raised Christ from the dead will also give life to your mortal bodies through His Spirit who dwells in you.

The Holy Spirit is a deposit or down payment or guarantee of your inheritance in Christ, according to Ephesians 1:14 and Corinthians 1:22; 5:5.

> Who is the guarantee of our inheritance until the redemption of the purchased possession, to the praise of His glory.

Who also has sealed us and given us the Spirit in our
hearts as a guarantee.

Now He who has prepared us for this very thing is
God, who also has given us the Spirit as a guarantee.

When you come to Jesus, you no longer base your relationship
with God upon obeying laws and regulations as a means of pleasing
God. Romans 10:4 says that Christ is the end of the Law for everyone
who believes. Anyone who has truly found Jesus comes to realise
that all the seeking and searching for the truth stops because the soul
comes to a rest; the longing, the thirsting, the panting of the soul
ceases. The void and the emptiness in the soul is filled, as explained
in Psalm 42:1–2. Your debt was fully paid on the cross, and all fear
is gone and replaced by a confident assurance and a sigh, a relief, as
if the soul is saying, 'This is it, this is what I have been searching for
all this time,' according to Romans 5:1; 8:1.

Therefore, having been justified by faith, we have
peace with God through our Lord Jesus Christ.

Therefore, there is now no condemnation for those
who are in Christ Jesus. (NIV)

Henceforth, we understand that all the promises of God are
realised in him, as declared by 1 Corinthians 1:20.

For all the promises of God in Him are Yes, and in
Him Amen, to the glory of God through us.

You are empowered to change your circumstances, your family,
and the world around you, according to Philippians 4:13.

I can do all things through Christ who strengthens me.

You are an heir of God and a joint heir with Christ of all that belongs to God, according to Roman 8:17.

> And if children, then heirs—heirs of God and joint heirs with Christ, if indeed we suffer with Him, that we may also be glorified together.

Resurrection power never gives up because it always believes that the best is yet to come. Your best days are not behind but ahead of you. The resurrection defies nature because what goes down is supposed to stay down, but the resurrection makes the impossible possible to him who believes, because with God, all things are possible. He has destroyed the devil, who used the fear of death to terrorise mankind by his own death. As a believer, death should be the last thing to fear because it has been transformed into your servant to bring you to your heavenly Father and, hence, your eternal inheritance. Death has become a shadow through which we can walk without any fear, with no power to hurt a believer.

His resurrection is guarantee that you also will rise from the dead, according to John 11:25–26.

> Jesus said to her, 'I am the resurrection and the life. He who believes in Me, though he may die, he shall live. And whoever lives and believes in Me shall never die. Do you believe this?'

As the song writer said, 'Because He lives, we can face tomorrow.' Hallelujah.

THE HEALING POWER OF JOY

Jesus said in John 15:11, 'That my joy may be in you and that your joy may be complete' (NIV); in John 16:22, 'And no one will take away your joy'; and in John 17:13, 'That they may have the full measure of my joy.'

Isaiah prophesied in Isaiah 12:3, 'With joy shall ye draw waters from the well of salvation.'

The dictionary defines joy as 'lively emotion of joy and gladness evoked by a success or of well-being' or 'to experience great pleasure or delight in a thing'. An essential ingredient of joy is the expression or manifestation of emotion or a deep-settled confidence that God is in control.

The Hebrew dictionary teaches that joy means 'to brighten up, to cheer up, to be merry, to bring pleasure'. The Greek dictionary teaches that joy means 'cheerfulness and gladness'.

Joy is a gift from God. 'My joy shall be in you' (John 15:11, NIV). Joy doesn't depend upon circumstances. Jesus said, 'No one will take away your joy' (John 16:22). The 'quality' of people will be seen in their joy. The actions of other people often attack your joy and would drain you of all joy and emotional energy if you let them.

Proverbs 17:22

A merry heart does good, like medicine, But a broken spirit dries the bones.

The above scripture is saying that joy has a medicinal effect on the body, but its absence brings on sicknesses and disease to the body. Proverbs 4:20–23 echoes the same thought.

Philippians 2:17–18; 4:4–7; 1:3–6

> Yes, and if I am being poured out as a drink offering on the sacrifice and service of your faith, I am glad and rejoice with you all. For the same reason you also be glad and rejoice with me.

> Rejoice in the Lord always. Again I will say, rejoice!

> Let your gentleness be known to all men. The Lord is at hand.

> Be anxious for nothing, but in everything by prayer and supplication, with thanksgiving, let your requests be made known to God; and the peace of God, which surpasses all understanding, will guard your hearts and minds through Christ Jesus.

> I thank my God upon every remembrance of you, always in every prayer of mine making request for you all with joy, for your fellowship in the gospel from the first day until now, being confident of this very thing, that He who has begun a good work in you will complete it until the day of Jesus Christ.

From the scriptures above, it is apparent that joy, rejoice, joyful, and its many derivatives are the major theme of the book of Philippians, most likely written by the apostle Paul during his first Roman imprisonment in about AD 60 and of the Bible as a whole. Joy is a deep personal emotion that resides in the spirit of man. Unlike happiness, joy does not depend on what is happening around us but the condition of the heart. That is why you cannot really tell whether a person is joyful on the inside. Joyful people are able to smile and laugh deeply easily, as it is a matter of regurgitating what is already on the inside of them. The Bible declares that the joy of the Lord is our strength, according to Nehemiah 8:10.

Numerous medical studies have discovered a direct correlation between laughter and the functioning of the immune system. Laughter is said to have lots of health and healing benefits by boosting the immune system and reducing dangerous stress hormones in the human body. People with an optimistic outlook on life and a good sense of humour experience overall 'less stress and better health'.

The story has been told of Norman Cousins, journalist and former editor of the *Saturday Review* who developed an extremely painful disease called ankylosing spondylitis, and doctors gave him up to die. Then he remembered an article he once read about negative emotions and their deadly effects on the human body. He wondered, 'Could positive emotions help?' and proceeded to watch funny movies to make himself laugh. Laughter improved his sleep after watching the funny movies for some time and eventually healed him completely of his condition. Laughter is known to ventilate the lungs and leave the muscles and nerves and heart warm and relaxed, giving the same benefits as an aerobic exercise or jogging or a deep massage. Just like in aerobic exercise, laughter temporarily speeds up the heart rate, increases blood pressure and breathing, expands circulation, and helps the flow of oxygen in and out of the body. A good laughter also exercises the upper torso, lungs and heart, shoulders, arms, abdomen, diaphragm, and legs. It makes the brain work better. Laughter is infectious. You can learn to laugh by first choosing to smile. Laughter comes on the heels of smiling. Even if you don't feel like smiling, smile anyway.

JOY AND HAPPINESS

Happiness and joy are not the same. Happiness is a feeling of pleasure, contentment, or well-being that comes from what is happening on the outside. It is temporary and depends on external factors, including what others say and do.

Joy, on the other hand, is abiding and enduring. It comes from a feeling of contentment from deep inside a person. It comes from an inner sense of value, purpose or fulfilment, and satisfaction. It is from God. Pleasure that produces happiness comes through the five senses; eating a delicious ice cream, listening to a beautiful piece of music, compliment from a respected or valued person, receiving a gift from a cherished one, moving into your dream home, or driving your dream car for the first time, or even finding a good bargain on sale. Unfortunately, these can be addictive if care is not taken. Sex, gambling, prescription drugs, eating, alcohol, etc., all have the capacity to induce a feeling of pleasure, but they can all be addictive. If your goal is to find happiness through pleasure via the five senses, you will never be fully satisfied, as it will take more and more doses of indulgence to get the next and corresponding highs. Marriage is tough work compared to the easy short-term thrill of an affair or a noncommittal relationship, but there is in the ultimate, greater long-term joy and satisfaction, according to 1 Corinthians 7:28, 33 and Hebrews 13:4.

> But even if you do marry, you have not sinned; and if a virgin marries, she has not sinned. Nevertheless such will have trouble in the flesh, but I would spare you.

> But he who is married cares about the things of the world—how he may please his wife.

> Marriage is honorable among all, and the bed undefiled; but fornicators and adulterers God will judge.

Marriage has the potential to distract from focus on God if the couple does not maintain a united focus. But the verdict of the Bible, overall, is that it is a good thing for a couple to commit to make it work. It leads to better overall health, greater financial stability and wealth, and much greater sexual and emotional satisfaction and fulfilment. All these have the potential for a greater life expectancy.

Joy, on the other hand, does not flow from situations but from your will and emotions from deep within. You can literally choose to be joyful or you can choose to be miserable.

WHY PEOPLE LOSE THEIR JOY

People may lose their joy for a number of reasons including some of the following:

A negative home environment riddled with criticism and fault-finding can easily drain you of your joy.

In the same way, if you allow yourself to be overburdened with too much responsibilities, obligations, and pressures of tight deadlines and targets, too heavy workloads, then you will lose your joy when you fail to meet all those impossible expectations. The result of all these will be exhaustion, burnout, and disappointments.

Not setting goals that are challenging enough to stretch you and bring out the best in you could also do violence to your joy and self-satisfaction. I once read the story of a couple in their nineties that took a ship trip from Europe to Australia to begin a new life. Talk of optimism, this couple had no plans for dying, and death certainly has a kind of respect for people with that kind of attitude.

Many are losing their joy and lives over unhealthy relationships. Sometimes, the best way forward may be the least bad option in a situation, which may actually be a separation or even a divorce. But don't see this as the first recourse or even an option in any situation until all avenues are explored. Never resolve a temporary problem with a permanent solution. Every problem has a solution somewhere, and it all depends on where you have been looking.

Many people, too, take life too seriously and have never seen anything funny about life. Do not take yourself too seriously and have a laugh at some of your own gaffes from time to time. Learn to laugh at yourself. See your work and whatever you do as fun or play and try to enjoy it. Be like a child and pursue your passion in life. To a child, everything is like play. Perhaps that is what the Lord meant when he said unless we become like little children, we cannot enter the kingdom of God.

Seek also to bring joy to others in all your interactions. Give compliments and affirmations and praise for little things. This means you should always be looking out for the best in people so that you can give genuine praise. Look for the positives in your spouse, children, work colleagues, and all those you interact with. They will respond in kind and will always love to be in your presence. This will certainly enhance your image of yourself and increase your joy. Everybody loves a nice compliment, but nobody loves their critics, even those that may be constructive and warranted. This is the surest way to get couples to open up to each other emotionally and is even more crucial in getting teenage children to open up to their parents. Joy towards others will engender joy towards you.

The more you give away joy in the form of smiles, compliments, and words of encouragement to others, the more you will feel joy welling up in you. Just try it and see. Make your mind up to ignore the little quirks in other people's behaviours and look out for the best in them, ready to compliment and praise and hug and see what it would do for your own joy. In football management, as in any other, the best managers are the ones who know how to lift up their players with optimism and self-belief after a crushing defeat whilst still making everyone know who is boss. Husbands, in particular, need to learn how to do this and compliment and appreciate their wives a lot more for their many contributions to making the house a home and enriching their lives.

Maintain a strong hope, faith, and confidence in God and his faithfulness because his Word is the anchor to your soul in trying times, according to Hebrews 6:19.

> This hope we have as an anchor of the soul, both sure
> and steadfast, and which enters the Presence behind
> the veil.

Meditating in the Word of God will greatly increase your joy and ability to meet all kinds of challenges.

The apostle Paul had one of the most challenging yet most fruitful ministries of all time. But because of his strong confidence in God, he was always in full control of every situation and circumstance he found himself in whether he was being hounded by his Jewish countrymen, stranded in the middle of the ocean, or shackled in chains in some dark prison. To him, God was a very present help in time of trouble, as he wrote on several occasions in Galatians 1:1, 15; 2:20; and elsewhere in the scriptures.

> Paul, an apostle (not from men nor through man, but through Jesus Christ and God the Father who raised Him from the dead), and all the brethren who are with me.

> But when it pleased God, who separated me from my mother's womb and called me through His grace, to reveal His Son in me, that I might preach Him among the Gentiles.

> I have been crucified with Christ; it is no longer I who live, but Christ lives in me; and the life which I now live in the flesh I live by faith in the Son of God, who loved me and gave Himself for me.

Experts tell us that not only does laughter make our serious lives lighter but also it helps to reduce or control pain in at least four ways:

- by distracting our attention from the pain,
- by reducing the tension we are having to live with as a result of the pain,
- by changing our expectations, and, finally,
- by increasing the production of endorphins, the body's natural painkillers.

Laughter, strange as it may be, turns our minds from our seriousness and pain and actually creates a degree of anaesthesia. By diverting our attention from our situation, laughter enables us to take a brief excursion away from the pain. Sometimes, the cause may not be literal pain but a mindset that is too serious. When our worlds become too serious, we need momentary interruptions of just plain fun—a surprising day off, a long walk in the woods, a movie, a pillow fight with the grandkids, or a relaxed and enjoyable evening with a loved one over a bowl of popcorn.

If you are married, see your marriage as an adventure, not as a problem to solve. Perhaps you are in the 'if only' group of people whose mantra is 'I will laugh if only I had more money, if only I had more talent, if only I was more beautiful, if only I had a more fulfilling job.' Just as more money never made anyone more generous, and more talent never made anyone more grateful, more of anything never made anyone more joyful. A joyful countenance has nothing to do with one's age or occupation or geography or education or marital status or good looks, or circumstances. It is a matter of choice. It is a matter of one's attitude that stems from a deep confidence in God—confidence that God is in full control of what is happening or will happen in one's life. I learnt this the hard way when I went to spend some time with my friends in Ghana a couple of years ago. To them, everything happening has one refrain, 'God is in control.' It got to a point where I was frustrated with that cliché that I began to answer back, saying that is just an escape from personal responsibility. But upon careful reflection, they are right—'God is in control' because he has final say over the big picture, and the more we believe he is in control even in challenging situations, the more likely we are to believe him to resolve those challenges.

This is how David, the psalmist king of Israel, puts it in Psalm 46:1–2.

God is our refuge and strength,
A very present help in trouble.
Therefore we will not fear,

> Even though the earth be removed,
> And though the mountains be carried into the midst
> of the sea.

The choice could not be more clear: either we fix our minds on God and his Word and determine to laugh again in the midst of life's challenges, or we focus on ourselves and wail and whine our way through life and keep complaining that we never get a fair shake at life. The contrast between the two positions cannot be clearer in Psalms 1, 91, and 23.

Have broad enough shoulders to let things be and leave room for differences. Everybody does not have to conform or even agree with your opinions and personal idiosyncrasies. As Paul said in Philippians 1:15–18, what if some preach with wrong motives—who cares? What are you going to do about that? Would you try to stop them, all of them? Paul's answer was that what really matters is that Christ is being preached and rejoices for that.

> Some indeed preach Christ even from envy and strife, and some also from goodwill: The former preach Christ from selfish ambition, not sincerely, supposing to add affliction to my chains; but the latter out of love, knowing that I am appointed for the defense of the gospel. What then? Only that in every way, whether in pretense or in truth, Christ is preached; and in this I rejoice, yes, and will rejoice.

Your only answer to this is to preach the truth and do it as forcefully as you possibly can. No matter what you do, people will preach lies to deceive, and others will preach with wrong motives. Unfortunately, some people will love to hear that, as that is what soothes their itching ears.

Jesus had a very simple solution for the tares sown by the enemy amongst the wheat in Matthew 13:30.

> Let both grow together until the harvest, and at the time of harvest I will say to the reapers, 'First gather together the tares and bind them in bundles to burn them, but gather the wheat into my barn.'

At the harvest, we can tell the difference from the fruit each bears. At the harvest, true wheat will bow, heavy with fruit, while tares will continue to stand upright and erect because there is no fruit on the stalk. Herein lies the difference between the wheat and the tares. It is important not to clutter one's mind with borderline legalistic thoughts that will zap your emotional energy and steal your joy. Understand what is worth our passionate concern and what is not. Most things are not worth the trouble, even though some are. I once heard the story of a well-intentioned young man who took upon himself to correct every injustice at his work place. This guy, like they say, had his heart in the right place and was burdened by the slightest injustice or the minutest foibles of others to the degree that he was always fighting mini battles on several fronts. Eventually, he developed a reputation for being quarrelsome and not a team player. He was right most of the time, though his only problem was that he did not know which battles to ignore and which ones were worth his sweat. Not all battles are worth your sweat. Not all wrongs are worth your attention. Refuse to be crippled by other people's words and refuse to submerge yourself in self-pity and refuse to take criticism personally. 'The longer I live, the more I become convinced that our major battle is not with age but with maturity.' We have no choice about growing older, but our challenge is whether we grow up. Growing

G. K. Chesterton was never more correct than when he wrote, 'Madmen are always serious, they go mad from lack of humour.'

It is always good to look at the fun side of life and not take things too seriously beyond what is normal. It starts with a healthy appreciation of nature, the beautiful clouds, the rainbow, the starry night sky, the soaring eagle, the wildlife in their natural habitat, the beauty and power of the waterfall, the beautiful spring flowers, and the beautiful lights as you fly over a city at night. There are really endless marvels of creatures out there to be admired and worship God for. As someone who originally came from a hot climate, I was and I am still fascinated by the winter snow. Back home, we only read about snow in books, but here I am seeing it for real. I still love the snow blanket that covers the ground, especially in the eerie night when there are no movements on the roads. Flying at night over the meandering Nile River is another spectacle for me. Keep it simple and enjoy the marvels of nature.

Here are some Bible verses that can help you understand the deep power of joy. It is important to meditate on these repeatedly to witness the upwelling of joy in your heart.

Joy is more than just a happy feeling—it is a spiritual power! Through the power of Jesus, we can be joyful in mind and attitude, even when we are not feeling happy. The Bible talks about joy a lot.

> Do not be grieved, for the joy of the Lord is your strength. (Neh. 8:10)

> The thief does not come except to steal, and to kill, and to destroy. I have come that they may have life, and that they may have it more abundantly. (John 10:10)

> Be glad in the Lord, and rejoice, O righteous, and shout for joy, all you upright in heart! (Ps. 32:11)

> The meek shall obtain fresh joy in the Lord, and the poor among mankind shall exult in the Holy One of Israel. (Isa. 29:19)

> For God has not given us a spirit of fear, but of power and of love and of a sound mind. (2 Tim. 1:7)

> Delight yourself also in the LORD, And He shall give you the desires of your heart. (Ps. 37:4)

Great is my boldness of speech toward you, great is my boasting on your behalf. I am filled with comfort. I am exceedingly joyful in all our tribulation. (2 Cor. 7:4)

You will keep him in perfect peace, Whose mind is stayed on You, Because he trusts in You. (Isa. 26:3)

And we know that all things work together for good to those who love God, to those who are the called according to *His* purpose. (Rom. 8:28)

Strengthened with all might, according to His glorious power, for all patience and longsuffering with joy; giving thanks to the Father who has qualified us to be partakers of the inheritance of the saints in the light. (Col. 1:11–12)

Your words were found, and I ate them, And Your word was to me the joy and rejoicing of my heart; For I am called by Your name, O LORD God of hosts. (Jer. 15:16)

Arise, shine; For your light has come! And the glory of the LORD is risen upon you. (Isa. 60:1)

But let all those rejoice who put their trust in You; Let them ever shout for joy, because You defend them; Let those also who love Your name Be joyful in You. (Ps. 5:11)

But the fruit of the Spirit is love, joy, peace, longsuffering, kindness, goodness, faithfulness. (Gal. 5:22)

THE POWER OF YOUR THOUGHTS

Philippians 4:6–8, 13 is our key bible verse for this study.

There is a battle raging all around us, but it is not a battle over a piece of land but a battle for our minds. The devil knows that if he can control our minds and our thoughts, he will control the whole of our lives. This is because our thoughts determine our attitudes, and our attitudes determine our actions, and our actions determine our habits, and our habits, our character, ultimately determine our destiny. Yes, we need to watch what enters our lives through our eyes and ears, but more importantly, through our minds. The devil knows that if he can get you to dwell on depressing thoughts, you will end up having a depressing life. If he can get you to dwell on angry thoughts, you will end up having an angry life. That explains why some people are perpetually angry, sometimes without knowing what they are really angry about. For such people, it does not take much to explode into a fit of rage because what triggers their anger is not the real cause of their anger. If you continually think negative thoughts, you are going to end up a negative and sarcastic person attracting negative and sarcastic people into your life. Such negative people do not only attract negative people into their lives but also attract negative activities and negative philosophies and will develop a negative lifestyle overall. Such people believe all kinds of conspiracy theories about nations and races and all kinds of weird stuff. Your life will always follow the direction of your dominant thoughts. Like a magnet, we draw in what we think about rather effortlessly. If you are a person given to happy, joyful, positive thoughts, you will surely attract happy, upbeat, and positive people into your life. Our thoughts will also affect our emotions. Whatever you dwell on will end up flavouring your emotions, for good or for bad. You will feel according to the way you think. It is impossible to be happy when you are thinking negative thoughts. To be happy, you must first think happy and positive thoughts. In fact, when you begin to express joy whilst thinking negatively, it is as though your mind will ask you, what are you happy about? Because that emotion is not consistent with what you are thinking.

Consequently, it is impossible to remain discouraged for long whilst your mind is thinking positive and upbeat thoughts. So much of what we call success or failure begins in our minds.

SET YOUR MIND ON HIGHER THINGS

Colossians 3:2, 'Set your mind on things above, not on things on the earth.' Perhaps you do not realise it, but we can all choose the thoughts we dwell on. Nobody can make you think about something you don't want to think about, not God and certainly not the devil. That is why the above scripture invites us to set our minds on heavenly things. The things above are the positive things of God. The mind is like the thermostat that we can regulate and set at a certain level or on something, the same way a thermostat is set to regulate the room temperature. You decide what you entertain in your mind and your thoughts. Oh yeah, we can all have fleeting negative thoughts, but to dwell on them is our choice to make. We can dismiss any negative thought that flashes through our minds, usually by speaking the opposite positive word out aloud. It is like turning on the switch, and the darkness will instantly disappear. Simply because the devil plants a discouraging, negative thought in your mind does not mean you have to own it, 'water' it, nurture it, coddle it, and help it to grow. You can choose to cast it down and dismiss it from your mind. If you make the mistake and start dwelling on negative, discouraging thoughts, they will soon poison your emotions, your attitudes, and, hence, your actions, bringing discouragement and depression and end up zapping your emotional energy and strength. Very often, when you see bitter, disrespectful people, they are also dissatisfied, unhappy people. Very often, these people will vent their unprovoked vitriol on any authority figure in sight, be they the police, government leaders, the clergy, royalty, or even men in general or even people of a different race they perceive as 'oppressors'. I was horrified to witness one such incident when, without provocation, an angry lady emptied her poisonous verbiage on a picture hanging on the wall because she saw that class of people the picture represented as enemies of the people. What a miserable way to live, fighting shadows and pictures.

The more we dwell on the enemy's thoughts, the more garbage he dumps into our minds, as if we have erected a signpost over our minds saying, 'Rubbish here!' We all get knocked down temporarily, but we don't have to stay down permanently. The Bible lists the examples of people who had to endure serious setbacks in their lives and careers, including Paul and Silas in Acts 16, Paul in Acts 27, David in 2 Samuel, Daniel in Babylon, Moses, Jacob, and Joseph, but triumphed over their adversity in the end. If you are depressed, unhappy, negative, bored, sarcastic, or uncooperative or have a sour and sullen attitude, it is important to remember that nobody is responsible for your misery but yourself. You have to realise that you are the only person who can pick yourself up and get back up from that situation. The moment we get into making excuses and blame our family, our environment, past relationships with others, or our circumstances and even blame God, the devil, or anything else, we will never be truly free and be emotionally healthy. We need to take responsibility for our actions in life. Blaming others for our predicament will birth in us a victim mentality. Yes, we may suffer adverse life circumstances, but they need not define us and dictate our emotions. It is not your circumstances and experiences that have you down. It is your thoughts about your experiences that have you down. The way you respond to your experiences is infinitely more important than the experience per se. You could be in the biggest storm of your life and still be filled with joy and peace and victory if you learn how to choose your thoughts. It is time to think about what you are thinking about. Yes, bad things do happen to good people just as good things do happen to bad people. Yes, we need to be realistic and admit our problems, but we should focus on the One who has the solution, as the Bible declares in 2 Timothy 1:7, 'For God has not given us a spirit of fear, but of power and of love and of a sound mind.'

Are you sick? Admit it, but focus on the healer, the solution of the problem, who is Jesus. Are you tired and weighed down by the cares of life? Look up to the one who said, 'Those who wait on the Lord shall renew their strength.' Yes, Jesus said that in this life, we will have trouble but 'be of good cheer because I have overcome the world'. Choose to believe that your God is bigger and greater than every storm in your life. Whatever storm you may be going through now, remember that storms never last forever; also at the end of every storm is a great calm. Weeping may endure for the night, but joy always comes in the morning. Your day of joy is around the corner. As you dwell on the promises of God, you'll be filled with hope, faith, and a positive attitude that will draw in the victory you need. Philippians 4:4–7 enjoins us to take everything to God in prayer in a joyful, positive, and expectant attitude. We should not allow worry and anxiety to cloud our thinking and attitude. In a problem situation, what we need the most to move forward with God is peace, above all else. When we calm down and replace anxiety of spirit and mind with the calmness and peace of God, then we are within earshot of the desired solution from God.

Rejoice in the Lord always. Again I will say, rejoice!

Let your gentleness be known to all men. The Lord is at hand.

Be anxious for nothing, but in everything by prayer and supplication, with thanksgiving, let your requests be made known to God; and the peace of God, which

surpasses all understanding, will guard your hearts
and minds through Christ Jesus.

You must cheer up first before God shows up and turns your situation around. You are to strip off the old man and put on the new man and be renewed in the spirit of your mind, according to Ephesians 4:23. The scripture exhorts us that if our father and mother reject us, the Lord will sure receive us. What all these seek to establish is that we must first win the victory in our minds. When you think thoughts of failure, you are destined to fail. When you think thoughts of mediocrity, you are destined to perform below your true potential. On the other hand, when you dwell on God's promises of victory, favour, faith, power, and strength, nothing can hold you down. When you think positive and excellent thoughts, you will be propelled towards greatness, increase, promotion, and God's supernatural blessings on every side. Do not focus on people and problems and what and who caused it. That would only make you bitter and prolong your pain needlessly, draining you of all emotional power needed for forward momentum. Stop playing the blame game for anything, past, present, or future. As Buddy Hackett, the comedian once said, 'I never hold grudges; while you are holding grudges, they are out dancing.' Keep your mind positive and refuse to criticise, complain, or condemn, even when you think you have reason enough to do so.

We must be especially determined when you are going through a period of adversity and times of personal challenge. When trouble strikes, our first thoughts are not necessarily higher or noble or positive, but negative thoughts bombard us from all angles, but this is when we stand firm and decide to trust God. If you will transform your mind and begin to think positive thoughts, God will transform your life. The Bible says we should take every thought captive and cast down every imagination. God has a lot of confidence in his children, and it is time we have confidence in ourselves because of he that is in us. Begin to see greatness in yourself because of your God. We have to agree with the apostle Paul that we too can do all things through Christ who strengthens us.

Romans 12:2

> And do not be conformed to this world, but be transformed by the renewing of your mind, that you may prove what is that good and acceptable and perfect will of God.

Have a mental picture of success, victory, and breakthrough because that is God's will for you. It does not matter what has gone on before; remember God always saves his best for last. I once heard the story of a Christian lady who complained to God, unlike others who are always giving great testimonies of what God has done in their lives. But God replied to her, 'You have a testimony. I kept you from all that.'

POSITIVE ATTITUDE IN TRIALS

How you handle the low points in your life will be the defining moments in your life. It is during the low points that you prove your love for God and put your faith to work. It is during the low points that the devil visits you. During those times, do not allow your mouth to utter any negative word or your frustrations. Do not say anything you do not want in your future. Refuse to allow yourself (mouth) to be an instrument of satanic voice. You can write down your frustrations and speak your faith. You will have what you say. Do not say what you have. Say what you want, not what you have if what you have is not what you want or desire.

Always remember that life itself is a war zone, and the moment you accepted Jesus as your Lord and Saviour, you enlisted in the army of the Lord and declared war on the devil and his kingdom, whether you knew this or not. Everybody, at some point in their lives, goes through one battle or another.

According to 1 Peter 4:12–13,

> Beloved, do not think it strange concerning the fiery trial which is to try you, as though some strange thing

happened to you; but rejoice to the extent that you partake of Christ's sufferings, that when His glory is revealed, you may also be glad with exceeding joy.

According to 1 Corinthians 10:13, the believer is not necessarily exempt from the normal temptations and vicissitudes of life. Issues to do with marriage and relationships, wayward children, health, finance, and on-the-job issues always ensure that at every point in one's life, you may be entering, stuck in, or emerging from one battle and crisis or another. The Bible says that after Jesus's temptation, 'the devil left Him for a season'. The pressure is relentless, and you are not alone. That is why we are admonished to be strong in the Lord and in the power of his might. Fight with the strength and power of the Lord because most of it is spiritual in origin and do not respond to physical weapons. And the enemy you are fighting is not flesh and blood neighbours. Remember that your adversary, the devil, has a dedicated professional army of principalities and powers and rulers of the darkness of this world to do his fighting with subtlety and cunning deception. But the victory is assured and promised.

No temptation has overtaken you except such as is common to man; but God is faithful, who will not allow you to be tempted beyond what you are able, but with the temptation will also make the way of escape, that you may be able to bear it. (1 Cor. 10:13)

But the good news to remember is that as a child of God, when the devil attacks you, God takes it personally and expects you to engage his services and use his prescribed weapons and battle instructions and strategies to guarantee your victory. The battle is really the Lord's. They may plan and plot and scheme in secret, but God says, 'Be still and know that I am God.' Hide behind the choir and sing, 'Praise the Lord, for His mercy endures forever,' and watch him rout the enemy, as stated in 1 John 5:4–5.

> For whatever is born of God overcomes the world.
> And this is the victory that has overcome the world—
> our faith. Who is he who overcomes the world, but he
> who believes that Jesus is the Son of God?

God has assured his children of victory in life's battles in his Word, and we have to believe them and act on them. Victory was part of the original package we inherited in Christ, the Lion of the tribe of Judah, the conquering Saviour and Lord Supreme. See what he says to you in John 16:33 and be encouraged:

> These things I have spoken to you, that in Me you may
> have peace. In the world you will have tribulation; but
> be of good cheer, I have overcome the world.

It is finished.

It has long been discovered that all riches, material or intangible, originate in the mind. Poverty is a state of mind, as much as excellent social standing in friendship, family, physical health, self-discipline all have their roots in the mind. That is why we are commanded to guard our minds and our thoughts and cultivate the mind of Christ in the scriptures. The state of your mind will end up determining the direction of your life. That is why I have always believed that the best help to give people struggling to meet life's basic needs is not necessarily more, and more had outs even though that may be the convenient starting point. It is information and knowledge about taking control of their attitudes and thinking, and the possibilities open to them. We have all witnessed the scenario where the government builds state-of-the-art modern apartments with all the state-of-the-art security gadgets and conveniences and moved people from some run-down slum area to this new gated community only to discover that within a matter of a couple of years, these ultramodern facilities have been thrashed and reduced to what is normal to them. People will always bring things down to their concept of 'normal'. If you do not change internally no matter what happens to you on the outside, sooner or later, you will return to normal for you. Studies have found that most all who win big on lotteries, sums in the millions of dollars, eventually lose it all and return to normal, penniless. You need to change the kind of treasure that is inside your heart. This treasure is made up of your thoughts, beliefs, assumptions, doctrines, and teachings you accept as true. Your daily life, even if you are not aware, emanates from this treasure trove. You are not just in a bad mood; rather, it is the way you think, rather negatively. It has been said that the man who is not master of himself may not be master of anything. To understand others, you must first understand yourself. Strangely, the world stands aside for them to pass and come to the aid of people who move with a definite purpose in life. To achieve enduring success, you must have a success consciousness. Successful people become successful because they have acquired the habit of thinking in terms of success. God did not put in Philippians 4:13, 'I can do all things through Christ who strengthens me,' in there just to tickle your fancy but to get you to reorientate your mind into possibility thinking. Yes, recognise the obstacles on your way to success, but not as stop signs, but as a test of your resolve to achieve and that they are there to be overcome and make you stronger after you have subdued them. With Jesus in your corner and the Word of God on your lips, and by the power of the Holy Spirit, you have all the spiritual arsenal to overcome any problem. If you do not ride the horse of life, life will ride you as a horse. The choice cannot be any clearer. Choose to win in life because you are wired for success.

Determine to move away from the blame culture. Ours have become a culture of blame, complaint, and nonresponsibility. It is always someone else's fault, and we sedate ourselves with excuses as if they give us the reason, if not the right, to fail. Even obvious failures in behaviour and character defects are blamed on our genetics, environment, and, certainly, parenting. This leads people to claim credit for their successes in life but not their failures. As renowned author and motivational speaker Zig Ziglar once noted, 'We have all heard of the self-made success but not the self-made failure.'

Winston Churchill, the late British prime minister, once remarked with characteristic insight, 'Responsibility is the price of greatness. The sooner you accept that the number one person responsible for all your woes is yourself, the quicker you will begin to make decisions that will change your life.'

Leadership expert and trainer John Maxwell noted in his book *Developing the Leader within You* that 'choices, life choices are significant. What we do affect who we are and where we will end up. Our futures are flexible.'

Others can slow us down or even try to put road blocks on our way to our potential, but we are the only ones who can stop the car or change direction. Achievers take control of their lives. You are an achiever waiting to happen.

THE POWER OF GOD'S GRACE IN YOUR LIFE

Grace is God's free, eternal, unmerited, undeserved favour towards his creatures. All of God's dealings with his creation and all his benefits and his blessings towards us are based on his grace or benevolence alone. Grace is also God's divine ability working in man and making him able to do what he cannot do in his own ability. His grace is his divine influence on our lives to make us able beyond our human ability. God's grace is always aggressive and relentless in its pursuit as when he located David, a shepherd boy in some remote woodland, and laid hold of him, transforming him into the sweet psalmist and Israel's greatest warrior king. God seems to have a flair for picking armed robbers, murderers, idol worshippers, and whoremongers and turning them into his instruments of choice for his glory, as he did in the case of Abraham, Jacob, Moses, Rahab, David, and many modern-day heroes of faith. What else would cause a couple who has had a bitter divorce several years earlier to hear the message of grace and fall back in love all over again? His aggressive grace is best illustrated in the story of the wealthy father of the prodigal son who was always on the lookout for his wayward son and ran to meet him when he saw him come back after his riotous experience. His love for us is the reason he does us good, but his grace is the vehicle for making that love available to us. Where sin abounds, his grace super abounds. It is like where sin has done its dirtiest work, his grace rises to its highest degree. He supplies the amount of grace commensurate with the need. All of God's dealings with his creation are rooted in his grace, even when it is not readily apparent to us. For instance, Noah's flood by which the then world was destroyed by water, saving only eight people in the process, was an act of his grace. Had he not destroyed mankind and start over again with Noah, the entire human race would have been polluted (gene-wise) by the Nephilim, and the promised Messiah could not have come into the world as a perfect human species to redeem mankind. He had to destroy the polluted race to preserve our redemption. The same is true of his instructions for the Jews to destroy the polluted Canaanites to preserve the coming of the Messiah to redeem us all. The same consideration of his grace demanded that he banish Adam and Eve from the Garden of Eden so they could not lay hands to eat of the tree of life and remain immortal in their sin and sickness-ravaged bodies. Can you imagine living in this corrupted body for a thousand years, not to think of forever? What about slaying an innocent animal not just to cover Adam and Eve's nakedness? But foreshadowing the atonement his Son Jesus Christ was to provide for man's sin and to bring justification and imputed righteousness to man. Even behind every one of the seemingly harsh Old Testament laws such as stoning for adultery and fornication was his grace to protect the unborn baby from the curse of illegitimacy and ensure that every child in Israel had a biological father and mother growing up. And when enlightened New Testament Christians read it, if they do at all, they dismiss it as archaic Old Testament stuff that was given to ancient Israel and, therefore, does not apply to us. Just look at how far our touted enlightenment has brought us. Families lay in ruins, and societies are tearing themselves apart. Our bodies are riddled with unnameable ailments, and our neighbourhoods have become war zones simply because we got smarter than God.

His entire creation was an act of grace as much as his continuing sustenance of the same. In the New Testament, we were all called in grace, as in Galatians 1:6, 15–16.

I marvel that you are turning away so soon from Him who called you in the grace of Christ, to a different gospel, which is not another; but there are some who trouble you and want to pervert the gospel of Christ

But when it pleased God, who separated me from my mother's womb and called me through His grace, to reveal His Son in me, that I might preach Him among the Gentiles, I did not immediately confer with flesh and blood.

Isaiah 49:1, 5

Listen, O coastlands, to Me,
And take heed, you peoples from afar!
The LORD has called Me from the womb;
From the matrix of My mother He has made mention of My name.

And now the LORD says,
Who formed Me from the womb to be His Servant,
To bring Jacob back to Him,
So that Israel is gathered to Him
(For I shall be glorious in the eyes of the LORD,
And My God shall be My strength).

Jeremiah 1:5

Before I formed you in the womb I knew you;
Before you were born I sanctified you;
I ordained you a prophet to the nations.

Romans 1:16–17; 3:22–24, 28; 5:8; 9:10–13

For I am not ashamed of the gospel of Christ, for it is the power of God to salvation for everyone who believes, for the Jew first and also for the Greek. For in it the righteousness of God is revealed from faith to faith; as it is written, 'The just shall live by faith.'

Even the righteousness of God, through faith in Jesus Christ, to all and on all who believe. For there is no difference; for all have sinned and fall short of the glory of God, being justified freely by His grace through the redemption that is in Christ Jesus.

But God demonstrates His own love toward us, in that while we were still sinners, Christ died for us.

And not only this, but when Rebecca also had conceived by one man, even by our father Isaac (for the children not yet being born, nor having done any good or evil, that the purpose of God according to election might stand, not of works but of Him who calls), it was said to her, 'The older shall serve the younger.' As it is written, 'Jacob I have loved, but Esau I have hated.'

Other useful scriptures on God's grace include Ephesians 1:4–17 and Genesis 25:23.

WE HAVE RECEIVED THE FULLNESS OF HIS GRACE IN CHRIST

John 1:16–17 says,

And of His fullness we have all received, and grace for grace. For the law was given through Moses, but grace and truth came through Jesus Christ.

God's grace has always been available to his creatures, but with the coming of Christ, we have received the fullness of God's grace or grace upon grace. Jesus and his atoning sacrifice is the embodiment of God's grace. We live in a period of God's extended mercy. That is why it appears as if God is overlooking sin and wickedness. He is not overlooking sin and wickedness, but he is long suffering towards us, not willing that any should perish but all should come to repentance, as Peter explained in 2 Peter 3:9.

There are degrees of grace, and all grace is not received at once because of a lack of knowledge and faith on our part. According to our knowledge, we have faith, and according to our faith, we receive grace or God's favour. In Exodus 34:6–7, God unveiled a glimpse of his grace to his servant Moses in the wilderness.

> And the LORD passed before him and proclaimed, 'The LORD, the LORD God, merciful and gracious, longsuffering, and abounding in goodness and truth, keeping mercy for thousands, forgiving iniquity and transgression and sin, by no means clearing the guilty, visiting the iniquity of the fathers upon the children and the children's children to the third and the fourth generation.'

Accept the fact that you serve a God with a big heart, who is kind, merciful, gracious, and compassionate. He loves you so much to die for you, according to Ephesians 2:8–9.

> For by grace you have been saved through faith, and that not of yourselves; it is the gift of God, not of works, lest anyone should boast.

Look back at the great Bible characters who were mightily used by God and you will see it is all an act of God's grace.

Moses was a murderer, Jacob cheated Esau and Laban, Abraham tricked King Abimelech, David was an adulterer and murderer, Peter denied his master three times, John and James fought for the highest position in his kingdom, and Paul was a persecutor.

As if that was not enough, all the four women mentioned in Jesus's genealogy had issues about them. Tamar slept with her father-in-law but was mentioned in the Lord's genealogy. Bathsheba, the wife of Uriah, was an adulteress, but she is also mentioned. So is Ruth, the Moabitess, the idol worshipper from Jordan. Rahab was the harlot of Jericho. All these are in the family tree of Jesus. God put them all there to tell you that it does not matter your background, where you have been, and what you have done in the past; you can also call upon him just to prove that, according to Romans 5:20.

> Moreover the law entered that the offense might abound. But where sin abounded, grace abounded much more.

In fact, God has proven over and over again that he uses the rejects, the despised, the outcasts, and the nobodys of society for his maximum glory, as he declares in 1 Corinthians 1:26–29.

> For you see your calling, brethren, that not many wise according to the flesh, not many mighty, not many noble, are called. But God has chosen the foolish things of the world to put to shame the wise, and God has chosen the weak things of the world to put to shame the things which are mighty; and the base things of the world and the things which are despised God has chosen, and the things which are not, to bring to nothing the things that are, that no flesh should glory in His presence.

The beauty of grace is that it takes the discarded useless things and recycles them into excellent beauty and usefulness. This is cause for hope for you and me.

Sometimes we hear the testimony of people who were lucky to be born to Christian parents and, hence, do not go through some of the things us ordinary mortals have to suffer in life, and we envy them. But know that the Bible says where sin abounds, grace abounds much more. Those people have not needed the grace we have needed to bring us this far. So we know God on another level because we know that we would not be here had it not been for his watchful eye over us, even before he claimed us for himself. There is more grace for the prostitute, the adulterer, the murderer, and the repentant thief than the one who has not been through any of these situations. It is our chequered careers, our sinfulness, our degradation, our shame, and our filth that became the grace of God on the cross. After being rescued from the gates of hell, we come to have a deeper understanding and a personal, experiential encounter with his grace. The deeper the hurt, the greater the destiny. You might as well stop asking God why you hurt so much and start asking him why he trusts you so much. Our hurts have become our schooling and preparation, our training for high ministry, and our scars, the points from which his anointing flows out to bless others, according to Colossians 2:14–15.

> Having wiped out the handwriting of requirements that was against us, which was contrary to us. And He has taken it out of the way, having nailed it to the cross. Having disarmed principalities and powers, He made a public spectacle of them, triumphing over them in it.

After we have had a brush with death, life assumes new meaning for us. Grace always provokes an attitude of gratitude. We become more appreciative and do not take things for granted anymore. We develop a more healthy fear for the Lord for the lifeline he threw us. Romans 11:6 declares that grace and law were given for different purposes under different dispensations and do not mix. That is a major problem in the church today because we take a bit of grace and mix it with a bit of law, and what happens is confusion as they neutralize each other.

And if by grace, then it is no longer of works; otherwise grace is no longer grace. But if it is of works, it is no longer grace; otherwise work is no longer work.

But under the New Covenant, we are told we have the fullness of grace or grace after grace. The Old Testament saints, who were under limited grace, strove to obey the Old Testament laws and to do outward works of goodness and to earn righteousness with God. But listen to Paul's verdict on all his labouring as a good and observant Pharisee, to obey the Law under the Old Covenant, according to Philippians 3:1–11.

> Finally, my brethren, rejoice in the Lord. For me to write the same things to you is not tedious, but for you it is safe.

> Beware of dogs, beware of evil workers, beware of the mutilation! For we are the circumcision, who worship God in the Spirit, rejoice in Christ Jesus, and have no confidence in the flesh, though I also might have confidence in the flesh. If anyone else thinks he may have confidence in the flesh, I more so: circumcised the eighth day, of the stock of Israel, of the tribe of Benjamin, a Hebrew of the Hebrews; concerning the law, a Pharisee; concerning zeal, persecuting the church; concerning the righteousness which is in the law, blameless.

> But what things were gain to me, these I have counted loss for Christ. Yet indeed I also count all things loss for the excellence of the knowledge of Christ Jesus my Lord, for whom I have suffered the loss of all things, and count them as rubbish, that I may gain Christ and be found in Him, not having my own righteousness, which is from the law, but that which is through faith

in Christ, the righteousness which is from God by
faith; that I may know Him and the power of His
resurrection, and the fellowship of His sufferings,
being conformed to His death, if, by any means, I may
attain to the resurrection from the dead.

Paul is saying he did everything required of him as an observant
Pharisee, zealous to the point of persecuting Christians, coming from
the royal tribe of Benjamin; but in the end, all these were worthless
as far as knowing God was concerned, because the more I did, the
emptier I felt on the inside. Now I have come to the point where I am
happy to lose all these so I may gain Christ because I have realised
that good works and personal effort do not cut with God. I have
realised that everything I am and do is his working in me by his grace
alone. This is what he is saying in 1 Corinthians 15:10.

But by the grace of God I am what I am, and His
grace toward me was not in vain; but I labored more
abundantly than they all, yet not I, but the grace of
God which was with me.

Paul is saying that now, with the fullness of grace, power would
no longer be defined by high position in politics, victory in warfare,
social standing or heritage, even performance of the miraculous, but
by the emptying of self so he can fill it, by the denying of self so he
can live through us and get the glory, by reliance upon him so he can
manifest his power through us, by service unto others so he can love
through us, and by humility so he can reign through us. It is only
when we are weak that we can be strong in him. It is no longer our
power, but we are strong in him and by the power of his might. His
message to you and me is, 'You do not have to prove anything to
me. Just obey me and rely on me.' This is the beauty of grace. I got
asked recently by a fellow minister, 'Do you think anybody can live a
sinless life?' God is not demanding perfection from us because that is
not attainable on this side of eternity. You do not have to be perfect in

your self-effort to go to heaven. But Jesus wants you to rely on him, on his grace, and on his power, which alone will keep you from sin. And if you do sin, then come to him in true repentance and receive his ready forgiveness and move on. As you walk in obedience with him, his grace will cover every aspect of your life. You are going to heaven not based on your works of righteousness but based on his gift of righteousness, which alone is the perfect righteousness acceptable to God, as declared in 2 Corinthians 5:21 and Romans 5:17–20.

> For He made Him who knew no sin to be sin for us, that we might become the righteousness of God in Him.

> For if by the one man's offense death reigned through the one, much more those who receive abundance of grace and of the gift of righteousness will reign in life through the One, Jesus Christ.

> Therefore, as through one man's offense judgment came to all men, resulting in condemnation, even so through one Man's righteous act the free gift came to all men, resulting in justification of life. For as by one man's disobedience many were made sinners, so also by one Man's obedience many will be made righteous.

> Moreover the law entered that the offense might abound. But where sin abounded, grace abounded much more.

The verdict is clear out there. You only enter heaven because he has qualified you by his blood and his gift of righteousness. You only disqualify yourself by playing smart with the Lord and hiding things from him as if that were possible. He knows everything, but he says, 'If you sin or mess up, just come to me in a penitent heart and tell me about it, and my forgiveness is ready waiting,' as he says in 1 John 1:9.

> If we confess our sins, He is faithful and just to forgive
> us our sins and to cleanse us from all unrighteousness.

Whilst this may be referring to a repentant sinner coming to the Lord for the first time, the principle applies equally to our continuing walk with the Lord. That was the power and secret of David's successful walk with the Lord. You will notice that David had the same weakness of flesh as most of us do, but he let God be God and kept short accounts with the Lord in his moments of weakness. His confessions and repentance were immediate and heartfelt, and so he always met with God's forgiveness and grace. And God said, 'This man may have many flaws and weaknesses, but I can do business with him.' That is what God expects from all his children.

2 Corinthians 9:8

> And God is able to make all grace abound toward you,
> that you, always having all sufficiency in all things,
> may have an abundance for every good work.

God's grace covers every aspect of our lives, including the material, physical, spiritual, and financial. His grace replaces our fear with his boldness, our poverty with his riches, our sicknesses with his health and healing, our curses with his blessing, and our weaknesses with his strength and power. He does all these because on his cross, he took all these on himself on our behalf and died our death so that we can live with him in his resurrection power and life. Love is God's greatest attribute; in fact, it is the essence of his being and the sole motivation of all he does, but it is his grace that makes that love available to you. May his grace be sufficient for you in all your life's endeavours as it was for Paul and the early Christians, as eloquently explained in 2 Corinthians 2:9–10.

And He said to me, 'My grace is sufficient for you, for My strength is made perfect in weakness.' Therefore most gladly I will rather boast in my infirmities, that the power of Christ may rest upon me. Therefore I take pleasure in infirmities, in reproaches, in needs, in persecutions, in distresses, for Christ's sake. For when I am weak, then I am strong.

May you take pleasure in your weaknesses, knowing that his grace is sufficient for you and his strength only comes to the fore in our weaknesses. As you rely upon him, your need will provide occasion for his grace. I can personally attest to the fact that when everything seems normal and all is tranquil in your life, you will hardly sense his presence and grace, but let any form of danger threaten your life, then you will know that he has been present all the time, ready to intervene and deliver you from danger. So like the apostle Paul asked rhetorically in Romans 8, what shall we say to all these? How do we respond to the abundance of his grace in our lives apart from thanking him for his goodness! Grace must engender an attitude of gratitude in our lives.

Be encouraged that he has not left you alone to fend for yourself, as he said in John 14:18, 'I will not leave you orphans; I will come to you.' Before he went away, he gave us his last promise in Matthew 28:20, 'And lo, I am with you always, even to the end of the age.'

Amen.

BIBLICAL FINANCE: HOW GOD BLESSES HIS PEOPLE FINANCIALLY

God has his chosen ways to bless his children financially, including the following:

SOWING AND REAPING: GIVING AND RECEIVING

God first established his controlling law of kingdom economics and kingdom prosperity in Genesis 8:22 when he declared,

> While the earth remains, Seedtime and harvest, Cold and heat, Winter and summer And day and night Shall not cease.

This is the controlling law of kingdom economics popularly referred to as giving and receiving, or sowing and reaping. It is the only thing that unlocks the door to increase. Covenant practice is the only guaranteed bailout of this and every economic downturn. It is not praying and receiving or even fasting and receiving, even though these worthwhile Christian disciplines may come in support of the process. It is giving and receiving, or sowing and reaping. Whatever God puts into your hands, whether it is a salary or profit or interest or a gift or any form of windfall, you are the one who decides whether it is a seed or harvest. You can sow it as a seed and expect a harvest, or you can eat or spend it as your harvest. There is no moral judgment with the choice you make, as you are perfectly free to use it as you choose. According to 2 Corinthians 9:10, you become a sower or an eater depending on what you choose to do with what God gives you.

> Now may He who supplies seed to the sower, and bread for food, supply and multiply the seed you have sown and increase the fruits of your righteousness.

If you choose to eat what you have been supplied, it blesses you once and then end of story. However, if you choose to sow it or a part of it, it becomes seed, which multiplies to your account, as the verse above teaches.

In Acts 20:35, the apostle Paul reiterates the Lord Jesus, the ultimate giver, saying, 'It is more blessed to give than to receive.' Of course, when you receive, you are blessed; but when you give, you the giver is blessed because you have opened the door for God to bless you for your obedience to him and for the receiver to thank and bless you as well. The receiver is blessed as his need is met, and he blesses the giver and God, who answered his prayer, and God receives thanksgiving from you both and is thereby blessed as well. So there is blessing all around.

IT IS GOD WHO GIVES YOU THE POWER TO GET WEALTH

According to Deuteronomy 8:18,

> And you shall remember the LORD your God, for it is He who gives you power to get wealth, that He may establish His covenant which He swore to your fathers, as it is this day.

According to this and several other passages of the Bible, God is the source of our material and financial blessings. He blesses us so we can, in turn, finance his work on earth. God does not need our earthly currencies in heaven, and whatever we turn over to him, he sows back into the earth to get our family and friends saved, to get evangelists and preachers to come with his healing messages to get us healed, and to have outreaches that bring good drinking water and mobile clinics to people in remote areas. It is important for God's people to understand that we are the instruments for getting his work and mission out there, and he is counting on us to be faithful partners with him in this.

He gives talents, skills, abilities, creativities, aptitudes, know-hows, favours, dexterities, and what have you to individuals in the forms of good looks and physical attraction, mental acumen, slick of speech, beauty, strength, vitality, etc., for our and the world's benefit. You may dig the gold, but God says, 'I provided the shovel.' And guess who put the gold, the diamond, and the oil there underground in the first place? He gives you life, strength, energy, and wisdom to go to your job or business daily. We all know people richer, more educated, more beautiful, socially better placed and connected, but no more, dead and gone, often in the prime of life. He says remember why he has blessed you for his covenant; so you will keep the door of the temple open, so others may come into the kingdom. His empowerment is not the stuff per se but rather the anointing to attract the stuff, whatever form it may take. He may anoint your hands so that whatever you touch turns to gold. He may anoint your feet so that every ball you kick is a goal. He may anoint your mouth and lips so that whatever you declare comes to pass. For some, it is the grace to write words that bless people. When we are thus endowed, we are in a position to attract wealth, but we should not forget that is not just for ourselves. We are always blessed to be a blessing. He gives us so we can give back where he needs it. So long as we remember this, that we are his resource conduit to get resources to where he needs them, our supply will never run dry.

HOW ARE WE TO GIVE?

The Bible is pretty clear on how we are to give.

We are first and foremost to give willingly. Giving must not be forced or done under duress or fear. People must not be pressured to give under any circumstance.

Exodus 25:2, 35:5; Deuteronomy 15:7–11

> Speak to the children of Israel, that they bring Me an offering. From everyone who gives it willingly with his heart you shall take My offering.

> Take from among you an offering to the LORD. Whoever is of a willing heart, let him bring it as an offering to the LORD: gold, silver, and bronze.

We are to give cheerfully. Closely related to the first is the injunction to give cheerfully. Giving to God should be an occasion for joy. It is our recognition of the fact that he owes our very lives and all that we have. It is a celebration of his good generosity to us in giving us life, health, strength, and wisdom to acquire whatever it is we work at. In 2 Corinthians 2:9, he says,

> So let each one give as he purposes in his heart, not grudgingly or of necessity; for God loves a cheerful giver.

We are to give bountifully. This is talking about the size of our giving. We are encouraged to give as much as we possibly can afford. Luke 6:38 encourages us to give in proportion to the size of the harvest we expect to receive back.

> Give, and it will be given to you: good measure, pressed down, shaken together, and running over will be put into your bosom. For with the same measure that you use, it will be measured back to you.

We are to give sacrificially, according to 2 Corinthians 8:3, 7. Sometimes we can give beyond what we are able when we give sacrificially.

For I bear witness that according to their ability, yes, and beyond their ability, they were freely willing.

But as you abound in everything—in faith, in speech, in knowledge, in all diligence, and in your love for us—see that you abound in this grace also.

Luke 21:1–4 (Mark 12:41–44)

And He looked up and saw the rich putting their gifts into the treasury, and He saw also a certain poor widow putting in two mites. So He said, 'Truly I say to you that this poor widow has put in more than all; for all these out of their abundance have put in offerings for God, but she out of her poverty put in all the livelihood that she had.'

God looks at our affordability, not just the size of our giving. This poor widow's mite was all she had, and it made a far bigger impact on God than the much bigger sums the rich and wealthy must have given that day.

We are to give tirelessly and repeatedly, according to Philippians 4:10, 15–17.

But I rejoiced in the Lord greatly that now at last your care for me has flourished again; though you surely did care, but you lacked opportunity.

Now you Philippians know also that in the beginning of the gospel, when I departed from Macedonia, no church shared with me concerning giving and receiving but you only. For even in Thessalonica you sent aid once and again for my necessities. Not that I seek the gift, but I seek the fruit that abounds to your account.

The Philippians supported Paul's evangelistic ministry again and again on a continuous basis. That is how we are to give. It should be our continuing lifestyle.

We are to give expectantly or in expectation of the harvest. Your giving is what God multiplies, and your expectation or faith is why he multiplies it, according to Galatians 6:7–9.

> Do not be deceived, God is not mocked; for whatever a man sows, that he will also reap. For he who sows to his flesh will of the flesh reap corruption, but he who sows to the Spirit will of the Spirit reap everlasting life. And let us not grow weary while doing good, for in due season we shall reap if we do not lose heart.

Even though much of this verse is contrasting carnal hedonistic behaviour with spiritual, what is being discussed here is equally applicable to seed sowing in expectation of a harvest. You need the grace of God to give because it is the anointing that destroys the spirit of selfishness, which is a destiny destroyer, according to 2 Corinthians 8:7.

> But as you abound in everything—in faith, in speech, in knowledge, in all diligence, and in your love for us—see that you abound in this grace also.

However, Proverbs 11:24 teaches that to increase and have more, you must give away first. When you recognise God as the source of all that you are and have, you begin to see yourself as his conduit and steward.

> There is one who scatters, yet increases more;
> And there is one who withholds more than is right,
> But it leads to poverty.

God is saying we need that generous spirit to give liberally to prosper. It is only in the kingdom of God that one increases by giving away. The world's system is the exact opposite where you are supposed to hoard and stack up and have it compounded multiple times as much as possible to increase. In God's kingdom, holding what you have close to your chest leads to poverty and ruin. I have witnessed stingy Christians literally come to financial ruin from one terrible crisis to another simply because they decided to play by their own rules and would not be told what to do. That attitude is not the best for God's kingdom life because over there, even as a beloved heir of all things, Daddy still calls the shots. It is a straight choice: keep your life and lose it, or lose your life in Christ and gain it never to lose it again. He says, 'My yoke is easy and my burden is light.' Compare that with the so-called liberty and freedom of the world and be your own judge. Wisdom gives what it cannot keep to gain what it cannot lose.

WHATEVER HE SAYS, DO IT

This most saintly advice was given by the blessed Mary, the mother of Jesus, in John 2:5 at the wedding feast in Cana of Galilee.

His mother said to the servants, 'Whatever He says to you, do it.' If only Christians will heed this saintly advice, our walk with the Lord will be much simpler and blessed. Amongst the things the Lord said to us all is that it was more blessed to give than to receive. How complicated is that? And also those who bless Israel he will bless, and those who pray for the peace of Jerusalem he will prosper, and that if we want a harvest, then we should see what he puts into our hands as seed to sow for a greater harvest instead as bread to fill our stomachs for once. Rather, we prefer to fast and pray and do all kinds of religious ritual to be blessed.

According to Job 29:12–17, the secret to Job's prosperity was that he gave to the poor and the fatherless and those who had no helpers.

Because I delivered the poor who cried out,

The fatherless and the one who had no helper.

The blessing of a perishing man came upon me,
And I caused the widow's heart to sing for joy.
I put on righteousness, and it clothed me;
My justice was like a robe and a turban.
I was eyes to the blind,
And I was feet to the lame.
I was a father to the poor,
And I searched out the case that I did not know.
I broke the fangs of the wicked,
And plucked the victim from his teeth.

As I have said elsewhere, the proof of our righteousness is our love for people. You demonstrate to people that you are a righteous person by the way you love and treat people, saved and not yet saved. Like God says in his Word, professing love for God, whom you cannot see, if it is not matched by love for neighbour, whom you can see, is meaningless hypocrisy. When Job made a lifestyle of giving to the needy and helpless in his society, God made him the wealthiest person in the east in his days. With the wealth came power and influence in his society.

Job 1:3

Also, his possessions were seven thousand sheep, three thousand camels, five hundred yoke of oxen, five hundred female donkeys, and a very large household, so that this man was the greatest of all the people of the East.

What is God's purpose for giving us all this detail about Job's lifestyle? God is trying to get our attention as it were, saying, 'This is the way you prosper with me.' Instead of asking the Holy Spirit for cars and houses and such material things, he is saying, 'Listen to my instructions for prospering you, and when you do and obey them, these will be integral.' The instructions you obey will create the future you desire.

Blessing the poor and needy in society also attracts God's favour and blessing, as the experience of Job illustrates. This is further reiterated in Psalm 41:1–3.

> Blessed is he who considers the poor;
> The LORD will deliver him in time of trouble.
> The LORD will preserve him and keep him alive,
> And he will be blessed on the earth;
> You will not deliver him to the will of his enemies.
>
> The LORD will strengthen him on his bed of illness;
> You will sustain him on his sickbed.

God is saying that if we bless the poor and vulnerable in society, which may include orphans and widows, the physically and mentally challenged, the homeless and the destitute, we will attract his protection, preservation, victory over enemies, and healing. Make it a habit of blessing others who are less privileged than yourself and see what God will do in your life and that of your family.

In Genesis 26:1–2, 12–14,

> There was a famine in the land, besides the first famine that was in the days of Abraham. And Isaac went to Abimelech king of the Philistines, in Gerar.
>
> Then the LORD appeared to him and said: 'Do not go down to Egypt; live in the land of which I shall tell you.'
>
> Then Isaac sowed in that land, and reaped in the same year a hundredfold; and the LORD blessed him. The man began to prosper, and continued prospering until

he became very prosperous; for he had possessions of flocks and possessions of herds and a great number of servants. So the Philistines envied him.

When he obeyed God's instructions to stay in Gerar, contrary to all scientific investment advice because of the ravaging famine and the parched land, God blessed him with a hundredfold harvest. This was more crucial because it was not long ago that his father Abraham had taken his whole family to Egypt to escape a similar famine. Even though Isaac carried the anointing to prosper, he still had to follow God's instruction to sow in obedience to trigger that anointing. In Genesis 28:22, Jacob, the son of Isaac, had to trigger the same anointing of prosperity by making a vow to God when he had nothing in his hand to sow.

> And this stone which I have set as a pillar shall be God's house, and of all that You give me I will surely give a tenth to You.

This is a great principle in faith and a trust in God's faithfulness. You can sow what you do not have through a vow, trusting in God's faithfulness, and he is sure to come good for you.

In Genesis 12:7, 8; 14:20; 22:1–19, we see our father Abraham as the great worshipper and giver that sealed his destiny and place in history.

> Then the LORD appeared to Abram and said, 'To your descendants I will give this land.' And there he built an altar to the LORD, who had appeared to him. And he moved from there to the mountain east of Bethel, and he pitched his tent with Bethel on the west and Ai on the east; there he built an altar to the LORD and called on the name of the LORD.

Then they came to the place of which God had told him. And Abraham built an altar there and placed the wood in order; and he bound Isaac his son and laid him on the altar, upon the wood. And Abraham stretched out his hand and took the knife to slay his son.

But the Angel of the LORD called to him from heaven and said, 'Abraham, Abraham!'

So he said, 'Here I am.'

And He said, 'Do not lay your hand on the lad, or do anything to him; for now I know that you fear God, since you have not withheld your son, your only son, from Me.'

Here we see this extraordinary patriarch seal his destiny and his place in history by literally sacrificing his only begotten son and heir, Isaac, to God. When you obey God's promise and meet the conditions thereof, it graduates into a covenant. It means it is your obedience that obligates God to perform and fulfil his part of the promise. The moment Abraham passed the test of offering up Isaac, it sealed God's hand to offer his Son, Jesus Christ, in the fullness of time. What a debt of gratitude we all owe this great patriarch Abraham. No wonder everybody wants to relate to him and have a bit of his heritage.

Psalm 112:1–2

Praise the LORD!
Blessed is the man who fears the LORD,
Who delights greatly in His commandments.
His descendants will be mighty on earth;
The generation of the upright will be blessed.

No wonder Abraham's descendants are mighty on earth till this day.

Ephesians 4:28

> Let him who stole steal no longer, but rather let him labor, working with his hands what is good, that he may have something to give him who has need.

According to the above scripture, the purpose of work is so you will have something to give to him who has need. If your income is not enough to meet your needs, it is not your harvest. It is your seed. You will need to sow it or at least part of it to obtain your harvest. May you abound in the grace of giving so that you can give beyond your ability and see the untold riches of Christ abound to your account. As long as you are willing to open your hand, God is willing to open his heart. The spiritual law is that the physical always comes first and then the spiritual. Abraham had to offer his son, Isaac, and then God responds and sacrifices his Son, Jesus, for the world. So the sequence is as follows: sowing and then reaping; giving and then receiving; cause and then effect; action and then consequences.

In the same way, nothing leaves heaven until something leaves your hand. God said to one of his servants regarding sowing for a harvest, 'I have a harvest in mind when I talk about a seed.' If you can't trust God with your money, why on earth will you trust him with your life, your eternal destiny? Obedience to God's instructions is the only expression of your faith, and that is the only thing that opens the door to your harvest.

Compare Genesis 12:2–3, where God gave the promise to Abraham, and Genesis 22:15–18, when Abraham seals the promise with his obedience by 'sacrificing' his only son, Isaac.

> I will make you a great nation; I will bless you And make your name great;

And you shall be a blessing. I will bless those who bless you,

And I will curse him who curses you; And in you all the families of the earth shall be blessed.

You see a complete change in God's attitude and demeanour, to the extent that now he is swearing upon oath, not just promising, to bless Abraham.

Then the Angel of the LORD called to Abraham a second time out of heaven, and said: 'By Myself I have sworn, says the LORD, because you have done this thing, and have not withheld your son, your only son—blessing I will bless you, and multiplying I will multiply your descendants as the stars of the heaven and as the sand which is on the seashore; and your descendants shall possess the gate of their enemies. In your seed all the nations of the earth shall be blessed, because you have obeyed My voice.'

Hebrews 6:13–18 takes this up in the most beautiful way possible, saying,

For when God made a promise to Abraham, because He could swear by no one greater, He swore by Himself, saying, 'Surely blessing I will bless you, and multiplying I will multiply you.' And so, after he had patiently endured, he obtained the promise. For men indeed swear by the greater, and an oath for confirmation is for them an end of all dispute. Thus God, determining to show more abundantly to the heirs of promise the immutability of His counsel, confirmed it by an oath, that by two immutable things, in which it is impossible for God to lie, we might have

strong consolation, who have fled for refuge to lay
hold of the hope set before us.

In Genesis 12, God made a promise to Abraham, which he
certainly intended to honour in the fullness of time. But when
Abraham followed this up with his incredible superhuman obedience
of sacrificing his only son, Isaac, unto God, God said, 'Now you
have passed the test.' God said, 'Not that my Word of promise is
not good enough, but to make you double sure, I will add my oath
to it,' and he swore by himself. And the Bible declares that these are
two things in which it is impossible for God to lie, his Word and his
oath. God's counsel or his decision is immutable or unchangeable.
God cannot say one thing and do the opposite. That is why whenever
you receive any word that contradicts any part of his Word, simply
bin it; it is no good. God is not double-tongued. In the same way, if
any other religion comes up with any word that contradicts what the
God of Abraham, Isaac, and Jacob has said in his Word, the Bible, it
cannot be the same God speaking. We surely do not serve the same
God, no matter how politically correct that may sound. One of them
must be an imposter, claiming to be God. Talking up on Abraham's
obedience, God says, 'By myself, I have sworn.' Your obedience to
God's instructions will seal your destiny in him.

Abraham sowed an uncommon seed. So what makes a seed
uncommon?

A seed is anything that has the capacity to bless someone. By
this definition, your talents and skills are seeds when used to bless
someone. So are your time, your material possessions, and, certainly,
your money. Money has assumed a special place amongst seeds
because of its liquidity. This means that when you give someone
money, they can convert it into water, food, transport, medicine,
shelter, knowledge, or whatever they need at the time. But it is by no
means the only seed. God reacts to uncommon seed. The uncommon
seed is the one that costs the giver the most, such as Abraham giving
Isaac, or God giving his Son Jesus. God could have sent one of his
highest-ranking angels to rescue us, but that would not have cost God

nearly enough as Jesus, his only Son. In the same way, Abraham could have sacrificed one of his devoted servants, say, Eliezer of Damascus, but that would not have hurt nearly enough as Isaac, another only son. It bears repeating that your seed is what God multiplies, but your expectation is why he multiplies it. So you, too, like God, whenever you sow a seed of any kind, have a harvest in mind. Sow in expectation to receive back. When you sow expecting a harvest, you are not being carnal or unspiritual because it is God himself who promised to bless your seed with a good harvest. Rather, you are denying him an opportunity to bless you so that his name would be glorified. That is being unscriptural and disobedient.

A seed sown during a crisis in your life is an uncommon seed.

Philippians 4:14–19

Nevertheless you have done well that you shared in my distress. Now you Philippians know also that in the beginning of the gospel, when I departed from Macedonia, no church shared with me concerning giving and receiving but you only. For even in Thessalonica you sent aid once and again for my necessities. Not that I seek the gift, but I seek the fruit that abounds to your account. Indeed I have all and abound. I am full, having received from Epaphroditus the things sent from you, a sweet-smelling aroma, an acceptable sacrifice, well pleasing to God. And my God shall supply all your need according to His riches in glory by Christ Jesus.

Paul was moved by the generosity of the Philippian brethren who supported him financially at the beginning of his ministry when nobody knew him, and, hence, funds were scarce to come by. It is fashionable to support a worldwide, popular ministry that is raking in the dollars by the millions. But for an obscure or young ministry that nobody has heard of, it takes real faith to put your money in on a regular basis. There is a family like that in my ministry who have supported my ministry over the last several years, and my prayer for them is 'May God supply all their need according to his riches in glory by Christ Jesus.'

Luke 6:38; 1 Kings 17:10–14

> So he arose and went to Zarephath. And when he came to the gate of the city, indeed a widow was there gathering sticks. And he called to her and said, 'Please bring me a little water in a cup, that I may drink.' And as she was going to get it, he called to her and said, 'Please bring me a morsel of bread in your hand.'
>
> So she said, 'As the LORD your God lives, I do not have bread, only a handful of flour in a bin, and a little oil in a jar; and see, I am gathering a couple of sticks that I may go in and prepare it for myself and my son, that we may eat it, and die.'
>
> And Elijah said to her, 'Do not fear; go and do as you have said, but make me a small cake from it first, and bring it to me; and afterward make some for yourself and your son. For thus says the LORD God of Israel: "The bin of flour shall not be used up, nor shall the jar of oil run dry, until the day the LORD sends rain on the earth."'

This widow immortalised her place in the halls of faith by her sacrificial giving to the Prophet. She was in a time of distress, but she stepped out in faith and met the need of the prophet of God and received a great harvest as a result.

The size of the seed will make it uncommon, as illustrated in Matthew 26:6, 7, 13 and Mark 12:42–44.

And when Jesus was in Bethany at the house of Simon, the leper, a woman came to him having an alabaster flask of very costly fragrant oil, and she poured it on his head as he sat at the table.

> Assuredly, I say to you, wherever this gospel is preached in the whole world, what this woman has done will also be told as a memorial to her.

This woman with the alabaster oil came in at the exact time the oil was needed, the night before Jesus's crucifixion and burial. The timing made it uncommon as much as the fact that it was very costly, maybe something that took her a whole year to save for her wedding. And she 'wasted' it on Jesus. No wonder she is memorialised in the gospels.

> Then one poor widow came and threw in two mites, which make a quadrans. So He called His disciples to Himself and said to them, 'Assuredly, I say to you that this poor widow has put in more than all those who have given to the treasury; for they all put in out of their abundance, but she out of her poverty put in all that she had, her whole livelihood.'

Jesus must have loved this old lady for sure. From the account narrated by the Lord Jesus, this lady had nothing left after giving the little she had. Such sacrificial giving; no matter how small is sure to move God. Some wealthy dudes must have given out of their abundance, but as a proportion of wealth, she gave the highest because she must have given 100 percent of her wealth, the whole lot.

So is a seed planted in obedience to the voice of God is uncommon, according to Genesis 26:2–3, 12–13 and 22:1–2.

> Then the LORD appeared to him and said: 'Do not go down to Egypt; live in the land of which I shall tell you. Dwell in this land, and I will be with you and

bless you; for to you and your descendants I give all these lands, and I will perform the oath which I swore to Abraham your father.'

Then Isaac sowed in that land, and reaped in the same year a hundredfold; and the LORD blessed him. The man began to prosper, and continued prospering until he became very prosperous.

God gave Isaac direct instructions to stay in Gerar and not go down to Egypt as his father had done in his day during the famine. He obeyed and sowed in the famine-ravaged land, and God blessed his faith and obedience with a hundredfold return.

Now it came to pass after these things that God tested Abraham, and said to him, 'Abraham!'

And he said, 'Here I am.'

Then He said, 'Take now your son, your only son Isaac, whom you love, and go to the land of Moriah, and offer him there as a burnt offering on one of the mountains of which I shall tell you.'

Abraham offered his son, Isaac, in obedience to God's command, and when he obeyed, God swore an oath to bless him and his family and, through him, all humanity.

From the foregoing, it is obvious that nobody can sow your seed for you. It is something you have to do personally. It is also important that you give your seed an assignment. What are you sowing the seed for? You can sow a seed for any need to be met in your life. Very often it is the seed you need to unlock a particular door instead of prayer. You can create your desired future with your seed by sowing your way into your destiny. The seed that leaves your hand goes into your future to create that desired future.

The seed can be sown into a church or a ministry, into a charitable organisation, especially one with a religious flavour, or into the life of a man or woman of God.

The four things that affect your financial success

The tithe, as an acknowledgement that God is your source, according to Malachi 3:8–10, Hebrews 7:8, and Matthew 23:23.

> Will a man rob God? Yet you have robbed Me! But you say,
> 'In what way have we robbed You?' In tithes and offerings.
> You are cursed with a curse, For you have robbed Me, Even this whole nation. Bring all the tithes into the storehouse,
> That there may be food in My house, And try Me now in this,'
> Says the LORD of hosts, 'If I will not open for you the windows of heaven
> And pour out for you such blessing. That there will not be room enough to receive it.'

God says if we keep the tithe, we are robbing him, and we are cursed, because it does not belong to us but to him. I have seen financial catastrophe after catastrophe fall upon Christians who refused to tithe even though they have a clear understanding of it and what God says about it. You may be saying that the tithe belongs under the Old Testament Law, but that is not correct because Abraham paid a tithe to Melchizedek in Genesis 14, thousands of years before the birth of Moses and the Law. In addition, the tithe is the key subject of Hebrews (7:7–9) and Matthew (23:23), both of which encourage us to pay. If, for whatever reason, you do not pay the tithe, don't feel bad about it. Like most things that have to be caught by revelation, some people will always look for reasons to justify their disobedience, but those who catch the revelation will look for reasons to obey, of which there are many. When a certain man of God asked Jesus in a vision why he did not make the tithe crystal clear that we should all pay it, his characteristic reply was 'Even if I said plainly in the New Testament that all should pay tithes, not all would obey. I do not cast my pearls before swine. That is why most of the key doctrines of the faith are caught by revelation. The deity of Christ, salvation by faith, divine healing, tithe, and baptism in the Holy Spirit are all doctrines that one has to catch by revelation, and it is reserved for those who have a heart to obey.' Those are the master's words. No more comment.

Hebrews 7:8 says, 'Here mortal men receive tithes, but there he receives them, of whom it is witnessed that he lives.'

Matthew 23:23

> Woe to you, scribes and Pharisees, hypocrites! For you pay tithe of mint and anise and cummin, and have neglected the weightier matters of the law: justice and mercy and faith. These you ought to have done, without leaving the others undone.

Both of the above verses are clearly saying that we are to pay the tithe.

Honouring one's parents as God's vehicle for bringing them into the world, according to Ephesians 6:1–3.

> Children, obey your parents in the Lord, for this is right. 'Honor your father and mother,' which is the first commandment with promise: 'that it may be well with you and you may live long on the earth.'

Honouring the child-parent relationship is crucial to financial success and success in every facet of life. The rupturing of the relationship between children and parents, especially fathers, is one of the main causes of the crises amongst young people, especially murders and homicides that have reached crisis proportions in many nations of the world today. Fathers, your children need you to be around and to be actively involved in their lives more than you care to know. Their lives literally depend on it.

Obedience to your assignment on earth, as explained in John 12:24.

> Most assuredly, I say to you, unless a grain of wheat falls into the ground and dies, it remains alone; but if it dies, it produces much grain.

We must discover our God-given assignment and fulfil it to be really fulfilled in life. The moment you discover your assignment and walk into it, you will discover that money is waiting for you there. Money is the scriptural reward for obedience to your assignment, as whatever God calls you to do will bless people for which they will be prepared to reward you back financially accordingly.

The seed you sow, according to Luke 6:38, will determine the future you create for yourself.

> Give, and it will be given to you: good measure, pressed down, shaken together, and running over will be put into your bosom. For with the same measure that you use, it will be measured back to you.

This follows one of the most powerful laws God instituted in his universe: the law of sowing and reaping, or the law of reciprocity. If you sow, you are bound to reap. It may not come from the same source or place where you sowed or even in the manner and form you expected it, but come it surely will.

Obedience brings the blessing

It is important to understand that God has the ability and willingness to bless his children exceedingly financially. It is equally important that when we support God's work on earth financially, he turns the money around and use it on us and our fellow humans, since heaven has no need for dollars or any earthly currency. So essentially, we are not giving to a taker but to a receiver, who would only receive what we give so he can bless us. A taker takes for himself, but a receiver is a conduit, a channel used by God. So you and I need a lot of discernment when it comes to giving. Not all soils are fit for sowing your seed in them. Some are infested with mice and rodents, which will quickly devour any seed sown on them. There are a lot of takers around, and you have to identify them and stay away from them.

When it comes to many of the Christian disciplines, many believers will wait until a crisis hits them before they begin to pray or tithe or give in the emergency. But you do not rush to the ground to sow your seed in an emergency. No seasoned farmer does that. Emergency time is the time to call in the harvest. Like King Hezekiah in 2 Kings 20:1–3,

> In those days Hezekiah was sick and near death. And Isaiah the prophet, the son of Amoz, went to him and said to him, 'Thus says the LORD: "Set your house in order, for you shall die, and not live."'
>
> Then he turned his face toward the wall, and prayed to the LORD, saying, 'Remember now, O LORD, I pray, how I have walked before You in truth and with a loyal heart, and have done what was good in Your sight.' And Hezekiah wept bitterly.

When the king reminded God of how faithful and loyal he had been with God over the years, he was essentially calling in his harvest of healing based on the good seed he had sowed with God over the years, and God responded promptly and overturned his condition and healed him. The great object lesson this godly king was teaching us all was that you have a big part to play in your prosperity. You cannot live anyway you want and do anything you want and expect God to bless you or bail you out in a crisis. All of God's dealings with us are based on an ongoing relationship of love and obedience.

The three things God requires from his children to bless them are obedience, faith, and the seed. All three are closely related because if you have faith in God, you will have no problem obeying him, and then you will have no fear sowing your seed because you trust in his faithfulness. Obedience is the proof of faith. When you are not walking in obedience, your faith is called into question. Obedience pleases God above all else because when we walk in obedience, it is our recognition that not only is he God but also he is faithful and has our best intentions at heart as our Father. This was the trait that stood Abraham apart from all men who ever walked with God. He trusted God with his all. And today, the blessing of Abraham has come upon us to free us from the curse of the Law, which meant sickness, poverty, and spiritual death. That is why the Bible says that godliness is profitable unto all things physical, material, financial, emotional, and spiritual for time and eternity. Look at how God blessed Abraham in Genesis 24:35 as narrated by his servant.

> The LORD has blessed my master greatly, and he has
> become great; and He has given him flocks and herds,
> silver and gold, male and female servants, and camels
> and donkeys.

Abraham became great not just materially but also spiritually and generationally. In those days, camels and donkeys were like government bonds, or treasury bills and the ISAs of today. His ancestry stretches from the Arab nation, the Jews, and the Christians all over the world. We all see him as our father and trailblazer of our faith. God even calls him his friend in Isaiah 41:8 and 2 Chronicles 20:7. He demonstrated his faith by his instant obedience, even in the most challenging circumstances. He was a doer of the Word, not just a hearer. From God's first instructions to leave his native Ur of the Chaldees, to let his first son Ishmael go, to the sacrifice of his beloved Isaac, this man was tested to the hilt, in ways most of us would listen with gaping bewilderment, and he passed every one of these tests. We are all proud to be his children.

Unfortunately, many Christians have substituted knowing with doing. But knowing is not doing. It is good to know, but it is better to go one step forward and do what you know, as that is the only way to get blessed. They know all about prayer but hardly pray, all about tongues but hardly speak, all about tithing but hardly give, all about fasting, all about giving, but very few do these, at least on a regular basis. That is why God says to obey is better than sacrifice. Go ahead and do what you know, no matter how little you know.

A NOTE OF CAUTION ON MONEY AND RICHES

When it comes to life goals, it appears most people are primarily motivated by money and the things money can buy, especially in their youthful days. Check this out on daytime TV shows promising bounty scoops of cash for worthy contestants. Remember, whatever a person hungers for, Satan is always on hand to offer in exchange for a spiritual compromise, whether it is sex, automobiles, great wealth, popularity, fame, or adulation of men. But we are warned in 1 Timothy 6:9 about the dangers of pursuing money and wealth as a means in themselves.

> But those who desire to be rich fall into temptation
> and a snare, and into many foolish and harmful lusts
> which drown men in destruction and perdition.

Not only are we potential prey to wild-eyed get-rich schemes and shady deals that never deliver what they promise, but we may actually be putting our heads in the scope of the devil's rifle. Even if we are lucky to achieve this promised wealth, we soon come to realise that this does not satisfy our need for significance. No amount of money can do that. In our lifetime, we have witnessed the tragedy of some of the most famous and wealthiest individuals on earth live and die lonely, unloved, miserable, agonizing deaths. There has to be a better reason for living than the accumulation of wealth and things. Jesus kept returning to the theme of money over and over in his ministry for a reason. He was underlying the fact that a great spiritual danger accompanies the pursuit and the achievement of wealth. He explained why in Matthew 6:21, saying simply but poignantly, 'For where your treasure is, there your heart will be also.'

He says your heart will follow your money and wealth. It is impossible to detach your heart from where you put your money. This truth became real in my life and ministry when, years ago, I had to leave a ministry I had helped groom to start a new work on the orders of the Lord. My family and I were amongst the few tithe payers who had given our tithes and resources to accumulate a healthy bank balance for this church, and now we were to leave all that behind and go start a new work with nothing in the bank. No, not that I wanted any of that money for myself, but it nonetheless had a pull on my heart. But the Lord gave us the grace to leave that and everything else behind for a new person to take over, trusting him to bless us in our new assignment.

It is important to give the Lord first place in everything in our lives including our finances, because he will not settle for second place in anything. He is either Lord of all or none at all. When your focus and passion are set on your money or anything for that matter, it would not be long before God becomes almost an irrelevance in your life.

This understanding does not prohibit us from earning a living, having a savings account, or having a nice home and car. We are required specifically to provide for our families and to have something to give to the needy, according to 1 Timothy 5:8 and Ephesians 4:28.

> But if anyone does not provide for his own, and
> especially for those of his household, he has denied
> the faith and is worse than an unbeliever.

Wealth is not evil in and of itself. It can be a great force for good in the hands of the right person, in the same way as it can be a great force for evil in the wrong hands. Most of the Bible characters who walked faithfully with God accumulated great wealth and riches. Such patriarchs like Abraham, Isaac, Jacob, David, Solomon, and Joseph were all men of immense wealth. The apostle Paul clarifies this for us that money itself is not the problem but the love of it in 1 Timothy 6:10.

> For the love of money is a root of all kinds of evil, for which some have strayed from the faith in their greediness, and pierced themselves through with many sorrows.

We get into trouble when our possessions become our God. We are in danger when money becomes more important than our health, than human life, than our family, our marriage, and our children.

These four principles should define our attitude to and pursuit for money

We should recognise that the money belongs to God and that we are his stewards. We should therefore seek his opinion on all our spending decisions.

We should understand that there is always a trade-off between our time and effort and the money we earn. We spent our lives acquiring the money, so we should spend it wisely.

Since we do not have unlimited amounts of cash, we should always spend our money on the most important needs first.

We must also be willing to postpone spending on things we cannot really afford instead of buying on-hire purchase and credit cards with their crippling interests that will have implications on our lives and families later on. This means we should avoid living in debt as much possible, especially for perishable items. We should always endeavour to live within our means and spend less than we earn.

This is what the Lord says about the trappings of success in Jeremiah 9:23–24.

> Thus says the LORD:
>
> 'Let not the wise man glory in his wisdom,
> Let not the mighty man glory in his might,
> Nor let the rich man glory in his riches;

> But let him who glories glory in this,
> That he understands and knows Me,
> That I am the LORD, exercising loving kindness,
> judgment, and righteousness in the earth. For in these
> I delight,' says the LORD.

The Lord always gives good advice, and the above is a good example. Whatever we do should be motivated by our desire to serve him and his kingdom, the only thing that carries an eternal significance. Whatever we do, we should do all for the for the glory of God, as the apostle Paul advised in 1 Corinthians 10:31.

> Therefore, whether you eat or drink, or whatever you
> do, do all to the glory of God.

This is very clear and straightforward, isn't it? Our purposes are not our own. They are his. If you live long enough, you will trash your trophies and certificates. There was a time that I looked at my certificates with some real pride, but with time, these have held less and less significance till now I don't even know where they are and cannot really be bothered about them anymore.

Like King David's final words to his son, Solomon, and other dignitaries in 1 Chronicles 28:9, 'Know God' and serve him.

> As for you, my son Solomon, know the God of your
> father, and serve Him with a loyal heart and with a
> willing mind; for the LORD searches all hearts and
> understands all the intent of the thoughts. If you seek
> Him, He will be found by you; but if you forsake Him,
> He will cast you off forever.

> If you seek God you will find Him, but if you forsake
> Him he will cast you off.

How true and prophetic this sweet psalmist words are, even today.

GOD'S SEVEN WEALTH TRANSFER AND THE END OF THE AGE

As we approach the end of the age and the coming worldwide harvest of souls, it is my sincere conviction, based on solid biblical evidence, that God is going to shift massive amounts of finance and other resources from the world to his children in the church. Of course, it is not everyone in the church who is going to benefit directly from this coming wealth transfer but only those who have proven to be trustworthy receivers and conduits for financing his work on earth.

There is a difference between someone who has received a blessing and someone who carries the blessing. Abraham carried the blessing, but Lot received a blessing. In the same way, Jacob carried the blessing whilst Laban received a blessing. Joseph carried the blessing, but Potiphar and Pharaoh both received blessings because of the presence of Joseph under their roofs. So long as Pharaoh and his country hooked up with Joseph and, later, Joseph's people, Egypt was blessed, but when they broke ranks with the Jews and started oppressing them, it was downhill from then on.

> For God gives wisdom and knowledge and joy to a man who is good in His sight; but to the sinner He gives the work of gathering and collecting, that he may give to him who is good before God. This also is vanity and grasping for the wind. (Eccles. 2:26)

So it is God himself who has assigned the sinner the task of gathering and collecting wealth so he will transfer this to the righteous for the sponsoring of his work on earth.

Proverbs 13:22 declares,

> A good man leaves an inheritance to his children's children,

> But the wealth of the sinner is stored up for the righteous.

Very often the best inheritance to leave for children are not necessarily bank accounts and brick and mortar, as care should be taken not to do anything that will deprive children the thrill of experiencing the challenges of life and developing the vital life principles necessary for succeeding in life. It is more crucial to bequeath to children the character principles for coping with life's challenges. Give children a good education and teach them the values of integrity, honesty, persistence, hard work, faith, and relationships; all of which will equip them with the right attitudes for life. The truth of the matter is that if these virtues and positive attitudes are absent, no matter how much you leave for children in businesses, bank accounts, and properties, they will go down the drain in a matter of one or, at the most, two generations. This is one of the greatest lessons and legacies our father Abraham left for all mankind. He did such an excellent job in teaching his children the ways of God and the positive attitudes of faith and hard work and thus successfully passed on his enduring attitude of perseverance, the promise of God on his life, and the anointing unto his children and the generations following so that eventually these became part of the genetic makeup of the nation of people that came after him.

In Genesis 1:28, man started on the best positive footing as God bestows blessings on Adam and Eve.

> Then God blessed them, and God said to them, 'Be fruitful and multiply; fill the earth and subdue it; have dominion over the fish of the sea, over the birds of the air, and over every living thing that moves on the earth.'

God blessed man with fruitfulness, multiplication, dominion, and rulership over the entire created order. But we know what happened when man sold out to the devil and lost it all. Now man was to sweat to eke out a mere subsistence.

Now, that era passes with disappointment on all sides, so come in the flood and then Noah and his family to have a fresh go. God blesses them after the flood and makes some incredible promises to man. But then it was not long, and it all falls apart at the tower of Babel, and God had to disperse men all over the world after dividing the world into the present continents (and nations) as we know them today, according to Genesis 10:25.

Then came Abraham through whom God promised to raise an evangelistic nation to give them his Word and teach his ways so, in turn, they could teach the rest of mankind. God was, henceforth, not going to deal directly with all mankind as he had done in the past but rather do that through Abraham and his descendants, who became the Jews or Israelites.

Abraham was a giver and a great conduit whom God could trust implicitly, as he proved in Genesis 22, when he offered up his son, Isaac, as a sacrifice to God. He was the first to receive God's wealth transfer from a Gentile, in Genesis 12:16 and 20:14, first, from Pharaoh and then from Abimelech, king of Gerar.

> He treated Abram well for her sake. He had sheep, oxen, male donkeys, male and female servants, female donkeys, and camels.

Then Abimelech took sheep, oxen, and male and
female servants, and gave them to Abraham; and he
restored Sarah his wife to him.

In both episodes, Abraham actually did not conduct himself in
the best possible way, but God actually went ahead and blessed him
so that he came off much richer and blessed. This was so much that,
in Genesis 24:35, his servant reported,

The LORD has blessed my master greatly, and he has
become great; and He has given him flocks and herds,
silver and gold, male and female servants, and camels
and donkeys.

Abraham was a giver, as we have established already, who
understood the key to wealth transfer, giving a tenth of his wealth to
Melchizedek, in Genesis 14:18–20.

Then Melchizedek king of Salem brought out bread
and wine; he was the priest of God Most High. And
he blessed him and said:

'Blessed be Abram of God Most High,
Possessor of heaven and earth;
And blessed be God Most High,
Who has delivered your enemies into your hand.'

And he gave him a tithe of all.

Isaac, the son of Abraham, was next in line to receive the wealth
transfer, him also from Abimelech, king of Gerar. God gave him
express instructions to stay in Gerar during a severe famine, when
everyone was fleeing with their families to safety. It was the same
kind of famine that had caused his father Abraham to move to Egypt
temporarily in his day. So it was only natural that Isaac followed the

family tradition and move to Egypt or somewhere else for safety. But no, God told him not to go, but 'stay in the land and I will bless you.' After dithering for a long time, he finally decided to stay and sowed in the famine-ravaged land. The moment he obeyed God, he triggered the blessing, and that same year, the Bible says, God released the perfect hundredfold blessing to him, according to Genesis 26:12–14.

> Then Isaac sowed in that land, and reaped in the same year a hundredfold; and the LORD blessed him. The man began to prosper, and continued prospering until he became very prosperous; for he had possessions of flocks and possessions of herds and a great number of servants. So the Philistines envied him.

The third person to receive the wealth transfer from the sinner was Jacob, the son of Isaac and the grandson of Abraham. In his case, God took away the livestock of his uncle Laban and gave them to Jacob. Notice that Jacob actually fled from his family empty and had nothing but a staff in his hand and a rock for a pillow at one time. But Jacob was a very smart, determined, and hardworking man. He served his uncle for fourteen years to marry the girl of his dreams, Rachel. That speaks volumes about a man who knows what he wants and how to get it. His uncle Laban changed his wages ten times, but he was unperturbed. This man had the anointing and favour of God upon him, if anyone ever did. In Genesis 30:27–28, his uncle acknowledged that God had blessed him because of Jacob and actually asked him to name his wages.

> And Laban said to him, 'Please stay, if I have found favor in your eyes, for I have learned by experience that the LORD has blessed me for your sake.' Then he said, 'Name me your wages, and I will give it.'

Let us disabuse our minds of the fact that God's blessing precludes hard work and perseverance because that is not true at all. All these patriarchs were very hardworking people who did not set out to be rich but were diligent and determined people who persevered in the face of severe odds but ended up succeeding against all odds. In Genesis 31:6–9 and 30:43, the Bible had this to say about Jacob:

> And you know that with all my might I have served your father. Yet your father has deceived me and changed my wages ten times, but God did not allow him to hurt me. If he said thus: 'The speckled shall be your wages,' then all the flocks bore speckled. And if he said thus: 'The streaked shall be your wages,' then all the flocks bore streaked. So God has taken away the livestock of your father and given them to me.

> Thus the man became exceedingly prosperous, and had large flocks, female and male servants, and camels and donkeys.

You would have noticed by now that the wealth these patriarchs accumulated went up a notch with every succeeding generation. Abraham was blessed greatly, Isaac was very prosperous, but Jacob became exceedingly prosperous, with a huge family of four wives and thirteen children, not to mention the fact that he was given the honour of fathering the nation that bore his name, Israel, and actually became one of God's favourite characters in all the Bible. Talk of divine elevation and favour.

Joseph, the son of Jacob and the great-grandson of Abraham, was the fourth in line for the wealth transfer from the wicked to God's people. Through the incredible gift of interpreting dreams and unfettered service and great acumen for economic planning, God elevated this young man to one of the highest positions of political influence and economic power ever bestowed on a man in the ancient world. Joseph became the richest and most powerful person in all of Egypt bar Pharaoh. This is a true story of 'prison to palace' and the stuff of which thriller movies are made. Remember that Egypt was the superpower of that day, the richest and most powerful nation of the time. Genesis 41:38–44 gives an account of the influence and power that this young Jewish ex-slave enjoyed in the host superpower nation.

> And Pharaoh said to his servants, 'Can we find such a one as this, a man in whom is the Spirit of God?'
>
> Then Pharaoh said to Joseph, 'Inasmuch as God has shown you all this, there is no one as discerning and wise as you. You shall be over my house, and all my people shall be ruled according to your word; only in regard to the throne will I be greater than you.' And Pharaoh said to Joseph, 'See, I have set you over all the land of Egypt.'
>
> Then Pharaoh took his signet ring off his hand and put it on Joseph's hand; and he clothed him in garments of fine linen and put a gold chain around his neck. And he had him ride in the second chariot which he had; and they cried out before him, 'Bow the knee!' So he set him over all the land of Egypt. Pharaoh also said to Joseph, 'I am Pharaoh, and without your consent no man may lift his hand or foot in all the land of Egypt.'

It is worth remembering that in all his troubles, Joseph never once complained about the injustice done him and always gave the best account possible of himself. In Potiphar's house, he was very hard working and served his master and his family with excellence. He had an impeccable moral streak that most of us Spirit-indwelt, New Testament, tongues-talking Christians would envy. Of all Bible characters, Joseph stands out as the one most resembling the Lord Jesus Christ in outlook and life experiences. It took a great character like Joseph to look his brothers in the eye and tell them, 'It was not you, but God who sent me to this place, to save your lives.'

In Exodus 12:35–36, the Jews, before departing Egypt, received a supernatural wealth transfer from the Egyptians overnight of unimaginable proportions. This was purely by God's supernatural favour and intervention, according to the Exodus account.

> Now the children of Israel had done according to the word of Moses, and they had asked from the Egyptians articles of silver, articles of gold, and clothing. And the LORD had given the people favor in the sight of the Egyptians, so that they granted them what they requested. Thus they plundered the Egyptians.

To plunder a wealthy superpower like Egypt must have meant a lot of stuff. I guess God calculated to the last cent all the wages they were denied for their slave labour for all those hundreds of years, with compounded interest, multiplied seven times, and, literally, all the substance in the houses of the Egyptians were heaped on the Jews the night before their departure. God is about to repeat this in our day. He is going to do that once again for the Jewish people in the end times as God finally humiliates their enemies who have harassed them for millennia and empty their treasures unto Israel.

In 1 Kings 10:14–29, God gives King Solomon the wealth of the nations, and he becomes the richest man of all time.

Solomon's Great Wealth

> The weight of gold that came to Solomon yearly was six hundred and sixty-six talents of gold, besides that from the traveling merchants, from the income of traders, from all the kings of Arabia, and from the governors of the country.

> And King Solomon made two hundred large shields of hammered gold; six hundred shekels of gold went into each shield. He also made three hundred shields of hammered gold; three minas of gold went into each

shield. The king put them in the House of the Forest of Lebanon.

Moreover the king made a great throne of ivory, and overlaid it with pure gold. The throne had six steps, and the top of the throne was round at the back; there were armrests on either side of the place of the seat, and two lions stood beside the armrests. Twelve lions stood there, one on each side of the six steps; nothing like this had been made for any other kingdom.

All King Solomon's drinking vessels were gold, and all the vessels of the House of the Forest of Lebanon were pure gold. Not one was silver, for this was accounted as nothing in the days of Solomon. For the king had merchant ships at sea with the fleet of Hiram. Once every three years the merchant ships came bringing gold, silver, ivory, apes, and monkeys. So King Solomon surpassed all the kings of the earth in riches and wisdom.

Now all the earth sought the presence of Solomon to hear his wisdom, which God had put in his heart. Each man brought his present: articles of silver and gold, garments, armor, spices, horses, and mules, at a set rate year by year.

And Solomon gathered chariots and horsemen; he had one thousand four hundred chariots and twelve thousand horsemen, whom he stationed in the chariot cities and with the king at Jerusalem. The king made silver as common in Jerusalem as stones, and he made cedar trees as abundant as the sycamores which are in the lowland.

Also Solomon had horses imported from Egypt and Keveh; the king's merchants bought them in Keveh at the current price. Now a chariot that was imported from Egypt cost six hundred shekels of silver, and a horse one hundred and fifty; and thus, through their agents, they exported them to all the kings of the Hittites and the kings of Syria.

Solomon's reputation of wealth and wisdom had survived him till today. He must have been wise and industrious, but at the heart of it, God gave it all to him. He was the sixth person to receive the wealth of the nations. The last and final transfer of wealth will not just be to an individual, like those of the past, but would be a mass transfer to multitudes of believers and even churches and ministries that are at the forefront of God's final evangelistic thrust to win the world for Jesus. According to Proverbs 13:22,

A good *man* leaves an inheritance to his children's children,
But the wealth of the sinner is stored up for the righteous.

God has watched the wicked store up a lot of wealth and other stuff that he is going to transfer to his children for the end-time harvest of souls. You are the seventh in line for the blessing and the coming transfer of wealth. Money will bring satisfaction and contentment only to the degree that it benefits others. Don't accumulate money for its sake. Use it to benefit others because its accumulation can become compulsively addictive and distort your view of the real essence and meaning of life.

To qualify for this coming wealth transfer, you must position yourself accordingly by demonstrating your financial integrity to God. There will be no time to hoard the coming stuff because of the time period we live in. Luke 6:38 advises us,

> Give, and it will be given to you: good measure,
> pressed down, shaken together, and running over will
> be put into your bosom. For with the same measure
> that you use, it will be measured back to you.

When Jesus asks us to give just one time, we are to expect to receive seven times, according to the above scriptures. When God tells you to give, his real focus is on you receiving the harvest and the fruit of your sowing. We should be harvest oriented and give with expectation. It is unscriptural and certainly not a sign of humility to give without expecting to receive back. Without expecting to receive back, you are literally raping your seed of the harvest and denying God the opportunity to bless you and demonstrate his good generosity and, hence, the praise and thanksgiving due him. It might actually be helpful to write down the harvest you expect to receive from the seed you sow so that when it does come in, you will know that the Word really works and that God is really faithful, watching over his Word to perform it. After sowing your seed, you are left to start praising God because praise is the language of faith. It is the evidence of your expectation of the harvest.

According to Deuteronomy 8:18, there is an anointing for prosperity, and my prayer for you is that as you demonstrate your faithfulness in small things, that anointing will come and abide on you.

> And you shall remember the LORD your God, for it
> is He who gives you power to get wealth, that He
> may establish His covenant which He swore to your
> fathers, as it is this day.

God gives you this anointing for wealth so that he can establish his covenant on earth. God's prosperity and anointing is always for a purpose, and once we identify where he is busy working and we get involved alongside with him, he will surely prosper us so we can be co-labourers with him. For some, he may have to take us out of debt and reposition us to be partners in his ministry. God always blesses so you can be a blessing. Begin to thank him because he has qualified you for a blessing, according to Colossians 1:12.

> Giving thanks to the Father who has qualified us to be partakers of the inheritance of the saints in the light.

He has qualified you by the precious blood of Jesus. It is a done thing.

WHY CHRISTIANS SHOULD
SUPPORT ISRAEL

It all started with the call of Abraham by God to leave his native Ur of the Chaldees to the land of Canaan, according to Genesis 12:1–3. Since the time God made this seminal declaration, the course of man's history on planet Earth has never been the same. This single statement of intent and all the ramifications that have resulted from it continue to shape the lives of humanity till today, and its effects will carry on into eternity future. Even though the enemies of God have sought to propagate their hideous cruelties and suffering on mankind, as they do with every good thing God has for man, the blessings, both physical and spiritual, that have resulted from God's simple command to Abraham and his obedient response against all odds continue to reverberate around the world. We cannot exhaust the implications and effects of this unfolding drama in all the volumes that could be written, as there will not be any earthly library big enough to stock them.

Now the LORD had said to Abram:

'Get out of your country,
From your family
And from your father's house,
To a land that I will show you.
I will make you a great nation;

> I will bless you
> And make your name great;
> And you shall be a blessing.
> I will bless those who bless you,
> And I will curse him who curses you;
> And in you all the families of the earth shall be blessed.'

Israelis are the people and nation that descended from Abraham, Isaac, and Jacob. The patriarch Jacob fathered twelve sons, who became the fathers of the Jewish people. God changed Jacob's name to Israel (a prince with God) when the latter wrestled with the Angel of the Lord in Genesis 32:28 at the river Jabbok.

> And He said, 'Your name shall no longer be called Jacob, but Israel; for you have struggled with God and with men, and have prevailed.'

The nation of Israel descended from four matriarchs, Jacob's wives—namely, Leah and her servant Zilpah and Leah's sister Rachel and her servant Bilhah.

Together they gave birth to the twelve sons, who became the fathers of the twelve tribes of Israel, and a daughter named Dinah. The twelve sons are Reuben, Simeon, Levi, Judah, Dan, Naphtali, Gad, Asher, Issachar, Zebulun (Dinah), Joseph, and Benjamin, in that order.

Israel is the only nation created by a sovereign act of God. God gave the title deed for the land of Israel to Abraham, Isaac, and Jacob and their descendants forever.

The following are some of the many scriptures that detail God's covenant to Abraham and his descendants after him regarding the land of Canaan: Genesis 12:7; 13:14–15; 15:7, 18; 17:2–8; and Exodus 19:5, 6.

Then the LORD appeared to Abram and said, 'To your descendants I will give this land.' (Gen. 12:7)

And the LORD said to Abram, after Lot had separated from him: 'Lift your eyes now and look from the place where you are—northward, southward, eastward, and westward; for all the land which you see I give to you and your descendants forever. (Gen. 13:14–15)

Then He said to him, 'I am the LORD, who brought you out of Ur of the Chaldeans, to give you this land to inherit it.' (Gen. 15:7)

On the same day the LORD made a covenant with Abram, saying:

'To your descendants I have given this land, from the river of Egypt to the great river, the River Euphrates.' (Gen. 15:18)

'And I will make My covenant between Me and you, and will multiply you exceedingly.' Then Abram fell on his face, and God talked with him, saying: 'As for Me, behold, My covenant is with you, and you shall be a father of many nations. No longer shall your name be called Abram, but your name shall be Abraham; for I have made you a father of many nations. I will make you exceedingly fruitful; and I will make nations of you, and kings shall come from you. And I will establish My covenant between Me and you and your descendants after you in their generations, for an everlasting covenant, to be God to you and your descendants after you. Also I give to you and your descendants after you the land in which you are a stranger, all the land of Canaan, as an everlasting possession; and I will be their God.' (Gen. 17:2–8).

Note how God emphasizes the fact that he has given the land of Canaan to Abraham and his descendants after him forever in an everlasting covenant, as an everlasting possession.

Notice also how God set the Jewish people apart for himself to be his special treasure and evangelistic nation to bless the rest of the world through them:

> 'Now therefore, if you will indeed obey My voice and keep My covenant, then you shall be a special treasure to Me above all people; for all the earth is Mine. And you shall be to Me a kingdom of priests and a holy nation.' These are the words which you shall speak to the children of Israel. (Exod. 19:5, 6)

> For you are a holy people to the LORD your God; the LORD your God has chosen you to be a people for Himself, a special treasure above all the peoples on the face of the earth. (Deut. 7:6)

> Also today the LORD has proclaimed you to be His special people, just as He promised you, that you should keep all His commandments, and that He will set you high above all nations which He has made, in praise, in name, and in honor, and that you may be a holy people to the LORD your God, just as He has spoken. (Deut. 26:18–19).

Ishmael, the father of the Arabs (who fathered twelve sons, the second son, Kedar, from whom the prophet Mohammed of Islam descended; Gen. 25:13) was excluded from the title deed to the land, according to Genesis 17:18–21.

And Abraham said to God, 'Oh, that Ishmael might live before You!'

Then God said: 'No, Sarah your wife shall bear you a son, and you shall call his name Isaac; I will establish My covenant with him for an everlasting covenant, and with his descendants after him. And as for Ishmael, I have heard you. Behold, I have blessed him, and will make him fruitful, and will multiply him exceedingly. He shall beget twelve princes, and I will make him a great nation. But My covenant I will establish with Isaac, whom Sarah shall bear to you at this set time next year.'

After Abraham had waited for almost twenty-five years without the promised son, Ishmael came along through the suggestion of Sarah to lay with her Egyptian maid Hagar. In the episode above, Abraham was pleading with God to fulfil his promised covenant through Ishmael, but God flatly said, 'No.' God went on to say that Sarah was going to beget a son through whom the promise would come. God also promised to bless Ishmael and his descendants, materially, of course, hence the incredible oil wealth the descendants of Ishmael have enjoyed over the years.

Therefore, modern-day Palestinians have no biblical mandate to own the land. If only the world will tell them the truth about their claims to the land of Israel, they will abandon their futile struggle for a land that was never theirs and never will. They are simply being used as unwitting pawns in a politico-cosmic war game with all the needless suffering that has entailed.

When God established the nations of the world, he began with Israel. Israel is the centre of the universe, in the mind of God.

Deuteronomy 32:8–10, Numbers 34:10–15, Joshua 11:16–22, Exodus 19:4–6

> When the Most High divided their inheritance to the
> nations,
> When He separated the sons of Adam,
> He set the boundaries of the peoples
> According to the number of the children of Israel.
> For the LORD's portion is His people;
> Jacob is the place of His inheritance.

The title deed to the land of Canaan, the Promised Land, was passed from Abraham, in Genesis 12:7 and 13:15; to Isaac, in Genesis 26:3; and from Isaac to Jacob, in Genesis 28:13, 15; 35:12; 48:3–5. According to Psalm 89:30–37; 105; and all the above scriptures, God's promise to Israel was unconditional.

> Dwell in this land, and I will be with you and bless
> you; for to you and your descendants I give all these
> lands, and I will perform the oath which I swore to
> Abraham your father.

It is worth remembering that Israel's title to the land is unconditional and eternal. This means the land is theirs whether they are living in it or not. However, the land use covenant, their use and enjoyment of the land, is conditional upon their obedience, according to Deuteronomy 28:1–2, 15, 64–65. This explains why anytime they disobeyed God, they were uprooted from the land and sent into exile, but even then, the land still belonged to them. Dispersion has never meant dispossession.

> Now it shall come to pass, if you diligently obey the
> voice of the LORD your God, to observe carefully all
> His commandments which I command you today, that
> the LORD your God will set you high above all nations
> of the earth. And all these blessings shall come upon
> you and overtake you, because you obey the voice of
> the LORD your God:

But it shall come to pass, if you do not obey the voice of the LORD your God, to observe carefully all His commandments and His statutes which I command you today, that all these curses will come upon you and overtake you:

Then the LORD will scatter you among all peoples, from one end of the earth to the other, and there you shall serve other gods, which neither you nor your fathers have known—wood and stone. And among those nations you shall find no rest, nor shall the sole of your foot have a resting place; but there the LORD will give you a trembling heart, failing eyes, and anguish of soul.

Of course, if you do not believe in the Bible and the God of the Bible, then this will not mean anything to you. But for those of us who take the Word of God to be the true, literal, inspired Word of the God who created and owns the whole world, this becomes your definitive law and truth. More importantly, you can see how every precept of the Word has been fulfilled to the letter. We have no doubt that any remaining and outstanding promise to Israel will happen exactly as prophesied in its time.

Christians owe a debt of gratitude to the Jewish people for their contributions that gave birth to the Christian faith. 'It pleased them indeed, for they are their debtors. For if the gentiles have been partakers of their spiritual things, their duty is also to minister to them in material things,' according to Romans 15:27. Jesus Christ, a prominent Jewish Rabbi from Nazareth, said, 'Salvation is of the Jews,' in John 4:22. It was through the Jewish people that salvation came to the world. Do you understand why the devil is hell bent on destroying them? He will not stop until the greatest Jewish man, Jesus of Nazareth, comes to destroy him, chain him, and cast him into prison.

Consider what the Jewish people have given to Christianity.

The sacred scriptures is a Jewish book that shows man the way of salvation and exposes all the devices of the devil, the archenemy of God and man. No wonder they have been subjected to the most intense oppression and persecution since they became a nation in Egypt until this day. Anti-Semitism is demonic, and Satan is behind it all. But he will fail, as he always has.

The prophets are all Jewish.

The patriarchs are all Jewish.

The twelve disciples were all Jewish.

The apostles were all Jewish.

The Messiah was Jewish. If Jesus showed up in a Western church today, he would not be wearing a three-piece suit tailored in Savile Row but a Jewish prayer shawl with tassels on each corner and black-and-white borders.

Christianity, for the first twenty or so years, was an exclusively Jewish 'sect' or religion. Judaism does not need Christianity to explain itself, but you cannot explain Christianity without the Jews and Judaism. They are the root, and we but grafted branches.

Jesus said, 'Salvation is of the Jews,' according to John 4:22. They were God's instrument for bringing salvation to the world.

All these people, like their master, Jesus, were martyred for their faith.

Mary, Joseph, and Jesus of Nazareth, the first Christian family, were Jewish.

The Bible says if we have received of the Jew's spiritual blessings, then our duty is to share with them our material blessings. That is the least we can do.

Romans 9:1–5; 1:3

> I tell the truth in Christ, I am not lying, my conscience also bearing me witness in the Holy Spirit, that I have great sorrow and continual grief in my heart. For I could wish that I myself were accursed from Christ for my brethren, my countrymen according

to the flesh, who are Israelites, to whom pertain the adoption, the glory, the covenants, the giving of the law, the service of God, and the promises; of whom are the fathers and from whom, according to the flesh, Christ came, who is over all, the eternally blessed God. Amen.

Concerning His Son Jesus Christ our Lord, who was born of the seed of David according to the flesh.

The Jewish people have paid a great price to hand down to us the preserved Word of God and Christianity as a whole. Many of them have made the ultimate sacrifice to hand down to us the promises of God that we as New Covenant believers enjoy today. Remember, all the promises in the Old Testament, carried over to the New were given initially and exclusively to the Jewish people. It is not possible to say you are a Christian and not love the Jewish people. How can we love Jesus and David and the apostles and prophets and call Abraham our father and hate the living Jews. To claim to love the dead Jews, we must first demonstrate love towards the living Jews and bless them accordingly both in word and deed. In Matthew 25:40, 45, during the judgment of the nations, individuals and nations will be judged according to how they have treated the Jews in their dire time of need in the tribulation. This is how serious God takes antisemitism, hatred for the Jewish people. It will literally send multitudes to hell.

And the King will answer and say to them, 'Assuredly, I say to you, inasmuch as you did it to one of the least of these My brethren, you did it to Me.'

Then He will also say to those on the left hand, 'Depart from Me, you cursed, into the everlasting fire prepared for the devil and his angels: for I was hungry and you gave Me no food; I was thirsty and you gave Me no drink; I was a stranger and you did not take Me in, naked and you did not clothe Me, sick and in prison and you did not visit Me.'

Then they also will answer Him, saying, 'Lord, when did we see You hungry or thirsty or a stranger or naked or sick or in prison, and did not minister to You?' Then He will answer them, saying, 'Assuredly, I say to you, inasmuch as you did not do it to one of the least of these, you did not do it to Me.'

Jesus is saying here that whatever you do for his brethren, the Jewish people, you are doing it for him. And whatever you do against the Jewish people, you are doing it against him, and each will be recompensed accordingly. I will hate to go on the wrong side of the Lord on any issue.

Jesus was born a Jew to Jewish 'parents', and he never renounced his Jewishness. He was born a Jew, circumcised on the eighth day, had his bar mitzvah on his thirteenth birthday, kept the Law of Moses, wore the prayer shawl and the kippah (the Jewish skull cap), worshipped in the temple, observed the Sabbath, and ate kosher as the Law of Moses commanded all Jewish men. He died on the cross with the inscription over his head, 'King of the Jews.' He said repeatedly that he came to fulfil the Law of Moses, not to destroy it, according to Matthew 5:17 and Mark 5:27–28.

Do not think that I came to destroy the Law or the Prophets. I did not come to destroy but to fulfil.

When she heard about Jesus, she came behind Him in the crowd and touched His garment. For she said, 'If only I may touch His clothes, I shall be made well.'

Jesus considered the Jewish people his family and called them his brethren, according to Matthew 25:40, 45. 'And the King will answer and say to them, "Assuredly, I say to you, inasmuch as you did *it* to one of the least of these My brethren, you did *it* to Me.'"

Christians are to support Israel because it brings the blessings of God to them personally and corporately as God promised Abraham in Genesis 12:1–3. In Psalm 122:6, King David commands us to 'pray for the peace of Jerusalem' and adds, 'May they prosper who love thee.' God's prosperity is tied to blessing Israel and the city of Jerusalem.

Why did Jesus Christ take time off his busy schedule to go to the house of Cornelius in Capernaum and heal his servant who was at the point of death? He went because that Gentile was deserving of the blessing of God by demonstrating his love for the Jewish people by building them a synagogue, as explained in Luke 7:1–7.

> Now when He concluded all His sayings in the hearing of the people, He entered Capernaum. And a certain centurion's servant, who was dear to him, was sick and ready to die. So when he heard about Jesus, he sent elders of the Jews to Him, pleading with Him to come and heal his servant. And when they came to Jesus, they begged Him earnestly, saying that the one for whom He should do this was deserving, 'for he loves our nation, and has built us a synagogue.'

Then Jesus went with them. And when he was already not far from the house, the centurion sent friends to him, saying to him, 'Lord, do not trouble Yourself, for I am not worthy that You should enter under my roof. Therefore I did not even think myself worthy to come to You. But say the word, and my servant will be healed.'

I can hear some people protesting that nobody deserves anything from God because grace gives us what we do not deserve. Well said; perhaps you need to read the above scripture extract again to see what it says. Remember that the centurion sent Jewish elders to Jesus, and they obliged and went. He must be on very good terms with them, being a Roman officer. When the elders came to Jesus, they pleaded for him to come with them; their reason was that he, the centurion, loved the Jewish nation and the Jewish people and had actually built them a temple to worship in. And because of his love for the Jewish people and his kindness towards them, he was 'deserving of God's blessing'. Have you noticed that Jesus did not protest saying, 'No. I will come with you to heal his servant because I am willing. Nobody is deserving of my blessing. It is all by my grace alone.' Rather, when they said the man was deserving, Jesus just got up and went with them, no questions asked. Your actions and obedience can qualify you for grace and for favour. If believers will take the Word of God literally, without complicating it, and do as it says, life will be a lot simpler and better for us all. God says that if you bless the Jewish people, he, God himself, will bless you in turn. Does anyone need an expository Bible and a concordance to understand this? As a believer, you are entitled to the grace of God, but you do not receive all his grace because you believed. Your growth in the knowledge of his word and your subsequent obedience will determine the amount of grace and favour you will enjoy in your life. You cannot believe for what you are ignorant about. And you cannot have what you know about but do not incorporate in your life by your obedience. Obedience releases both grace and favour. We know about Philippians 4:19 'And my God shall supply all your need according to his riches in glory by Christ Jesus' and forget that the Philippian believers did verses 10- 18 to qualify for verse 19. God says if you bless the Jewish people, he will bless you. So do your part and watch him do his.

How does one bless the Jewish people?

Well, the Bible says the centurion loves our nation. So I guess we can all love Israel and the Jewish people—I mean the ones in Israel today who are under so much murderous threats from much of the world. This includes the ones you meet in particular places in your town or city with their distinctive dressing and hairstyle and skull caps. Love them because they are the children and surviving descendants of Abraham, Isaac, and Jacob. The centurion did not just show affection towards them in his heart; he did practical things to help them. He himself may not have been a proselyte, a Gentile convert to Judaism, so he might not personally have needed the temple, but he built one for them.

So you can support them in tangible ways by supporting Jewish charities that are helping poor and elderly Jews with food and clothing and medicines in many parts of the world including Ethiopia, the former Soviet Union, Russia, India, and Israel itself. Many of these are very old Holocaust survivors, often without any close family members, having lost all their family in the Holocaust. Some of the familiar Jewish charities and organisations I am acquainted with Include the International Fellowship of Christians and Jews, founded and led by Rabbi Yechiel Eckstein, based in Washington DC, USA. Amongst their favourite programmes one could support are On Wings of Eagles, which helps Jews who want to migrate to Israel, based on Exodus 19:4. Then there is Stand for Israel, based on Isaiah 62:1. Then there is Guardians of Israel, providing comfort for Israel, based on Isaiah 40:1 and Isaiah 58. Your support for each of these and the many other charitable outreaches would mean you have become God's instrument for the fulfilment of prophecy. Yes, if God was ever to write a second edition of his book, your name would be in there.

There is also Jewish Voice Ministries International, founded and led by Rabbi Jonathan Bernis, who does similar outreaches as above with emphasis on evangelistic and medical outreaches for Jews and others in very remote places in Ethiopia, India, and many other places. Do you know what it means to help get Jewish people saved and healed? Like he did for Cornelius in Acts 10:2, 4, 31, he will heal you and your loved ones and get your unsaved family saved. You help save his family, he will save yours.

There is also Christians United for Israel, founded and led by the 'Gentile Rabbi' Pastor John Hagee of Cornerstone Church in San Antonio, Texas, who has done perhaps more than most in showing the Jewish people that our love for them is real and authentic, for which the nation of Israel honoured him, and rightly so, on the seventieth anniversary of the nation's founding on May 14, 2018. CUFI hosts the annual Washington Israel Summit and night to remember Israel in

Washington DC for all lovers of the Jewish nation and peoples. This author has had the unforgettable privilege to attend a couple such summits and they are priceless. There is something powerful in being together with thousands of lovers of Israel and the Jewish people. I will venture to believe that this is the one annual family gathering on Jesus calendar that he never fail to attend in person.

You can get more information on any of these Jewish charities online and take it from there.

You can also elect to intercede for Israel and the Jewish people, and for the city of Jerusalem over which the world is on a collision course to self-destruction and mass suicide. Pray as we are commanded in Psalm 122:6 and Isaiah 40:1–2. Pray for peace with her neighbours, but certainly pray for Israel to be victorious should anyone attack them. Pray for their prosperity and pray for their national leaders, especially their prime minister, that courageous son of Benjamin, who has one of the most difficult, if not impossible, jobs in the world. Pray for God to guide his mind and his hand in all he and his government and all the leaders of the Jewish nation do. You see, Israel is going to be a superpower and wealthy nation (if they aren't already) after they have been duly tried in God's furnace. It would be a privilege to avail yourself as God's instrument of prophetic fulfilment with all the blessings that entails.

In Acts 10, we read about another Cornelius, another Roman military officer. God himself sent an angel from heaven to go tell this Gentile centurion how to get saved. Certainly, God is interested in the salvation of mankind, but I guess this does not happen often where God sends an angel from heaven to get one specific individual saved. He must have been arguably the first recorded Gentile to be saved, and certainly under these circumstances. A devout military officer? Well, not impossible, but you would not meet one at every street corner, especially in those days. God gave this Gentile officer the heavenly red carpet and gave the reasons for such in the following Bible verses. According to Acts 10:2, 4, 31,

A devout man and one who feared God with all his household, who gave alms generously to the people, and prayed to God always.

And when he observed him, he was afraid, and said, 'What is it, lord?'

So he said to him, 'Your prayers and your alms have come up for a memorial before God.'

And said, 'Cornelius, your prayer has been heard, and your alms are remembered in the sight of God.'

If you are a pastor or minister of the gospel, preach and teach your congregation about God's covenant with the Jewish people and how we are blessed through them, not only in the person and ministry of Jesus Christ but through the Jewish nation as a whole. Let your congregation come to appreciate the crucial importance of this nation in God's redemption plan for mankind and our relationship with them as adopted sons of Abraham through our common father Abraham.

Display Jewish paraphernalia such as the Jewish national flag, the Star of David, the prayer shawl, and the skull cap, both in your houses and in church as evidence of your support for them. Teach your members about the demonic origins of anti-Semitism and the need for them not to get involved in criticizing the Jews but to defend and bless them at every opportunity. Encourage your members to go on holiday (or pilgrimage, if you like) to Israel as a practical demonstration of your support and solidarity for them. Contrary to the news headlines, Israel is one of the safest places to visit and one of the most nostalgic on earth. Go to Jerusalem to understand why the whole world is fixated on it and will eventually commit collective mass suicide for it. It is neither the most beautiful, the biggest nor the most prosperous city on the planet, yet there is none like it because it is the one city the King of kings has chosen for his dwelling place on earth. Hence the furore over Jerusalem. When you go shopping, look out for and patronise made-in-Israel goods and products of which there are loads, ranging from agricultural products to electronics, to medical etc and are amongst the very best in the world. Use whatever influence you have to get policy makers in your nation to be favourably disposed towards Israel, especially in the UN and in your nation's foreign and trade policies. Explain to them the blessings that follow such policies for your nation and its citizens. Let policy makers understand the dangers of taking an anti-Israel stance in their policy and international affairs. In short, be an ambassador for Israel and the Jews.

These combined scriptures prove that prosperity (Gen. 12:3; Ps. 122:6), divine healing (Luke 7:1–5), and the outpouring of the Holy Spirit (Acts 10:44–48) came first to Gentiles who blessed Israel and the Jewish people in a practical manner.

We see the same phenomena repeated in the experience of Jacob with his uncle Laban in Genesis 30:27, and Joseph and his experience, first, with Potiphar and then with Pharaoh, king of Egypt (Gen. 39:2–5; 41:37–38). This experience of Gentiles who host Jews and are hospitable to them are blessed all through the scriptures, both in the Old and New Testaments. This is true of individuals and families as in the case of Potiphar and Joseph, Jacob and Laban, and in the case of nations as in the case of Egypt and Joseph and Daniel and Babylon. The promise in Genesis 12:3 is still valid today and one that this author can testify to. God still blesses those that bless the Jewish people. It works because God's Word is eternal and his promises are yeah and amen.

HOW ISRAEL CONTINUES TO BLESS THE WORLD

Children in the Syrian civil war continue to receive life-saving treatment in Israel. Israel is almost always the first on site at disaster-hit areas with doctors and nurses, rescue workers, medical supplies, and equipment, often travelling around the globe to do this even in nations that still refuse to have diplomatic relations with the Jewish nation. They were on site in Haiti when that impoverished nation was hit with a devastating 7.0 magnitude earthquake with the largest and best-equipped field hospital. In the two weeks they were on the ground, they treated 1,110 patients, performed 319 successful surgeries, and delivered 16 babies, the mother of the first baby naming her child Israel in gratitude. In the last decade or so, they have provided humanitarian aid to 140 disaster-struck nations, including Peru in 2007; Myanmar in 2008; Burkina Faso in 2013; the Philippines in 2013; Japan in 2011; Turkey, Serbia, and Bosnia in 2014; Nepal; and others too numerous to enumerate.

The tragic circumstances they have had to endure over their short history with major wars and countless intifadas have forced them to hone their emergency response procedures to a fine art to protect their people. But it goes deeper than that. Through their concept of *tikkum olam*, literally, repairing the world, Israelis have an instinctive response to disasters, and their National Rescue Unit has lived up to its name—to repair the world and be a light to the nations as God designed them to be, according to Isaiah 49:6, which says, 'I will also give you as a light to the Gentiles.' Israel is indeed a light to the Gentiles.

According to Dr. Jim Eckman in his article 'Israel: A channel of God's blessing',

> There are about 18 million Jews worldwide—0.2% of the world's population. But Jews make up 54% of the world chess champions, 27% of the Nobel physics laureates and 31% of the medicine laureates. Within the United States, Jews make up but 2% of the US population, but 21% of the Ivy League student bodies, 26% of the Kennedy Center honorees, 37% of the Academy Award-winning directors, 38% of those on a recent Business Week list of philanthropists, and 51% of the Pulitzer Prize winners for nonfiction. Within the nation state of Israel itself, Tel Aviv has become one of the world's foremost entrepreneurial centers—a new silicon valley in fact. For example,

Intel is the largest private-sector employer in Israel, with more than 8,000 employees, four design centers and two manufacturing plants. The Israelis who manage the R&D centers are responsible for much of the microprocessor innovation over the past 20 years, developing chips for large desktop computers, laptops, tablets and smartphones. Columnist David Brooks writes that 'Israel has more high-tech start-ups per capita than any other nation on earth, by far. It leads the world in civilian research-and-development spending per capita. It ranks second behind the US in the number of companies listed on the NASDAQ. Israel, with 7 million people, attracts as much venture capital as France and Germany combined'. Israel has used the present financial crisis in the world to solidify the economy's long-term future by investing in research and development and infrastructure, raising some consumption taxes, promising to cut other taxes in the medium to long term. The financial giant Barclay's argues that Israel is 'the strongest recovery story in Europe, the Middle East and Africa'. Finally, the nation of Israel is nothing short of astounding in terms of its creativity, scientific genius and technological savvy. For example, between 1980 and 2000, Egyptians registered 77 patents in the US. Saudis registered 171. Israel registered 7,652 patents!! The current Prime Minister, Benjamin Netanyahu, argues that Israel will become the Hong Kong of the Middle East, with its economic benefits spilling over into the Arab world. There is indeed some evidence that this is already occurring in Jordan and in the West Bank. An astonishing example of this innovation is the Israeli company Netafim, a company that produced the world's first drip irrigation system, which consists of a series of plastic pipes with small holes that lie on the ground. This system revolutionized the way Israel made its desert bloom so that it became a leading supplier of fruits, vegetables and flowers to the European market. Today, Netafim is the number one provider of drip irrigation to the world and conducts business in 110 countries spanning five continents. This highly efficient system has helped nations produce 50% more crop yield while using 40% less water. Nations such as India, Vietnam and Philippines all benefit from this technology. However, nations such as Iran and its terrorist allies, Hezbollah and Hamas, despise the success and innovation of Israel seek to destroy it.

In 'History of the Jews', Rev. Eric Strachen writes,

It was Winston Churchill, the wartime prime minister who once commented, 'Some people like the Jews, and some do not.'

History certainly validates beyond question the truthfulness of Churchill's words, but the British bulldog went on to say, 'But no thoughtful man can deny the fact that they are beyond question, the most formidable and the most remarkable race which has appeared in the world.' What is equally remarkable, and should I say quite astonishing, about the Jewish people is that their achievements throughout centuries of world history are completely disproportionate to their size. With the current world population nearing 7.5 billion, Jewish people number a mere 14 million, which translates to 0.2 per cent of the global figure.

Despite this relative numerical smallness as a people they have blessed the world beyond measure in virtually every area of life. Take for instance the whole field of medicine. It was Richard Lewisohn, a Jew, who developed the technique by which blood could be stored by using an anticoagulant. Another Jew, Richard Weil devised how it could be refrigerated thus permitting the creation of the first blood banks. It was Lewisohn again, in partnership with another Jewish researcher, Karl Landsteiner, who is credited with inventing the modern blood transfusion. Their discoveries have saved billions of lives. It would be fair to say that if you've ever received a blood transfusion you've a Jew to thank for it.

Tuberculosis was once a deadly disease but Selman Waksman and Albert Schatz created streptomycin, the first effective antibiotic to combat TB. It was Paul Zoll who invented the cardiac defibrillator, the external pacemaker, and the cardiac monitor.

The list goes on and on. Henry Heimlich invented 'The Heimlich Maneuver' which when employed has prevented many from choking to death. In the 20th century Abel Wolman determined a means by which water worldwide could be chlorinated, and deaths due to cholera, dysentery and typhoid could be eradicated. Charles Kelman developed the technique for cataract removal and eye lens implantation. Three Jewish men in research partnership invented cancer chemotherapy. Jewish research and ingenuity by Barnett Rosenburg have now made testicular cancer in men 90 per cent curable.

Credit the Jews too with the development of the hepatitis-B vaccine, the Wasserman test for syphilis and the vaccines by Salk and Sabin that have virtually eliminated polio and are estimated to have prevented half-a-million new cases of lifelong paralysis each year.

The contribution made by Jews in the whole field of medicine is nothing short of astounding.

It is obvious that the four-thousand-year-old prophecy given to Abraham, the father of the Jewish people, is still working today. 'In you all the families of the earth shall be blessed.' With its primary application to the Lion of the tribe of Judah, the Jewish Messiah, the Lord Jesus Christ, who is the principal channel of God's blessing to the world, the promise is nevertheless true of the entire Jewish race. It is obvious that God has not finished with them, and they are yet to come into their golden age where they will be an even greater light and multiplied blessing to the Gentile nations.

The existence of the Jews, their survival through incredible odds, is proof certain that there is a God in heaven and the Bible is the true Word of God. They are a miracle of history and one that points man to the unfailing faithfulness of God.

You may be saying, but these people have turned their backs on God, so how could God still be blessing them? That may be the case, but more than anything, it proves the faithfulness of God. It proves his unsurpassed grace towards mankind. It proves that his Word and his promises can be trusted, even when we fail our part of the bargain. God's commitment to millennia-old covenant with the fathers of the Jewish people is a cause for hope and optimism for us all that eloquently testify that this is a God to be trusted.

Note that what a nation does to the Jewish people, God does likewise to that nation whether good or bad.

God judges Gentiles (nations) for their abuse and oppression of Jews.

God's foreign policy towards any nation is based on their treatment of the Jews, period. The way countries treat the Jewish people is an indication of their salvation, or their relationship with

God. It is not the basis of their salvation, but it shows whether they know the God of Israel. If a nation and its people really know the God of Israel, they are going to be favourably disposed towards his covenant people because they will come to understand Israel's role in God's redemption plan for the world. That nation's perspective towards them would change. They have helped the Gentile world to come to know God, while today, most of them are languishing in unbelief, in need to be evangelised by those they were initially called to evangelise. God expects you, a believer in the Jewish Messiah, to love his people and approach them with utter respect and sensitivity. Remember at all times as a Gentile believer that you stand by his grace and goodness alone.

It is instructive to know that nations that welcome Jews in their countries are blessed by God. Historically, all the world empires that had the most Jews within their borders or the most direct influence with the Jewish people were the most powerful nations (economically and certainly politico-militarily) on earth, and those same nations fell based on what they did to the Jewish people.

This is true of ancient Egypt, which rose to become the superpower of its day. It is also true of Spain in the fifteenth and sixteenth centuries which had the highest number of Jews anywhere in the world following their expulsion from their land by ancient Rome. Today, the USA has arguably the largest number of Jews (about seven million of the estimated twenty to twenty-three million with about eight million in the nation of Israel itself, April 2018) outside of the nation of Israel and the greatest influence with the Jewish nation and government and has been the most prosperous country ever in terms of their economic prosperity and unsurpassed military might. People surmise about other countries overtaking America as the next economic and military superpower, but listen to me good, this will never happen so long as America continues to stand with and support Israel. But when countries begin to oppress and harass its Jewish population, they had better watch out for God's strong hand of judgment and retribution. Empires have risen and fallen, most into extinction, all based on their handling of the Jews.

Let's begin with the Amalekites who descended from Esau, the twin brother of Jacob. Amalek attacked Israel at their very low point on their way from Egypt to Canaan, and that got God very angry with them and swore to wipe them off the face of the earth.

In Exodus 17:8; 13–16,

> Now Amalek came and fought with Israel in Rephidim.

> So Joshua defeated Amalek and his people with the edge of the sword.

> Then the LORD said to Moses, 'Write this for a memorial in the book and recount it in the hearing of Joshua, that I will utterly blot out the remembrance of Amalek from under heaven.' And Moses built an altar and called its name, The-LORD-Is-My-Banner; for he said, 'Because the LORD has sworn: the LORD will have war with Amalek from generation to generation.'

Following their attack on Israel, their blood cousins, God vowed to blot the remembrance of Amalek from under heaven. This he instructed the first king of Israel, King Saul, to carry out several years later in 1 Samuel 15:2, 3.

> Thus says the LORD of hosts: 'I will punish Amalek for what he did to Israel, how he ambushed him on the way when he came up from Egypt.

> 'Now go and attack Amalek, and utterly destroy all that they have, and do not spare them. But kill both man and woman, infant and nursing child, ox and sheep, camel and donkey.'

Today, Amalek is extinct.

The mighty ancient Egyptian Empire and the pharaoh who knew not Joseph. This cruel Pharaoh who did not know Joseph and how God had used his gifts to save the Egyptian nation from famine enslaved the Jewish people with cruel bondage and terrible oppression and murdered their male children en masse to exterminate them as a nation. In the end, God reduced his nation to rubble with the devastating ten plagues and destroyed Pharaoh and his entire elite military machine in the Red Sea. This is the theme of the book of Exodus. Egypt was never to rise again as a significant nation till this day because of their treatment of the Jews. And that cruel pharaoh drowned with his forces in the sea.

> Now there arose a new king over Egypt, who did not know Joseph. And he said to his people, 'Look, the people of the children of Israel are more and mightier than we; come, let us deal shrewdly with them, lest they multiply, and it happen, in the event of war, that they also join our enemies and fight against us, and so go up out of the land.' Therefore they set taskmasters over them to afflict them with their burdens. And they built for Pharaoh supply cities, Pithom and Ramses. But the more they afflicted them, the more they multiplied and grew. And they were in dread of the children of Israel. So the Egyptians made the children of Israel serve with rigor. And they made their lives bitter with hard bondage—in mortar, in brick, and in all manner of service in the field. All their service in which they made them serve was with rigor.

Did you notice that phrase tacked away in the text, 'The more they afflicted them the more they multiplied and grew!'? Just like today, the more Israel is pressured and oppressed by their enemies, the more they are prospering. With enemies like that, who needs friends!

Another scoundrel who sought to destroy the Jewish people was the infamous Haman, from the Persian Empire, which is Iran today. He and his entire family were hanged on the very gallows they had prepared for Mordecai and the Jews as reported in the book of Esther 7:9–10.

> Now Harbonah, one of the eunuchs, said to the king, 'Look! The gallows, fifty cubits high, which Haman made for Mordecai, who spoke good on the king's behalf, is standing at the house of Haman.'
>
> Then the king said, 'Hang him on it!'
>
> So they hanged Haman on the gallows that he had prepared for Mordecai. Then the king's wrath subsided.

So what difference does it really make whether Iran acquires nuclear weapons? They simply haven't learnt any lesson from history but have rather been blinded by their murderous hatred of the Jews. Psalm 121:4 puts it this way:

> Behold, He who keeps Israel Shall neither slumber nor sleep.

This is my confidence. We have read the end of the book, and though weeping may endure for a night, but joy comes in the morning. Israel may be undergoing intolerable pressure and persecution by most of the world today, but their joy is around the corner. He who promised is faithful, who also will do it. I trust the God of Israel to do it again.

Love the Jewish people if you can, but if you can't love them, do well to leave them alone, for your own good. It is a Jewish man, in the person of Rabbi Jesus Christ, who you will be meeting at the gate to heaven who will decide who gets into his house and who does not.

Heaven is his private kingdom, and he reserves the right as to whom to let in. Just be smart because truly blood is thicker than water. There is a marked and pronounced blessing on the Jewish people, and that is the reason for the relentless jealousy, hostility, and persecution towards them. But you do not help your cause by coming against someone who carries God's blessing. Hebrews 7:7 says, 'Now beyond all contradiction the lesser is blessed by the greater.' (The very same mistake some people in poorer countries make by constantly bashing rich nations, instead of finding out what they are doing right that we are not doing. Don't worry, you are never going to be rich by hating the rich and successful. Your life is only going to change by learning and replicating what others are doing right that is making them successful. People think nations are successful because the population is so clever or they have all the natural resources in the world, or simply, God has blessed them. Listen, God has given every nation what they need to thrive and be successful. What they do with it is up to them. Which continent in the world is as blessed as Africa? None even comes a close second. But what do we see but disease, famine, squabbling, decay, and death. The differences in economic well-being is the direct result of culture and mindset and the way the people have chosen to live and the type of economic model they have chosen to pursue. Communism decayed and crumbled because it is ungodly at its core. It took the practitioners decades to realise this, but thank God they did; otherwise, some of the most beautiful nations on the planet, with the most intelligent nationals, would still be driving 1960s scrapyard cars in the twenty-first century.) You align with them, and then the anointing on them rubs off on you. Look at conditions in all the Israel-hating nations today and draw your own conclusions. When we stand with Israel, we are not necessarily saying that we approve of everything they do. They are human, just as any other nation. We are simply acknowledging their position as God's covenant people who have been used to bless the world and continue to do so even today in more ways than one. The

Jewish people have blessed the world more than any other ethnic group and continue to do so even today. It is beyond the scope of this narrative to catalogue all their achievements and contributions to the welfare of humanity.

I heard the story some time ago about the late Libyan leader Col. Muammar Gaddafi, who, at the height of his rule, was getting carried away by the absolute power he wielded over the Libyan people and his growing influence in African and world affairs. He started meddling in the Arab Israeli conflict and started becoming critical of Israel. It is reported that his sister called and advised him not to 'mess with those people for his own good'. It is obvious he did not listen to that sound advice, sad to say.

Another infamous incident involved Daniel and his detractors, in the book of Daniel 6:24.

> And the king gave the command, and they brought those men who had accused Daniel, and they cast them into the den of lions—them, their children, and their wives; and the lions overpowered them, and broke all their bones in pieces before they ever came to the bottom of the den.

They too suffered the fate of all those who oppress and maltreat the Jews, the burning vengeance of the God of Israel.

Spain, under King Ferdinand and Queen Isabella, also brutalised the Jews in the fifteenth and sixteenth centuries with the March 31, 1492, Edict of Expulsion, forcing the Jews to convert to Catholicism, burning and looting their property and killing and expelling them from their country. At this time, most of the world's Jews lived in Spain, and it was arguably the superpower of the day. The mighty Spanish Empire fell and has never risen anywhere near its past glory. This expulsion of the Jews from Spain led to the discovery of America by Christopher Columbus, himself a Jew, sent by God ahead of the expulsion, to provide a place of refuge for the fleeing Jews.

The mighty British Empire has equally not treated the Jews well enough with their handling of the Balfour Declaration of 1917 in which Britain pledged to facilitate the resettlement of the Jews in their ancestral homeland in Canaan but later reneged in 1922 when the Arabs discovered oil and used it as a tool to block the resettlement of the Jews in their ancestral homeland under the UN mandate. They yielded to Arab pressure and gave away 75 percent of the land earmarked for Israel to the Arabs, including much of what is Jordan today. So Jordan is the country for the Palestinians. They also blocked Jewish emigration from Europe to Canaan when they were fleeing Hitler's death camps, returning many to Germany, and occupied Europe to their deaths. No wonder after the war, the British Empire on which the sun never set crumbled like dominoes until the rump that it has become today. It is obvious that Britain still cherishes nostalgic memories and flashbacks of her colonial days when it ruled the world from Australia to Zimbabwe. Just watch their body language in the commonwealth gatherings. Any nation that expels their Jewish immigrants, God will ensure you get the immigrants of your choice in return. Germany and much of Europe have got their immigrants of choice, and that is no accident. Let me add that on the same day that Israel became an independent nation, the Palestinians could have declared theirs as well, as provided under the UN (1947) mandate, but they rejected the opportunity to do so because they wanted it all for themselves. As noted Jewish diplomat Abba Eban said, 'The Palestinians never missed an opportunity to miss an opportunity.' They have had four opportunities to have their own state but have rejected each of them. Why is everybody baying for Jerusalem today? And where were they when it, and the land, lay in ruins and became a barren, treeless, malaria-ridden wasteland for hundreds of years?

One may legitimately look back and ask,

Where is the mighty Roman Empire today?

Where are the Turks?

Where is the Ottoman Empire?

Where are the Assyrians and Babylonians and Persians?

Where are the Midianites, the Philistines, the Moabites, and all the other ites?

Where are Adolf Hitler and his SS henchmen?

Today, America stands at the crossroads of history. Her final fate will be determined by how she treats the Jewish people and how she executes her divine mandate to be the human protectors of Israel until God himself takes over. America was established by God to become the powerful superpower she is for two express reasons. The first is to be the defender and protector of Israel when she became a nation. The second was to be God's main evangelistic instrument for the rest of the nations. So long as she faithfully executes these two divine assignments, she will continue to be the most powerful and most prosperous nation on earth, all her notable excesses notwithstanding. In recent times, America has flirted with danger by pushing Israel to give up its land for an elusive peace in the ill-conceived land-for-peace doctrine and forcing Israel to abandon the rebuilding of her wastelands, as the scriptures say should happen, according to Isaiah 49:8; 58:12; 61:4.

Thus says the LORD:

'In an acceptable time I have heard You,
And in the day of salvation I have helped You;
I will preserve You and give You
As a covenant to the people,
To restore the earth,
To cause them to inherit the desolate heritages;

Those from among you
Shall build the old waste places;
You shall raise up the foundations of many generations;
And you shall be called the Repairer of the Breach,
The Restorer of Streets to Dwell In.

And they shall rebuild the old ruins,
They shall raise up the former desolations,
And they shall repair the ruined cities,
The desolations of many generations.'

Thus, the so-called settlements that the international community views with so much horror and disdain are commanded by God. Israel has a divine mandate to rebuild its waste heritages because the land has never belonged to the Palestinians and never will. We are talking about Judea, Samaria, and Gaza, the very heartlands of the Jewish state. How historically illiterate the world's media is. Israel has never built any settlements on Arab land. Why is Israel the only nation on earth that gets condemned for building houses on land they have owned for well over three thousand years? (Does anybody know that Yasser Arafat was himself Egyptian, not Palestinian?) This global duplicity will have to end at some point. Why does everybody think that Israel is the cause of problems in the Middle East? How many planes have Israel ever hijacked in its history? Are they the reason we are body-searched and harassed at every international airport nowadays? How many wars have they initiated in their history, and why does anyone think they cannot or should not defend themselves against people who openly declare their intentions to wipe them off the map? What part did they have in the eight bloody years of warfare when Iran and Iraq slaughtered over a million of their own citizens? How do you really negotiate peace with someone who refuses to recognise your very existence? Certainly, Pres. George Bush's Road map was doomed to fail in its cradle because it failed to recognise the realities on the ground and appeared totally ignorant of the root causes of the problem. The West can deceive itself all it wants and call Islam a religion of peace and presume to know more about this religion than its spiritual leaders, but it won't change anything when the Ayatollah Khomeini of Iran declared that 'the purest joy in Islam is to kill and be killed for Allah' and Osama bin Laden declared that 'this is a war between Islam and Christianity'. He is also on record to have said, 'We love death—the Americans love life—and that is the difference between us.' In a videotape message following September 11,2001, he said, 'War is our best hobby. The sounds of guns firing is like music for us. We cannot live without war. We have no other way except Jihad . . . The Americans love Pepsi Cola; we love death.' You can sit in New York or Brussels and contradict them all you want, deluding yourself into thinking you know more about their religion than its devoted practitioners.

Proverbs 8:36 puts it this way, 'All who hate me love death.'

America's recent betrayal of Israel at the throes of the Obama administration was disgraceful, to say the least. The UN met in Paris on January 15, 2016, at the Paris Peace Conference on the two-state solution to force their two-state solution dogma on Israel and the Palestinians at a meeting where both parties were barred from attending. And this was five days before President Obama was to leave office. His parting legacy to Israel indeed. This was a follow-up to an earlier UN meeting in New York on December 23, 2015, that declared Israeli settlements illegal, at which the USA was to famously abstain. Friend and protector indeed.

1 Corinthians 10:12 puts it this way,

> Therefore let him who thinks he stands take heed lest
> he fall.

Thank God a new wind is blowing in the corridors of power in Washington once again. Pres. Donald Trump courageously recognised Jerusalem as the capital of Israel on December 6, 2017, and followed up and moved the American embassy from Tel Aviv to Jerusalem on May 14, 2018, on the seventieth anniversary of the Jewish nation, all in fulfilment of major Bible prophecies. No nation on earth has a more legitimate title to its capital than Israel has to Jerusalem. However, with our understanding of Bible prophecy, this move will serve, amongst other things, to bring the world against the city in a doomed effort to capture it, as foretold by the prophet Zechariah 12:2–9 and 14:1–2.

'Behold, I will make Jerusalem a cup of drunkenness to all the surrounding peoples, when they lay siege against Judah and Jerusalem. And it shall happen in that day that I will make Jerusalem a very heavy stone for all peoples; all who would heave it away will surely be cut in pieces, though all nations of the earth are gathered against it. In that day,' says the LORD, 'I will strike every horse with confusion, and its rider with madness; I will open My eyes on the house of Judah, and will strike every horse of the peoples with blindness. And the governors of Judah shall say in their heart, "The inhabitants of Jerusalem are my strength in the LORD of hosts, their God." In that day, I will make the governors of Judah like a firepan in the woodpile, and like a fiery torch in the sheaves; they shall devour all the surrounding peoples on the right hand and on the left, but Jerusalem shall be inhabited again in her own place—Jerusalem.'

The LORD will save the tents of Judah first, so that the glory of the house of David and the glory of the inhabitants of Jerusalem shall not become greater than that of Judah. In that day the LORD will defend the inhabitants of Jerusalem; the one who is feeble among them in that day shall be like David, and the house of David shall be like God, like the Angel of the LORD before them. It shall be in that day that I will seek to destroy all the nations that come against Jerusalem.

Behold, the day of the LORD is coming,
And your spoil will be divided in your midst.
For I will gather all the nations to battle against Jerusalem;
The city shall be taken,

The houses rifled,
And the women ravished.
Half of the city shall go into captivity,
But the remnant of the people shall not be cut off from
the city.

(Yes, it is true that Jerusalem has tremendous significance for Christians, but we do not want to take it away from the Jewish people as others do. It is their city, and we can visit it and fellowship with our brothers and sisters, the Jewish people, into whose family we have been adopted and become Abraham's descendants by covenant through the blood of Jesus. So let nobody use the argument that because it has relevance for Christians as well, we want to take it away from its rightful owners, the Jewish people, the natural descendants of our common father Abraham.)

This, in a sense, is a set up by the Lord, as it is he who brings the nations against Israel and Jerusalem in the last days to settle this question once and for all. God will destroy all the armies that come against Jerusalem who will come close to taking the city. In fact, the Bible declares that Jesus will descend from heaven to rescue the Jewish people when their power to defend themselves is completely shattered, according to Daniel 12:7.

> Then I heard the man clothed in linen, who was above the waters of the river, when he held up his right hand and his left hand to heaven, and swore by Him who lives forever, that it shall be for a time, times, and half a time; and when the power of the holy people has been completely shattered, all these things shall be finished.

This will put pressure on the surviving Jews to cry up to the God of their fathers, just prior to the coming of the Lord to destroy the invading armies and rescue the city and the entire nation and then reveal himself to them as their long awaited Messiah. At this point, the Jews will recognise Jesus as their Messiah, mourn the error of their ways, and then be saved as a nation, according to Zechariah 13:6.

> And one will say to him, 'What are these wounds between your arms?' Then he will answer, 'Those with which I was wounded in the house of my friends.'

Let us get this clear that being pro-Israel is not necessarily anti-Palestinian, far from that. We want the suffering of Palestinian women and children to end, but that will only happen when we tell the truth for what it really is. But it is clear that the touted two-state solution is a myth. First, the Palestinians are not interested in any state of their own. They want the destruction of Israel above all else to please Allah. The issue is not about the size of Israel but the very existence of Israel. To the enemies of Israel, even if you moved the Jewish people and settle them on the moon, the problem is far from solved. But it should be apparent by now that Allah has not got the power to deliver on his Word. They want to maintain the status quo, living off aid and playing the victim. And should they become a state, who would want such a state for their neighbour, with Hezbollah and Hamas in government? I hope this is the last we have seen of America's betrayal of Israel. You have done an unpopular but a good job so far, America, so hold on, as we do not have much to go, and he who watches over Israel himself will take over to deliver his own people.

As for the UN and the EU, they had better mend their ways regarding their attitude towards Israel, or it will all be resolved at Armageddon, the final arbitration, to see who is right and who is wrong. Russia, China, and every nation are in the dock today regarding how they treat Israel. The problem with the world body and the major nations is that they are trying to solve a conflict they hardly understand or whose origin they either do not know or choose to ignore.

As for the Arab and Islamic world, they have taken their stand on Israel to destroy her. They have been at it since the furore in the tents of Abraham in the book of Genesis 21:8–13, where it all started.

> So the child grew and was weaned. And Abraham made a great feast on the same day that Isaac was weaned.
>
> And Sarah saw the son of Hagar the Egyptian, whom she had borne to Abraham, scoffing. Therefore she said to Abraham, 'Cast out this bondwoman and her son; for the son of this bondwoman shall not be heir with my son, namely with Isaac.' And the matter was very displeasing in Abraham's sight because of his son.
>
> But God said to Abraham, 'Do not let it be displeasing in your sight because of the lad or because of your bondwoman. Whatever Sarah has said to you, listen to her voice; for in Isaac your seed shall be called. Yet I will also make a nation of the son of the bondwoman, because he is your seed.'

Let me just add that it has taken them an awfully long time to solve the Jewish problem. Or perhaps it is unsolvable. Have they forgotten 1947–1949, 1967, 1973, 1982, 2006, 2012, 2014, and the many others in between? Hatred has never won because it cannot. If they drop all their hatred and animosity towards this tiny state and embrace them as the cousins they really are, all the violence, oppression, subjugation of women, and bloodshed going on in their lands will cease, and their children will also come to have a normal life like any other. But if they persist, there are major wars coming after which they will not have much of a nation left. Read Psalm 83, Ezekiel 38/39, Isaiah 17:1, 14 amongst others. The future does not bode well for the enemies of Israel.

God promised that Israel would become a mighty nation, which has already come to pass, against all odds, and that his seed would someday own the Promised Land forever (Gen. 12:7; 13:14–17). So Israel rightfully owns all the land that God gave to Abraham by blood covenant. 'From the river of Egypt to the great river, the river Euphrates, and from the wilderness and Lebanon, even to the Western Sea,' according to Genesis 15:18 and Deuteronomy 11:24. Ezekiel 48:1 established the northern boundary of Israel as the city of Hamath, with the southern boundary established in Ezekiel 48:28 as the city of Kadesh. In modern terms, Israel rightfully owns all of present-day Israel, all of Lebanon, half of Syria, two-thirds of Jordan, all of Iraq, and the northern portion of Saudi Arabia. When the Messiah comes, the seed of Abraham will be given that land down to the last square inch. The entire world is in the valley of decision today, and it has all to do with this tiny nation on a tiny piece of land that refuses to go away. Like Nikki Haley, the current US ambassador to the UN, said recently, Israel won't go away. In fact, I will add that the Jewish nation has only just arrived. Yes, desolations are determined for her, but by the help of their God, the God of Abraham, Isaac, and Jacob, Israel will prevail, as they always have. It cannot be any other way because the end was declared from the beginning.

Listen to God's thoughts on the Jewish nation as reported by their prophet Jeremiah in Chapter 31:35-36 of his prophetic treatise:

> Thus says the Lord who gives the sun for a light by day
> The ordinances of the moon and the stars for a light by night,
> Who disturbs the sea, and its waves roar
> (The Lord of hosts is his name)
> If those ordinances depart
> From before me, says the Lord,
> Then the seed of Israel shall also cease
> From being a nation before Me forever.
> Shalom!

THE NEW HEAVEN, THE NEW EARTH, THE MILLENNIUM AND ETERNITY

THE RENOVATION OF THE EARTH BY FIRE

Contrary to popular belief, this world is not going to end or be annihilated. All of God's creation is eternal and will exist forever. According to the Bible, the islands (Ps. 78:69; 104:5), the heavens, and the mountains (Gen. 49:26; 125:1; Isaiah 42:10–12) are all eternal, as are the sun, the moon, the stars, and the earth itself, according to Jeremiah 5:22; 31:35, 36; Psalm 146:6; and Proverbs 18:29. The Bible teaches that God will make a new heaven and a new earth, but it is not new in the sense of beginning but new in the sense of appearance and look. It is going to be new in character and freshness. God is going to renovate the present heavens and the present earth by fire to make it as good as new in appearance. There will be natural men on earth during the millennium and for all eternity. Also, there is the inaccurate belief that Christians will spend eternity in heaven, but this is far from what the Bible teaches. Also animals will continue to exist even in eternity, as will the sea, the oceans, the rivers, and much of what we have in the world today. Only their form will be radically altered.

Revelation 21:1–3, 9–11, 23

> Now I saw a new heaven and a new earth, for the first
> heaven and the first earth had passed away. Also there

was no more sea. Then I, John, saw the holy city, New Jerusalem, coming down out of heaven from God, prepared as a bride adorned for her husband. And I heard a loud voice from heaven saying, 'Behold, the tabernacle of God is with men, and He will dwell with them, and they shall be His people. God Himself will be with them and be their God.'

Then one of the seven angels who had the seven bowls filled with the seven last plagues came to me and talked with me, saying, 'Come, I will show you the bride, the Lamb's wife.' And he carried me away in the Spirit to a great and high mountain, and showed me the great city, the holy Jerusalem, descending out of heaven from God, having the glory of God. Her light was like a most precious stone, like a jasper stone, clear as crystal.

The city had no need of the sun or of the moon to shine in it, for the glory of God illuminated it. The Lamb is its light.

Isaiah 65:17; 66:22

'For behold, I create new heavens and a new earth;
And the former shall not be remembered or come to mind.

For as the new heavens and the new earth
Which I will make shall remain before Me,' says the LORD,
'So shall your descendants and your name remain.'

All the above scriptures speak about a new heaven and a new earth, but this is talking about new as in appearance but not new as in origin. God will actually renovate the existing heaven and earth by fire on the day of the Lord, according to 2 Peter 3:10–13.

> But the day of the Lord will come as a thief in the night, in which the heavens will pass away with a great noise, and the elements will melt with fervent heat; both the earth and the works that are in it will be burned up. Therefore, since all these things will be dissolved, what manner of persons ought you to be in holy conduct and godliness, looking for and hastening the coming of the day of God, because of which the heavens will be dissolved, being on fire, and the elements will melt with fervent heat? Nevertheless we, according to His promise, look for new heavens and a new earth in which righteousness dwells.

This renovation or cleansing will happen after the millennium, after the battle of Gog and Magog, after the casting of Satan into the lake of fire, and after the Great White Throne Judgment, which is the final judgment at the end of the millennium, which takes place in heaven. At the Great White Throne Judgment, death and Hades and all their present inmates will be cast into the lake of fire, which will be the final place of torment for the devil and all the ungodly, according to Revelation 21:10–15.

> The devil, who deceived them, was cast into the lake of fire and brimstone where the beast and the false prophet are. And they will be tormented day and night forever and ever.

> The Great White Throne Judgment

> Then I saw a great white throne and Him who sat on it, from whose face the earth and the heaven fled away. And there was found no place for them. And I saw

the dead, small and great, standing before God, and books were opened. And another book was opened, which is the Book of Life. And the dead were judged according to their works, by the things which were written in the books. The sea gave up the dead who were in it, and Death and Hades delivered up the dead who were in them. And they were judged, each one according to his works. Then Death and Hades were cast into the lake of fire. This is the second death. And anyone not found written in the Book of Life was cast into the lake of fire.

This terrifying day calls for sober reflection for all mankind because it is surely coming as night follows day. It is a day of dread and trepidation, but whilst you are still alive on this earth, it is one you can avert.

The renovation, according to 2 Peter 3, will be by fire. Fire does not destroy anything out of existence but rather changes the state of the thing subject to the fire from one condition to another.

Peter says that this change will take place with great noise and the elements will melt with fervent heat. These elements are a reference to the sinful nature of the present world system such as the sinful nature of man, diseases and germs that cause diseases and maladies, corrupting spirits that corrupt people and cause them to sin, as well as everything man has made that does not qualify to go into God's eternal perfect kingdom, such as illicit businesses, drugs and cigarette factories, alcohol-making factories, brothels, abortion clinics, and arms factories. The world would be loosed from its bondage to decay and corruption, according to Romans 8:18–22. The idea of melting involves loosing, putting off, unbinding, untying, or setting free and dissolving all the bondage that has polluted the earth and release it into a new state. Heat or fire is the best means of cleansing known to man.

> For I consider that the sufferings of this present time are not worthy to be compared with the glory which shall be revealed in us. For the earnest expectation of the creation eagerly waits for the revealing of the sons of God. For the creation was subjected to futility, not willingly, but because of Him who subjected it in hope; because the creation itself also will be delivered from the bondage of corruption into the glorious liberty of the children of God. For we know that the whole creation groans and labors with birth pangs together until now. (Rom. 8:18–22)

Thus, this world would be changed into a new and better state where everything would be better and worthy of the presence of God amongst men for all eternity.

You may be wondering how God will use fire to renovate and purify the earth when men are still on earth. He will do it the same way the three Hebrew young men were thrown into Nebuchadnezzar's fiery furnace but did not burn, nor were they so much as signed by the burning flames in Daniel 3:25, 27.

> 'Look!' he answered, 'I see four men loose, walking in the midst of the fire; and they are not hurt, and the form of the fourth is like the Son of God.'
>
> Nebuchadnezzar Praises God
>
> Then Nebuchadnezzar went near the mouth of the burning fiery furnace and spoke, saying, 'Shadrach, Meshach, and Abed-Nego, servants of the Most High God, come out, and come here.' Then Shadrach, Meshach, and Abed-Nego came from the midst of the fire. And the satraps, administrators, governors, and the king's counselors gathered together, and they saw these men on whose bodies the fire had no power;

the hair of their head was not singed nor were their garments affected, and the smell of fire was not on them.

God has already got the technology to burn selectively and to preserve the things he wants preserved in the midst of the fire, and he will use it again.

He will do it the same way he caused the bush to burn in Exodus 3 but were not consumed by the fire. Thus, God has the technology to cause his fire to burn up only those things he wants burnt up, whilst everything else remains unaffected by the fire.

Much of the oceans as we know them today will disappear, as the heat will cause much of the waters to evaporate in the renovation process. The waters that came out of the heavens and the deep to deluge the earth during the chaos of Genesis 1 will be gathered back into storage. Instead, there will be an abundance of rivers, lakes, and mini seas all over the earth, as described in Psalm 72:8–10, 17; 97:1–6; and Isaiah 42:4. There will be an abundance of water on earth to make the earth fruitful, as waters will even spring up in the deserts, according to Genesis 8:22 and Isaiah35.

THE NEW HEAVEN AND THE NEW EARTH

The result of the renovation by fire would be a new heaven and a new earth that looks new in every respect, in character and freshness, and not new in existence, as described in Revelation 21:1–22:5.

There will be new peoples and new conditions on earth following the renovation. God's original plan was for man to live forever. In that sense, the fall of man has greatly delayed his plan and purpose, but it has turned to his advantage and gain. In the meantime, God has created a heavenly people to rule and reign with him for all eternity. He will actually move his tabernacle from heaven down to earth to be with his children, according to Revelation 21:3, so that his children shall see his face.

And I heard a loud voice from heaven saying, 'Behold, the tabernacle of God is with men, and He will dwell with them, and they shall be His people. God Himself will be with them and be their God.'

It is said that there will be perpetual joy in his presence as he will wipe away every tear from their eyes, according to Isaiah 25:8.

He will swallow up death forever,
And the Lord GOD will wipe away tears from all faces;
The rebuke of His people
He will take away from all the earth;
For the LORD has spoken.

In addition to wiping away every tear from their eyes, there will be no more death, neither sorrow nor crying nor pain, for the former things have passed away.

The bride of Christ, the New Jerusalem, the dwelling place of his saints, a heavenly city that will also be new in freshness, will come down from heaven to the earth's atmosphere, according to Hebrews 11:9–10, 16.

By faith he dwelt in the land of promise as in a foreign country, dwelling in tents with Isaac and Jacob, the heirs with him of the same promise; for he waited for the city which has foundations, whose builder and maker is God.

But now they desire a better, that is, a heavenly country. Therefore God is not ashamed to be called their God, for He has prepared a city for them.

It is also called the holy city. The New Jerusalem is called the bride of Christ, because that is the dwelling place of the bride. Thus, the bride has reference to both the city and its inhabitants, as you cannot have one without the other, according to Revelation 21:2, 9–10.

> Then I, John, saw the holy city, New Jerusalem, coming down out of heaven from God, prepared as a bride adorned for her husband.

> Then one of the seven angels who had the seven bowls filled with the seven last plagues came to me and talked with me, saying, 'Come, I will show you the bride, the Lamb's wife.' And he carried me away in the Spirit to a great and high mountain, and showed me the great city, the holy Jerusalem, descending out of heaven from God.

The bride of Christ is not only the New Testament church but includes all those who had a part in the first resurrection. This is made up of the Old Testament saints from Adam as well as all the New Testament saints, both of whom were resurrected, and those who were raptured alive as well as all the tribulation martyrs, including the 144,000 Jewish evangelists and the two witnesses of Revelation 11. Both the Old and New Testament saints were promised the same city by God, according to Hebrews 11:8–16, 40, so all must be the bride of Christ.

Actually, both Revelation 21:9 and Hebrews 11:40 say that the Old Testament saints would not be made perfect apart from or without the New Testament saints, implying they will be made perfect with them or together. This means that they share the same inheritance in God. Although different companies are saved at different ages, yet in the final analysis, all will become one as the final bride. God has only one family, and all have a stake in his estate, irrespective of when they were saved.

God having provided something better for us, that they should not be made perfect apart from us, according to Hebrews 11:40.

At the end of the millennium, God will destroy all rebels, sin, and death, and remove the curse from the earth. Those who live till the end of the millennium and do not rebel at the Gog and Magog war will be purged and will enter eternity and live forever, as was originally intended by God in the garden. This will end the probation of man to see if he will obey God. Man will never again rebel against God, and the two will live in eternal harmony.

THE TRUTH ABOUT LIFE IN HEAVEN

Heaven is a real place promised to those who believe in Jesus as Lord and Saviour, according to John 14:1–3.

> Let not your heart be troubled; you believe in God, believe also in Me. In My Father's house are many mansions; if it were not so, I would have told you. I go to prepare a place for you. And if I go and prepare a place for you, I will come again and receive you to Myself; that where I am, there you may be also.

Our citizenship is in heaven, where our names are recorded, according to Philippians 3:20 and Luke 10:20.

> For our citizenship is in heaven, from which we also eagerly wait for the Savior, the Lord Jesus Christ,

> Nevertheless do not rejoice in this, that the spirits are subject to you, but rather rejoice because your names are written in heaven.

That is why we are to set our minds on things in heaven because that is where we are headed for. In the eternal state, the New Jerusalem, which is the capital city of heaven, will come down to earth to become the eternal dwelling place of the saints of God.

For convenience, the Bible distinguishes at least three heavens— namely, the first heaven or the atmospheric heaven, where the clouds are; and then there is the second heaven or outer space, where the planets and stars are, and where angels, good and bad, operate; the third heaven is the dwelling place of God and the promised future home of believers.

Heaven is the capital of the universe, where God has his capital city, the New Jerusalem, the heavenly temple and his throne in the temple.

Heaven, according to the Bible, is located in the northern parts of the universe, according to Isaiah 14:12–14 and Psalm 48 (75:6–8).

> How you are fallen from heaven,
> O Lucifer, son of the morning!
> How you are cut down to the ground,
> You who weakened the nations!
> For you have said in your heart:
> 'I will ascend into heaven,
> I will exalt my throne above the stars of God;
> I will also sit on the mount of the congregation
> On the farthest sides of the north;
> I will ascend above the heights of the clouds,
> I will be like the Most High.'
>
> Great is the LORD, and greatly to be praised
> In the city of our God,
> In His holy mountain.

Heaven is inhabited by several creatures including common angels, archangels, seraphim, cherubim, living creatures, spirit horses, and chariot drivers (1 Kings 22:19; 2 Chron. 18:18; Matt. 18:10; 22:30; 24:36; Rev. 12:12; 13:6; 21:1–22:23).

It is a place of stunning beauty, like a bride adorned for her husband, according to Revelation 21:2, a magnificent city spanning over 1,500 miles in each direction. It is a city of pure gold. The streets are paved with gold, and the foundations are adorned with all kinds of precious stones.

The Holy Mount Zion is the topmost mountain, with God's palace on top of it, making it visible from everywhere in the city, and his glory beams over the whole city. It is a place not to be missed for anything.

Several natural people have gone to heaven and come back or will come back later. Enoch (Gen. 5:22) and Elijah (2 Kings 2) have been there for thousands of years and will be back as the two witnesses of Revelation 11 to witness to the Jewish people during the tribulation. Enoch has been in heaven for over five thousand years, and Elijah over 3,500 years, according to Zechariah 4:11–14.

> Then I answered and said to him, 'What are these two olive trees—at the right of the lampstand and at its left?' And I further answered and said to him, 'What are these two olive branches that drip into the receptacles of the two gold pipes from which the golden oil drains?'
>
> Then he answered me and said, 'Do you not know what these are?'
>
> And I said, 'No, my lord.'
>
> So he said, 'These are the two anointed ones, who stand beside the Lord of the whole earth.'

Paul (2 Cor. 1:1–4) and John (Rev. 4:1) both went to heaven but in visions. As the end of the age dawns upon us, heavenly visitations have become much more commonplace. The Lord is taking many people not only to heaven but also to hell itself to see the horrors currently going on there and sending these back to warn the inhabitants of the earth as to what awaits all Christ rejecters. This is the overflowing grace and abundant mercy of the Lord. He does not want anyone to go there because he knows what awaits those who do go there by choice. According to Paul, the invisible things of heaven are like the visible things on earth, since the things on earth are patterned after those in heaven, even though the earthly pattern is a poor shadow of what is in heaven, having been scarred by the fall and the curse.

What shall we be doing in heaven?

Heaven is a place of praise. We shall be praising and thanking God for what he has done for us, according to Revelation 5:9–10; 14:3; 15:3.

And they sang a new song, saying:

'You are worthy to take the scroll,
And to open its seals;
For You were slain,
And have redeemed us to God by Your blood
Out of every tribe and tongue and people and nation,
And have made us kings and priests to our God;
And we shall reign on the earth.'

They sang as it were a new song before the throne, before the four living creatures, and the elders; and no one could learn that song except the hundred and forty-four thousand who were redeemed from the earth.

They sing the song of Moses, the servant of God, and the song of the Lamb, saying:

'Great and marvelous are Your works,
Lord God Almighty!
Just and true are Your ways,
O King of the saints!'

Heaven will be a place of fellowship where we get to know each other, talk to the Old Testament saints, the prophets, Adam, Eve, Abraham, the apostles, and, certainly, the Lord Jesus himself.

Prepare to meet your favourite Bible characters in heaven. I am looking forward to meet my man, Jacob, who, though, did not have the most enviable start in his life's journey but finished well as one of God's favourite characters in all the scriptures. I can identify with his story, personally, and that is a source of hope in what the grace of God can accomplish. No matter where you are coming from, no matter your background or history, when you come to Jesus, not only does he wipe your slate clean but also he opens a brand-new page for you to begin writing your life story from scratch. That is really what it means to be truly born again. You are a new person with a fresh assignment to accomplish for him.

Heaven will be a place of serving both God and his people, according to Revelation 7:15; 22:3.

> Therefore they are before the throne of God, and serve Him day and night in His temple. And He who sits on the throne will dwell among them.

> And there shall be no more curse, but the throne of God and of the Lamb shall be in it, and His servants shall serve Him.

Heaven is a place of learning, according to 1 Corinthians 13:9–10.

> For we know in part and we prophesy in part. But when that which is perfect has come, then that which is in part will be done away.

It will be a place of absolute joy and perfection where there will be no more sorrow, no more pain, no more trouble. The former things will truly pass away.

It will be a place of unbelievable real estate, according to John 14:2.

In My Father's house are many mansions; if it were not so, I would have told you. I go to prepare a place for you.

THE MILLENNIUM OR THE DISPENSATION OF DIVINE GOVERNMENT

As the name implies, the millennium is a thousand-year period during which Satan will be bound from the earth and chained in the bottomless pit. During the millennium, Christ and the glorified saints would be ruling over the natural humans on earth directly from Israel. The natural people will likely be living in their present nations to repopulate the earth. King David will be ruling over Israel, which will be the leading nation on earth and will be the main evangelistic nation that God will use to evangelise the nations, as there will still be unsaved people on earth. Following the release of Satan at the end of the millennium, he will go and deceive the people of the earth for the last time, and God will cause fire to come down from heaven to destroy all the rebels, and Satan will be cast into the lake of fire where the beast and the false prophet are and he will be tormented forever and ever. God will allow Satan back on earth for a short period at the end of the millennium so that those born during the millennium would have the same opportunity as everyone else to exercise their free will to either accept Jesus as Lord and Saviour, or reject his offer and accept the lies of Satan, as all humans have had opportunity to do in every dispensation. Many will choose to follow Satan and rebel against God and will be destroyed by fire and sent straight to the lake of fire for all eternity. At the end of the millennium following the renovation of the earth and the descent of the New Jerusalem from heaven to earth, we enter eternity where God himself brings his throne from heaven to dwell with man forever and ever.

PLEASE DO NOT COME WHERE I AM: THE RICH MAN AND LAZARUS

This is based on the true story about the rich man and Lazarus as narrated by the Lord Jesus in Luke 16:19–31.

In the Middle East, there is a fable told of a merchant in Baghdad who sent his servant to the marketplace to run an errand on his behalf. On completing his errand, the servant turned a corner, and there standing to his horror and amazement was lady death. The look on her face so frightened him he ran quickly home to his master and told him what he had seen, death. He asked his master for the fastest horse to run as far away from lady death as possible, all the way to Samara, the farthest city from Bagdad, before nightfall. So the master obliged and gave the servant his fastest horse to flee to Samara, the farthest city. Later that same afternoon, the merchant himself went to the Baghdad marketplace, and there she was, lady death! The master mustered all the courage he could and asked death, 'Why did you startle and frighten my servant with that look this morning?' Death replied, 'I did not intend to startle and frighten your servant. I was the one who was surprised to see your servant in Baghdad this morning, because I have an appointment with him tonight in Samara.'

You and I have an appointment; perhaps it will be in London, New York, Kumasi, Helsinki, Gyampomani, Accra, or wherever, but it is the one appointment we cannot miss. The Bible says it is appointed for you. Crucially, God has hidden the time of our individual appointments from us. The apostle Paul puts it this way,

'It is appointed for men to die once, but after this the judgement,' according to Hebrews 9:27. This appointment will be kept by 100 percent of all humans who live before the rapture of the church. In the Old Testament, there is the story of two people who were taken to heaven without dying, Enoch and Elijah, but even in their case, their deaths were only postponed, not cancelled, as I believe these are the two witnesses sent back to the earth to prophesy in Jerusalem against the antichrist and then get killed in Revelation 11:7. It has to happen thus because the scriptures cannot be broken. The world yonder is more real and colourful and vibrant than this one. It is a world of peace and love where there is no worry, fear, or anxiety, or it is one of torment and sorrow and pain. We have the opportunity in this life to prepare for which one we choose to spend eternity in. That is the central issue of life on earth, a rehearsal for life in the next.

In Luke 16:19–31, we have the story of the rich man and Lazarus, who appear to have lived and died about the same time. This is not a parable as many have mistakenly concluded. In a parable, the characters are fictional as the story itself. But in this case, real people, whose names are given, are involved, making it an actual historical story. Jesus actually names Abraham, Moses, and Lazarus.

In Hades, this rich man, whose name we are not given, learns to pray, but, oddly, he does not ask to be let out of this underground prison of heat and flames, as he knew there was no possible escape. He prays rather for the living, saying, 'Please don't come where I am.' Certainly, the condemned souls in hell know the finality of their plight, and that sense of hopelessness must be the worst of all torments. I can only guess that the rich man's family was still feasting at his funeral, which must have gone on for a good many days, drinking, dancing, and feasting on the best this world has to offer. And why not? They could afford it. Even though his family did not know it, he was in a very acute distress and suffering. Like many rich people today, he discovered rather too late that their worldly influence could not save them, nor could their wealth, nor their reputation. Instead of victors, they are victims. Instead of bragging about their freedoms, they are prisoners and beggars.

The Rich Man in Hades

He was fully conscious immediately after his death. Memory, speaking, pain, and torment were all part of his experience in Hades. He had all his senses about him. In Hades, the alcoholic will thirst for a drop of liquor, but none will be given him. The drug addict will crave a shot of coke but will not have it. The immoral man or woman will burn with lustful desire but will never have the opportunity to satisfy himself or herself, according to Revelation 22:11.

> He who is unjust, let him be unjust still; he who is filthy, let him be filthy still; he who is righteous, let him be righteous still; he who is holy, let him be holy still.

There will be perpetual increased desire but no satisfaction. According to Proverbs 27:20,

> Hell and Destruction are never full;
> So the eyes of man are never satisfied.

The eternal destiny of man will be irrevocably fixed at the point of death. According to Revelation 22:11, whatever condition you exit the world into eternity in, the same will be magnified and perpetrated in all eternity. The sin condition will be your lot throughout all eternity, and, sadly, there is no opportunity for satisfying your lusts and cravings in hell. The righteous and holy will be more righteous and holy in heaven, but the depravity of the damned will be their craving for all eternity, according to Luke 16:26.

> And besides all this, between us and you there is a great gulf fixed, so that those who want to pass from here to you cannot, nor can those from there pass to us.

Whereas, the relatives of this rich man on earth can leave the funeral home, go out for dinner, or go on vacation; their friend in Hades is confined in this pit without any possibility of escape. As the big dudes say back home, 'Do you know who I am?' Well, Mr. Big Shot, over there, it does not matter who you are. Nobody even remembers your name. You are alone in the midst of the crowd working the boiling mud for all eternity.

This man knew himself very well enough to know that what he was experiencing was fair, just, and deserved, because he says nothing about how unjust it was for him to be there. He complains about the pain, but he does not complain about the injustice. He knows exactly what his living brothers had to do to avoid his own fate. This rich man knew that unforgiven sin led quite logically to a place of agony. With heightened perception and a better understanding, he could now see that his relationship with God should have been his highest priority. But alas, it was too late. That is why God in his mercy asks us, in Isaiah 55:6–7,

> Seek the LORD while He may be found,
> Call upon Him while He is near.
> Let the wicked forsake his way,
> And the unrighteous man his thoughts;
> Let him return to the LORD,
> And He will have mercy on him;
> And to our God,
> For He will abundantly pardon.

The opportunity is on the table right now, and you can grab it and make it yours and avert the sad fate of this man who lived his life majoring on the minors and neglecting what was most important. God reiterates his offer in Romans 10:11–13, thus,

> For the Scripture says, 'Whoever believes on Him
> will not be put to shame.' For there is no distinction
> between Jew and Greek, for the same Lord over all is

rich to all who call upon Him. For 'whoever calls on
the name of the LORD shall be saved.'

You may be regurgitating the popular opinion of the majority
without really thinking about the issue. Why don't you spend some
time examining the evidence for yourself before you make your mind
up on Jesus?

Where this rich man went, there were fire and raging flames, there
were torment and excruciating thirst, and his tongue was parched as
a result. But there is also nothing he could do about his plight. His
money and wealth were no good to him there. This man had no regard
for God's servants because he was richer than most of them. And he
thought that was the end of story. Obviously, he has infected his five
brothers with this cancer of disregard for God's servants and God's
Word. Not only is he richer than them, but also he lives in a better
house, lives in the best neighbourhood in town, drives the latest gas
guzzler, and can afford the best food and clothes. Lots of beautiful,
colourful birds must have been nesting in his patch. That is why he
needed a 'special man of God', one back from the dead to witness
to them before they will believe, because he had no regard for those
on earth. They were not his class. Very often I have great pity for
the well-heeled and high-classed in society. How do you reach those
people to tell them about the love of Christ/ For many of them, that
is not the proper subject of conversation. They have better things to
talk about than God talk.

He had a great influence on his brothers and certainly in his
family and community and could have used this influence to direct
them to God, but he did the opposite. He knew that all those who
came under his influence on earth would suffer the same fate as him
because of his ungodly example and corrupting influence. Even in
Hades, this spoiled brat was trying to get Lazarus to wait on him,
because he had servants and courtiers waiting on him on earth. That
is what he was used to. But the times have changed and the tables
have turned, and in his case upside down. Lazarus, the once beggar,
is now God's royalty, and the rich man is worse than a beggar.

Abraham's answer to this man is very instructive: 'If they do not listen to Moses and the prophets, neither will they be persuaded if someone rises from the dead.' How true, when Christ told this story, he had not yet been put to death and resurrected from the dead. He had not visited the nether world yet. Today, even though there is overwhelming evidence of the resurrection, many men and women still choose not to believe. Jesus came and lifted the curtain on the other side of the veil and told us all about the horrors and torments of hell, but people are still making excuses when it comes to their eternal destiny. As a certain wise man noted, 'A man convinced against his will is of the same opinion still.' Oh, the stupidity of confusing the unfamiliar with the improbable.

What about Lazarus, the believer?

Let it be noted that Lazarus did not go to Abraham's bosom because he was poor, neither did the rich man go to Hades because he was rich. They both ended up in their respective places based exclusively on their relationship with God. The rich man did not know God and was not saved. Lazarus believed in God and was saved. Poverty does not take you to heaven, nor is it a virtue, the same way as being rich is not a sin and does not disqualify you from heaven.

At the time of this story—that is, before Christ's death and resurrection—Hades had two regions, according to Luke 16:23, 26.

> And being in torments in Hades, he lifted up his eyes and saw Abraham afar off, and Lazarus in his bosom.

> And besides all this, between us and you there is a great gulf fixed, so that those who want to pass from here to you cannot, nor can those from there pass to us.

The place of torment for unregenerate departed souls, and Abraham's bosom or paradise was for the good guys or those who knew God. The two regions of Hades were separated by a deep chasm, and it was impossible to cross from one section to the other, even though from the Luke 16 account, the inhabitants could see and hear each other from their own domain.

Since the resurrection and ascension of Jesus to heaven, believers no longer go to Abraham's bosom on death, but they go straight to the presence of God in heaven, according to Ephesians 4:8–10.

> Therefore He says:
>
> 'When He ascended on high,
> He led captivity captive,
> And gave gifts to men.'
>
> (Now this, 'He ascended'—what does it mean but that He also first descended into the lower parts of the earth? He who descended is also the One who ascended far above all the heavens, that He might fill all things.)

On account of the large numbers of people pouring into hell every second, the Bible says that hell has enlarged itself. The fires have now spread to cover what was Abraham's bosom before, where the good guys went before. This is reported to be deep in the heart of the earth. But enough of this for now.

'We are confident, yes, well pleased rather to be absent from the body and to be present with the Lord,' according to 2 Corinthians 5:8.

This means that when a believer casts off this earth suite in death, he is instantly transported into the presence of God. Today, those who die in the Lord go straight into the presence of the Lord in heaven. Even though death for now appears to be man's greatest enemy, in the end, it will prove to be his greatest friend, according to 1 Corinthians 15:26, 'The last enemy that will be destroyed is death.'

This is so because it is only through death that we can go to God, according to 1 Corinthians 3:21–23.

> Therefore let no one boast in men. For all things are yours: whether Paul or Apollos or Cephas, or the world or life or death, or things present or things to come—all are yours. And you are Christ's, and Christ is God's.

Only death can give us the gift of eternity. It introduces us to the riches of eternity. That is why believers are said to fall asleep when they die, because we rest from our labours only to wake up in the morning in the presence of the Lord. Even though death can still terrify us, like the bee, Christ, through his own death and resurrection, has removed death's sting, according to 1 Corinthians 15:53–55.

> For this corruptible must put on incorruption, and this mortal must put on immortality. So when this corruptible has put on incorruption, and this mortal has put on immortality, then shall be brought to pass the saying that is written: 'Death is swallowed up in victory.'

> O Death, where is your sting? O Hades, where is your victory?

Death has no sting to harm the believer. Instead of being afraid of death, the believer could actually look up to the time of reunion with his Lord. If those in heaven could talk with us, what would they say? I guess they will say to us, 'Please do all you could to please God because he is so good.' They will certainly urge us to live on earth with heaven in mind.

Death is swallowed up in victory, according to 1 Corinthians 15:54–55.

> So when this corruptible has put on incorruption, and this mortal has put on immortality, then shall be

brought to pass the saying that is written: 'Death is swallowed up in victory.'

O Death, where is your sting? O Hades, where is your victory?

A bee whose stinger has been removed can do no harm. Christ has removed death's sting, so it poses no threat for his children.

Death in the New Testament is transformed from a monster to a minister, which frees us to go to God.

Like the Israelites following Moses, their leader, out of slavery through the Red Sea to the Promised Land, we follow our leader Jesus, who died and rose from the dead and leads us to heaven. There is nothing to fear on the way because our leader knows the way. 'Where I go you cannot follow me now, but you will follow me later,' according to John 13:36. He also said in John 14:6,

Jesus said to him, 'I am the way, the truth, and the life. No one comes to the Father except through Me.'

Death has become a restful sleep for the believer. The body (not the soul) sleeps until the day of the resurrection. It is a means of rest and rejuvenation to awaken in the arms of God.

According to Hebrews 2:14–15, he has destroyed the devil who used death to put fear into mankind, through his own death. Thus, death should hold no terror for the believer, neither should we let the devil terrorise us with the fear of death any longer.

Inasmuch then as the children have partaken of flesh and blood, He Himself likewise shared in the same, that through death He might destroy him who had the power of death, that is, the devil, and release those who through fear of death were all their lifetime subject to bondage.

It is the route to our final home, in heaven.

Sorrow and grief are to be expected. Christ wept at the tomb of Lazarus and agonized with 'loud crying and tears' in Gethsemane at his own impending death, according to Hebrew 5:7.

When you believe in Christ, you pass from death into life, according to John 5:24.

> Most assuredly, I say to you, he who hears My word
> and believes in Him who sent Me has everlasting life,
> and shall not come into judgment, but has passed
> from death into life.

This is so because when we receive his eternal life, there is no point in time when our life ceases. We only pass from one plane of existence into the other without a break. Our lives continue as the veil parts between this world and the next seamlessly. The moment you are absent from the body, you are present with the Lord just in the same instance, effortlessly.

We will never see death, according to Jesus's words in John 8:51.

> Most assuredly, I say to you, if anyone keeps My word
> he shall never see death.

Here Jesus is not talking about physical death but the spirit of death that comes to escort unbelievers into hell. This is so because at the point of departure, God sends his angels to escort the believer in a chariot of fire to the portals of heaven. You will not make the trip alone, but angels will be your escort to the bosom of your Lord. What a blessed hope we have in Jesus.

As a consequence of his death, we can walk through the shadows of death without any fear. Death has been reduced to a shadow, without any power to hurt God's children, according to Psalm 23:4 and 1 Corinthians 15:54–57.

Yea, though I walk through the valley of the shadow
of death,
I will fear no evil;
For You are with me;
Your rod and Your staff, they comfort me.

So when this corruptible has put on incorruption,
and this mortal has put on immortality, then shall be
brought to pass the saying that is written: 'Death is
swallowed up in victory.'

O Death, where is your sting?
O Hades, where is your victory?

The sting of death is sin, and the strength of sin is the
law. But thanks be to God, who gives us the victory
through our Lord Jesus Christ.

The believer's passage in death is a comforting experience
because he is never alone in the journey, because death has been
swallowed up in victory. It is announcing that this one has made it,
has fought the good fight, and can look forward to a welcome and a
reward from his Lord and Master, Jesus Christ.

God actually looks forward with anticipation to the day of our
reunion with him because he misses his children as much as we do
him, according to Psalm 116:15. 'Precious in the sight of the LORD is
the death of His saints.'

This is because of the beautiful reunion that awaits and the
completion of our redemption. It is when our redemption is completely
complete and perfectly perfected, according to Hebrews 10:14.

For by one offering He has perfected forever those
who are being sanctified.

After death and reunion with him, we cannot be corrupted anymore, there is no danger of backsliding and losing our salvation, and we shall never be separated from him.

> Who, in the days of His flesh, when He had offered up prayers and supplications, with vehement cries and tears to Him who was able to save Him from death, and was heard because of His godly fear.

We feel the pain of separation. When Stephen was stoned to death, 'some devout men buried Stephen, and made loud lamentation over him'. But ours are tears of hope and not tears of hopelessness because of the promised resurrection. If you meet Jesus here, you will surely meet him there where there are no funeral services, no tombstones, and, certainly, no tearful goodbyes, in the land of no more sorrow, no more crying, and, certainly, no more pain. If you are born once, you will die twice; but if you are born twice, you will only die once. According to Revelation 20:6 and 21:8, the second death, which is the lake of fire, has no power over us.

> Blessed and holy is he who has part in the first resurrection. Over such the second death has no power, but they shall be priests of God and of Christ, and shall reign with Him a thousand years.

> But the cowardly, unbelieving, abominable, murderers, sexually immoral, sorcerers, idolaters, and all liars shall have their part in the lake which burns with fire and brimstone, which is the second death.

The lake of fire is the final horrific destination of all the wicked dead. It is a place of unimaginable suffering and torment, which is actually beyond the scope of this book. For more detailed description of the horrors and agonies of the lake of fire, see my other book, *Destination Heaven: Strive to Enter through the Narrow Way.*

You may be saying, what about those who lived in the Old Testament days, especially Gentiles who did not have the Law of Moses as the Jews did?

Good question indeed that demands an exploration from the scriptures, as these are our distant ancestors and we are interested to know their fate in eternity. First of all, understand that God's judgment will take account of every situation and circumstance of every individual's life. One of the considerations will be the degree of knowledge and opportunity one had to know God. Someone born today has greater opportunity to know the truth about Jesus than someone born in the age of conscience who could still know about God but not with the same degree of enlightenment we have today.

According to Romans 1:19–20, these people who lived in a period called the age of conscience had the witness of nature.

> Because what may be known of God is manifest in them, for God has shown it to them. For since the creation of the world His invisible attributes are clearly seen, being understood by the things that are made, even His eternal power and Godhead, so that they are without excuse.

These people could know about God the Creator through nature or the created world that bore witness to the Creator.

In addition to nature, they had the witness of their consciences. Your conscience is the voice of your spirit within an individual and tells you what is right and what is wrong. It is like an inner law that, if followed, will help you make right choices. This is explained in Romans 2:14:15.

> For when Gentiles, who do not have the law, by nature do the things in the law, these, although not having the law, are a law to themselves, who show the work of the law written in their hearts, their conscience

also bearing witness, and between themselves their
thoughts accusing or else excusing them.

Whilst conscience is not a perfect guide, it is a fairly good guide
to behaviour if one would listen to it. If you listen to your conscience
often, it will be a good guide for your actions. On the other hand,
if you defy it often, doing what it warns you not to, it will become
distorted or calloused, and with time, it may cease speaking to you
altogether. It is very dangerous to have a seared or dead conscience
because it means you cannot tell between good and bad or right and
wrong. That is why it is more difficult to do the wrong thing for the
first time, but repeated offenses become progressively easier until you
can begin to do bad things without thinking about them whatsoever.

In addition, they had the promise of a Redeemer, as God had
promised to send the One who would defeat Satan and sin, according
to Genesis 3:15.

> And I will put enmity; Between you and the woman,
> And between your seed and her Seed; He shall bruise
> your head,
> And you shall bruise His heel.

This narrative would have entered the folklore and oral tradition
of all the early societies as the parents must have told them about
the fall of our great forebears Adam and Eve and God's promise of
a Redeemer. Remember that at the beginning of man's history, they
lived for hundreds and hundreds of years and must have shared this
story down the line over the centuries. So right from the very cradles
of society, mankind had been living in the expectation of the arrival
of the promised Saviour.

They knew the importance of sacrifice, according to Genesis 4:4.

> Abel also brought of the firstborn of his flock and
> of their fat. And the LORD respected Abel and his
> offering.

When God came into the Garden of Eden after Adam and Eve's sin, the first object lesson he taught them was the need for an atoning sacrifice. This knowledge they passed on to all their children and succeeding societies. Even though corrupted in most societies, the need for a sacrifice in heathen cultures to appease the gods and demon spirits is widely held and practised even today. This means that they could always go to God via a sacrifice, usually a blood sacrifice.

They had prophets even in those times, according to Jude 14–15.

> Now Enoch, the seventh from Adam, prophesied about these men also, saying, 'Behold, the Lord comes with ten thousands of His saints, to execute judgment on all, to convict all who are ungodly among them of all their ungodly deeds which they have committed in an ungodly way, and of all the harsh things which ungodly sinners have spoken against Him.'

If you hear the account and life of some of these godly saints, like Enoch, Noah, and Abraham, it is obvious that they had very intimate knowledge of the Creator God. It is obvious that these people, including others like David, Daniel, and Moses, and the prophets enjoyed a degree of knowledge and intimacy with God that we New Testament believers can only dream of with all our Spirit indwelling and baptism and complete cannon of scripture in 101 different translations in every conceivable dialect under the sun.

They had preachers such as Noah, one of eight people, a preacher of righteousness, bringing in the flood on the ungodly, according to 2 Peter 2:5.

They knew the difference between good and evil, certainly, according to Genesis 3:22.

> Then the LORD God said, 'Behold, the man has become like one of Us, to know good and evil. And

now, lest he put out his hand and take also of the tree
of life, and eat, and live forever.'

Though they knew the difference between good and evil, because
they had learnt it not from God but rather in disobedience to his
Word; they always had a propensity for the evil instead of the good.

Several years later, we see Joseph, a slave in Egypt, espousing
one of the highest moral standards anywhere in all the Bible not only
in his handling of Potiphar's wife but also in his diligence, honesty,
integrity, and capacity to forgive his wayward brothers, which was
only second to Lord Jesus himself, according to Genesis 39:9.

There is no one greater in this house than I, nor has
he kept back anything from me but you, because you
are his wife. How then can I do this great wickedness,
and sin against God?

This is a remarkable young man in very challenging circumstances
who kept a pure faith and an undefiled conscience. Obviously, it is
all by the grace of God, but he certainly must have availed himself.

They were acquainted with the ministry of the Holy Spirit, as we
learn in Genesis 6:3.

And the LORD said, 'My Spirit shall not strive with
man forever, for he is indeed flesh; yet his days shall
be one hundred and twenty years.'

The benevolence of God in his provision for man and all the
created order, according to Acts 14:17.

Nevertheless He did not leave Himself without
witness, in that He did good, gave us rain from heaven
and fruitful seasons, filling our hearts with food and
gladness.

This benevolence of God in his provision of good things for man's benefit and enjoyment was God's powerful way of bearing witness to himself. The warm sunshine in the daytime, the moon and the stars by night, the refreshing rain and winds, the seasons, and the vegetation and their colourful flowers, even the different colours of people and languages all over the world should serve as powerful reminders of the existence of God. In the face of all these, man makes a deliberate and determined effort to blot out the knowledge of God from his mind. Fortunately, not believing in God does not eradicate him. Not believing in heaven and hell does not abolish them. God says he is, and that he is, a rewarder of those who diligently seek him.

Live in humility of mind

In this life, we are all subject to trials, sorrow, and pain, and despite our apparent show of vigour and strength, we are all as vulnerable as the grass of the field; here today, gone tomorrow. In our vulnerability and pain, we are all searching for answers, especially in times of bereavement and grief. We may have more questions than there are answers, but we should not be ashamed to ask the questions and seek to understand more. But in all these, we should hold unto the only hope that Christ brought into the world and let that be our consolation. His death and resurrection is the greatest hope for all mankind. There is hope that sin and pain and death do not have the final word, neither have death and the grave and the lake of fire, over all those who put their trust in him.

For parents who live to bury their children, I can only imagine how horrible an experience this could be, but be consoled that at the end of the dark tunnel, there is the bright light of a glorious reunion in the New Day that we all await. Separation from loved ones, even momentary separation, can be painful, but there is the hope of a new dawn in the presence of our glorious Lord in which we shall forever be united with all our loved ones. Jesus resurrected as the first fruits to God, holding promise for your and my resurrection and that of all believers as well. That is why Jesus said to Martha in John 11:25–26,

I am the resurrection and the life. He who believes in Me, though he may die, he shall live. And whoever lives and believes in Me shall never die. Do you believe this?

As Mary and Martha trusted Jesus's Word and got their brother Lazarus back, you can equally trust him to deliver for you and your loved ones. He is the same, yesterday, today, and forever more. Like Jim Elliot wisely observed, 'He is no fool who gives what he cannot keep, to gain what he cannot lose.'

See the victory of the empty tomb as your personal victory over whatever you may be going through in your life. Sin does not win in the end; neither do sickness, pain, and the grave and death. His resurrection is your eternal security and hope to live an extraordinary life on earth for Christ. Grief is part of the journey of life and has its rightful place, but it should not define our lives. We are not to grieve as those who do not know Christ. Remember that when God sent his Only Son to suffer and die for man, he was sharing our common grief, and by it saying, 'I know your pain, I understand how it feels, but be comforted, because there is hope. The same way I got my Son back on resurrection Sunday, you will get yours back, because by giving my Son, I was telling our common story.' You are not in this alone. Lift up your eyes and see the light at the end of the tunnel. God did not just explain our suffering; he shared it. He empathised with us all. In Revelation 21:1–7, Jesus paints a glorious picture of a New Day coming for all his children.

Now I saw a new heaven and a new earth, for the first heaven and the first earth had passed away. Also there was no more sea. Then I, John, saw the holy city, New Jerusalem, coming down out of heaven from God, prepared as a bride adorned for her husband. And I heard a loud voice from heaven saying, 'Behold, the tabernacle of God is with men, and He will dwell with them, and they shall be His people. God Himself will be with them and be their God. And God will wipe away every tear from their eyes; there shall be no more death, nor sorrow, nor crying. There shall be no more pain, for the former things have passed away.'

Then He who sat on the throne said, 'Behold, I make all things new.' And He said to me, 'Write, for these words are true and faithful.'

And He said to me, 'It is done! I am the Alpha and the Omega, the Beginning and the End. I will give of the fountain of the water of life freely to him who thirsts. He who overcomes shall inherit all things, and I will be his God and he shall be My son.'

This is my only hope, may it be yours as well. Amen. Maranatha.

THE GOSPEL: HOW TO GET SAVED AND YOUR FAMILY SAVED

God is so kind and loving he has made complete provision in his Son Jesus for the salvation of every person who would accept his free offer of forgiveness and reconciliation. Sometimes, we Christians have made it appear that God is mad at the people who do not know him yet through his Son Jesus, but that is as far from the truth as anything can possibly be. Listen to the best news you will hear anywhere under the sun, as reported in 2 Corinthians 5:18–21.

> Now all things are of God, who has reconciled us to Himself through Jesus Christ, and has given us the ministry of reconciliation, that is, that God was in Christ reconciling the world to Himself, not imputing their trespasses to them, and has committed to us the word of reconciliation.

> Now then, we are ambassadors for Christ, as though God were pleading through us: we implore you on Christ's behalf, be reconciled to God. For He made Him who knew no sin to be sin for us, that we might become the righteousness of God in Him.

The scripture above is saying it was God who took the initiative to come looking for you to settle the strained relationship between you and him. Think of it, whilst we were all minding our businesses, actually rebelling against everything he stood for, with little or no thought for God, he sent his Son Jesus to be born into the world to die for our sins. Because God had said in his Word in Romans 6:23 that the wages of sin is death, and since we were all born sinners (and have compounded our problems by sinning some more), every one of us was guilty and a candidate for hell, with a death sentence over our heads, without exception. But like the verse above continues, the gift of God is eternal life in Christ Jesus our Lord. He decided that instead of each one of us dying for our own sins, which will still not meet the demands of his justice, anyway, he will rather let his Son Jesus, the only innocent, perfect man ever to set foot on earth, die in the place of all mankind. All we have left to do is to admit our sin and acknowledge the person and work of Jesus Christ on the cross as our substitute, and then he will exchange his righteousness for our sin.

Then he charged those of us who have come into a relationship with him through his Son Jesus to tell all the others that he is not angry with them, but, rather, a warm welcome awaits everyone who will come to him because the price has already been fully paid, on his account. He is literally imploring, appealing, and begging the world to take advantage of the free offer of a pardon that he has already provided. God wants a big family, which would include you and me and everyone who will come. He loves children (all of us are his children), and he wants His house full with his loving children.

LISTEN TO THE GOSPEL OR THE GOOD NEWS

Gospel means good news. It is good news because God paid all the debt we owed him on our behalf and gave us a free pardon. Oh yes, there was a cost, but we did not pay it because we could not. Listen to how the great apostle Paul presents the good news in 1 Corinthians 15:1–4.

> Moreover, brethren, I declare to you the gospel which
> I preached to you, which also you received and in

> which you stand, by which also you are saved, if you hold fast that word which I preached to you—unless you believed in vain.
>
> For I delivered to you first of all that which I also received: that Christ died for our sins according to the Scriptures, and that He was buried, and that He rose again the third day according to the Scriptures.

Paul says it is the gospel message that points us to Jesus for him to save us. He said that the gospel is first of all. We should not come with human arguments and discussions about religion and such stuff but tell people about the good news of salvation through Christ. He gives a simple three-point condensation of the gospel message, thus,

- Christ died for our sins,
- he was buried, and that
- he rose again the third day.

He says that all these are according to the scriptures. He is saying that in the matter of your salvation, what the scriptures say must be the beginning and end of all discussion. The scriptures is the final authority, not what anybody says or a particular church tradition or any other religious book no matter how holy it claims to be.

So how are we to respond?

First of all, admit that you are a sinner. As it says above, he died for our sins, not his own sins. So admit that you are a sinner, that it was your sins he died for. Romans 3:10, 12b; 6:23 declares,

> There is none righteous, no, not one;
> There is none who does good, no, not one.

So the first thing you need to do is admit you are a sinner. Once you admit that you are a sinner, you are also saying that you need a Saviour.

> For the wages of sin is death, but the gift of God is eternal life in Christ Jesus our Lord.

After acknowledging your sin, the next step is to believe that Jesus is Lord, as explained in Romans 10:9–10.

> That if you confess with your mouth the Lord Jesus and believe in your heart that God has raised Him from the dead, you will be saved. For with the heart one believes unto righteousness, and with the mouth confession is made unto salvation.

To believe that Jesus is Lord, you have to believe that he was born of a virgin and that he is the Son of God, or God himself.

The third and final step, according to the verse above, is to call upon his name to save you. This is where you articulate or confess with your own mouth whilst believing in your heart that Jesus is Lord and invite him to come into your heart and be your Lord and Saviour.

Romans 10:13 says, 'For whoever calls upon the name of the Lord will be saved.'

Once you have taken these three steps, you are born again, you are a child of God, and he has written your name in his book of life.

You can accept Jesus as your Lord and Saviour by saying this simple prayer and believing in Him in your heart. It is an example of what you have to say to invite Jesus into your heart.

Lord Jesus, I acknowledge that I am a sinner, I believe You are the Son of God, and that you died on the cross for my sins. I now invite you into my heart to be my Lord and Saviour. Thank you for saving my soul. Amen (Rom. 10:9–11, 13). After inviting Jesus into your heart, you will need to join a Bible-believing and teaching church where you can fellowship with other Christians who will encourage you and help you to grow in your new faith.

Are you a Christian? Then be assured of your salvation. Go on to develop an intimate relationship with the Lord. It is all about getting to know Jesus through spending time with him in the Word of God and through prayer. Remember, God will not admit any stranger into his heavenly abode. Make sure you confess and repent of all known sin. Don't ignore the destructive power of sin. It could wreck your eternal destiny, so don't play with sin or entertain it in any shape or form in your life. Yes, God does not demand perfection from any of us because it is unattainable on this side of eternity. But that is not the same as ignoring known sin to fester in your life.

2 Corinthians 13:5 says, 'Examine yourself as to whether you are in the faith. Test yourselves. Do you not know yourselves, that Jesus Christ is in you?—unless indeed you are disqualified.'

If you walk with the Lord in simple obedience and constant fellowship in the word and prayer, he will make sure his grace covers your weaknesses and bring you into his heavenly kingdom.

PRAY FOR UNSAVED RELATIVES TO BE SAVED

As a believer in the Lord Jesus, you are advantageously placed to pray for your unsaved relatives to be saved as well. This is so important we must approach it with all diligence. In Acts 2:39, Peter, under the inspiration of the Holy Spirit, was speaking on the day of Pentecost when he declared,

> For the promise is to you and to your children, and to all who are afar off, as many as the Lord our God will call.

He was referring to God's promise to give the Holy Spirit to all his children. Since one has to receive the Lord Jesus before they can have the Holy Spirit, Peter was in effect saying that you and your children can all be saved. But we know that this is not straightforward for everyone. Some people delight in making fun of the gospel or simply do not believe in God. In Acts 16:30–31, we have another reference to household or family salvation.

> And he brought them out and said, 'Sirs, what must I
> do to be saved?'
>
> So they said, 'Believe on the Lord Jesus Christ, and
> you will be saved, you and your household.'

This is another instance where God explicitly says he will save us and our family members. As we said earlier, some family members may not want in, so what can we do in that situation? It is instructive to know that, in most cases, there is a spiritual power stopping them from believing in and accepting Jesus as Lord and Saviour. Listen to the verdict of scripture in that situation, according to 2 Corinthians 4:3–4.

> But even if our gospel is veiled, it is veiled to those
> who are perishing, whose minds the god of this age
> has blinded, who do not believe, lest the light of the
> gospel of the glory of Christ, who is the image of God,
> should shine on them.

The Bible is saying that in most of those situations, it is a demonic spirit who is blocking and blinding the minds of those people from the truth about Jesus. So all the fancy arguments about why they think the Bible is not true and why they think there is no God and no heaven and hell and all the many other arguments are actually coming from the pit of hell. Of course, the person making those arguments does not know he or she is being influenced or being deceived in any way. It is up to you, the Christian who knows the truth about these things, to take authority over the evil spirits, bind them, and command their influence to be broken off the minds of those you are praying for. You may not have to do this in their presence, since they will think you are weird, but you can pray first before meeting them to tell them about Jesus.

When you meet them, simply give them the gospel as we have outlined clearly here and invite them to make a decision for Jesus. If it does not happen the first time, simply do not give up. Believe that once you have committed to pray for them, it will happen at some point in their lives. Some people are known to give their lives to Christ on their death bed. Only do not give up. You cannot begin to think about the other side of the good news. It is not simply bad news; it is horrible news, and that is the reason God himself is determined for all to get on his side.

ABOUT THE AUTHOR

Originally from Ghana in West Africa, I have lived in the UK for 35 years. I am married to Victoria Bosompimaa, a very industrious and talented woman, who has encouraged me to tell the world my story since the day we met. We have a daughter Chantelle Nyarko. Together we pastor a dynamic Word-based Church in Streatham, South London, Mount Zion Revival. I thank The Holy Spirit, the greatest teacher, for His grace on my life that enabled me write this and other books. How can fail to mention Mrs Vivian Sackey and Mrs Sheilagh Ashiley for their commitment, support and loyalty over the years. Pastor Michael Boadu Mensah of Spurgeon's College, London, deserves a mention for assisting with the I.T aspects.

I have been a teacher most of my life, starting first at the School of Administration, University of Ghana, Legon, in the early 80s, where I was a Teaching Assistant for a couple of years, after graduating with a Bachelor of Science in Administration Degree, and then in several Colleges in London where I have been teaching Business studies to young adults.

I have always enjoyed sharing with others, whether it's my food, money, clothes or knowledge. My greatest passion is to share the word of God with other believers. As a consequence, I have a passion for disciplining believers to mature in their walk with the Lord, apply the bible to their daily lives and to meet the standards of our high calling by the enabling power of the Spirit of God.

For over 2 decades, I ran the OPERATION HOPE charity to help disadvantaged children in my native Ghana, from my personal earnings as a teacher to sponsor their education at all levels of the educational strata, educating several hundreds, perhaps a few thousands, in the process. Before primary education became free in Ghana, I offered a scholarship for a number of years to all the children in my hometown, Gyampomani, to enable every child attend school. Through the charity, I also built a number of fully equipped computer suites in several communities and schools in Ghana, fifteen of them, to be precise. By the same token I shipped secondary level books to many schools in Ghana, refurbishing many libraries in the process with books withdrawn from UK college libraries. We were also able to supply photocopiers to several schools and colleges, as well as clothing and school uniforms to very needy schools and individual students and pupils.

From this I learnt that you don't have to be rich to be generous, and that you can always start where you are with what you have. At 63, I think I have learnt a few lessons in life to share with others in my writings, especially the young, in their life's journey. A good mentor could be worth more than a university degree, and that is what I hope to be to the many who would read my books. This I hope to pursue with the same passion and vigour as I have anything I have had to do in life. So help me God.

Regards, Mark Nyarko

Printed in the USA
CPSIA information can be obtained
at www.ICGtesting.com
JSHW022057190923
48548JS00001B/29